LOGISTICS MATTERS

Englisch für Kaufleute für Spedition und Logistikdienstleistung

von

Peter W. Oldham

sowie

Irene Eckart

in Zusammenarbeit mit der
Verlagsredaktion

Verfasser:	Peter W. Oldham
	Irene Eckart, Flensburg (KMK-Materialien)
Berater:	Irene Eckart, Flensburg
	Marlies Hemmer-Hiltenkamp Menges, Braunschweig
	Mike A. Anderson, Braunschweig
	Ruth Frerichs, Leer
Verlagsredaktion:	Merlene Griffin
Redaktionelle Mitarbeit:	Oliver Busch(Wörterverzeichnisse),
	Christine House, Hannah Hudson,
	Oliver Kenny, Christofer Pape
Bildredaktion:	Gertha Maly
Umschlagfoto:	Masterfile RF
Umschlaggestaltung:	Katrin Nehm
Layout und	
technische Umsetzung:	Yvonne Thron, Berlin
	Sabine Theuring, Berlin
Erhältlich sind auch:	Handreichungen für den Unterricht + Lehrer-CD + Audio-CD
	ISBN: 978-3-06-020073-3

Soweit in diesem Buch Personen fotografisch abgebildet sind und ihnen von der Redaktion Namen, Berufe, Dialoge und Ähnliches zugeordnet oder diese Personen in bestimmten Situationen dargestellt werden, sind diese Zuordnungen und Darstellungen fiktiv und dienen ausschließlich der Veranschaulichung und dem besseren Verständnis des Buchinhalts.

www.cornelsen.de

Die Links zu externen Webseiten Dritter, die in diesem Lehrwerk angegeben sind, wurden vor Drucklegung geprüft. Der Verlag übernimmt keine Gewähr für die Aktualität und den Inhalt dieser Adressen und Dateien und solcher, die mit ihnen verlinkt sind.

1. Auflage, 3. Druck 2014

Im 2. Druck wurden *KMK exam practice*-Seiten sowie ein *KMK mock exam* im Anhang eingefügt.

Druck: Mohn Media Mohndruck, Gütersloh

ISBN: 978-3-06-020071-9

PEFC zertifiziert
Dieses Produkt stammt aus nachhaltig
bewirtschafteten Wäldern und kontrollierten
Quellen.

PEFC
PEFC/04-31-1033   www.pefc.de

Vorwort

Logistics Matters ist die Neubearbeitung des bewährten Lehrwerks *Freight Matters*. Logistics Matters ist für die Ausbildung in Berufsschulen sowie innerbetriebliche Aus- und Weiterbildung konzipiert und deckt nicht nur die Themenbereiche des Ausbildungsberufes Kaufmann/-frau für Spedition und Logistikdienstleistung ab, sondern kann auch in Klassen für Fachkraft für Lagerlogistik eingesetzt werden.

Das Lehrwerk basiert auf Lehrplänen der Bundesländer für Berufsschulen.

Logistics Matters ist zugeschnitten auf Lernende, deren Englischkenntnisse den Anforderungen eines mittleren Bildungsabschlusses bzw. eines durchschnittlichen gymnasialen Grundkursabschlusses entsprechen. Darüber hinaus enthalten die Units 1–7 mit den *Extra Material* auch anspruchsvolleren Lernstoff für Lernende mit fortgeschrittenen Englischkenntnissen. Neu an *Logistics Matters* ist auch der Bezug einzelner Übungen auf die KMK-Zertifikatsprüfung in Englisch, die in einigen Bundesländern auch für Kaufleute für Spedition und Logistikdienstleistung angeboten wird.

Logistics Matters enthält 8 Units, die jeweils wichtige Aspekte des Speditionsgeschäfts behandeln. Die Units sind in sich geschlossen, sodass sie in beliebiger Reihenfolge bearbeitet oder auch einzelne Units ausgelassen werden können. Dennoch wird empfohlen, die vorgegebene Reihenfolge einzuhalten, um einen kontinuierlichen Aufbau des Fachvokabulars zu gewährleisten.

Logistics Matters zielt in erster Linie darauf ab, Fertigkeiten der Kommunikation im Speditionswesen, besonders in der mündlichen Kommunikation, zu vermitteln. Dazu werden in fallstudienartigen Units an der Praxis orientierte Gesprächssituationen wie Telefonate und Direktgespräche zwischen englischsprachigen Kunden bzw. Geschäftspartnern und Speditionskaufleuten simuliert. Das nötige Fachvokabular und wichtige Redewendungen werden anhand von Übungen gefestigt, um sie später handlungs-

orientiert *(Role play)* anwenden zu können. Außerdem wird der Umgang mit englischsprachigen Dokumenten sowie das Lese- und Hörverständnis und das eigenständige Verfassen englischsprachiger Geschäftskorrespondenz – Brief, E-Mail, Formulare – geschult.

Dem Ziel des praxisorientierten Lernens entsprechen die verwendeten Textarten: authentische Geschäftskorrespondenz, Internet-Seiten und Zeitungsartikel. Das für die Praxis notwendige sprachliche Hintergrundwissen wird mit abwechslungsreichen Übungen vermittelt. Zu den vielfältigen Übungsformen gehören: *Information gap*, Rollenspiel, das Herausfiltern wichtiger Informationen aus Dokumenten und Broschüren, Wortschatzerweiterung und reines Hörverstehen. Die Texte dazu befinden sich auf der den Handreichungen für den Unterricht beigelegten CD-ROM.

Der Anhang enthält dazu zwei Wörterlisten, die das schnelle Auffinden von Vokabeln ermöglichen, Dokumente, eine Liste der Europäischen Länder, Informationen zu *business letters* sowie die Incoterms® 2010.

*Neu an dem vorliegenden Druck ist die zusätzliche Vorbereitung auf die KMK-Zertifikatsprüfung. Dies geschieht anhand von *KMK exam practice*-Seiten sowie einem *KMK mock exam* im Anhang des Buches. Sie können die Hörtexte zu den KMK-Hörverstehensaufgaben anhören, indem Sie den jeweiligen Webcode im Webcode-Suchfeld auf www.cornelsen.de/matters eingeben. Die Transkripte und Lösungen zu den KMK-Materialien sind als Download auf der Cornelsen-Webseite unter Logistics Matters zu finden.

💿	Dialog bzw. Text auf der Audio-CD (in den Handreichungen für den Unterricht)		
KMK	Prüfungsrelevante Übung	🖥️ www	Recherche im Internet
👥	Partnerarbeit	👥	Gruppenarbeit
BE	Britisches Englisch	AE	Amerikanisches Englisch

Table of contents

Working in logistics

1 | Lyreco logistics centre, Barsinghausen

Merlene Murphy, a trainee from Ireland, is doing an internship at Lyreco Deutschland GmbH, the central logistics centre for Germany. Before she arrives, she receives a site plan of the buildings so that she knows where to go on her first day.

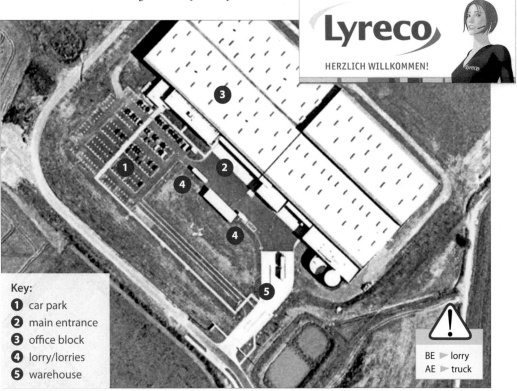

Key:
1. car park
2. main entrance
3. office block
4. lorry/lorries
5. warehouse

BE ▶ lorry
AE ▶ truck

 a **Work in a group and talk about the site plan. Look at the speech bubbles and useful terms and phrases box for help.**

> Where is the …?

> Can you see a/any/the …?

USEFUL TERMS AND PHRASES	Describing where things are
The … is/are …	opposite / in front of / behind the …
There is a/an …	beside / next to / near the …
There are (some) …	on the left/right-hand side of the …
I can see a/an/the …	to the left/right of the …
…	on the left/right.
	at the front/back of the …

b **Describe the building where you work with the help of photos and/or a site plan.**

2 Key figures

Merlene looks up some information about the company on its website.

⬈ Key Figures

Lyreco started in France as a small family-owned business in ...[1]. Since then we have grown into a major global operation and are active worldwide in the sale and delivery of office supplies. We have 10,000 employees in ...[2] countries and have four strategic alliances with forwarding agencies. We are one of the largest firms in Europe in this market sector.

Our central logistics centre for Germany is in Barsinghausen, a town near Hanover. It is not only one of the biggest logistics centres in the world, it is also one of the most modern and most technically advanced. This, together with its central position and access to an excellent transport system are guarantees of fast and efficient delivery to our customers. The logistics centre covers an area of 100,000 m², of which the warehouse alone takes up ...[3] m². It has 13,000 stocked articles, handles 4,000 consignments every hour and delivers ...[4] packages a month by van and lorry. The length of all the conveyor belts in the centre is ...[5] kilometres. We promise delivery within ...[6] hours of all orders placed before 5 p.m.

a   Use the numbers in the box below to complete the text.

> 1.7 • 24 • 29 • 1926 • 35,000 • 500,000

LANGUAGE   **Numbers and time**

In English we *write* ...		In English we *say* ...
numbers with commas:	230,000	two hundred and thirty thousand
decimals with dots:	1.7	one point seven
area:	... m²	... square metres
morning times:	a.m.	in the morning
afternoon/evening times:	p.m.	in the afternoon/evening
dates:	10 January 2010	the tenth of January two thousand and ten
years:	1948	nineteen forty-eight

b   Ask and answer questions with numbers using the information in the text.

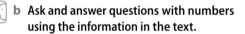

> How many people does Lyreco employ?

> Lyreco employs 10,000 people worldwide.

c Match the numbers (1–6) with the letters (a–f) to make terms associated with logistics. Then explain what each one is.

1 transport   a agency
2 conveyor   b article
3 market   c system
4 stocked   d centre
5 logistics   e belt
6 forwarding   f sector

REMEMBER   The simple present

1. Jane **goes** to work by bus every day.
2. I **work** here in the warehouse, but Danny **doesn't like** the noise.
3. He **has (got)** an interview for another job, but he **hasn't got / doesn't have** an appointment.
4. You **are** a warehouse packer. **Do** you **like** your job?

d Complete these sentences with the correct simple present form of the verbs in brackets.

1 Lyreco … *(not be)* a very old company. It was founded in 1926.
2 We … *(handle)* over 30,000 consignments every day.
3 … *(you / want)* your package delivered within 24 hours? Our company … *(guarantee)* fast and efficient delivery.
4 Our warehouse … *(cover)* an area of 35,000 m².
5 … *(Lyreco / employ)* people on other continents too?
6 Sharon … *(not have)* an identification number for this customer.

e **PRESENTATION: Introduce your firm. Say where it is and what it does, and present some key figures.**

See appendix, p. 101, for more tips on how to give a presentation.

3 About Lyreco

On Merlene Murphy's first day of her eight-week internship at Lyreco Deutschland GmbH, Jan Baumgarten, the Logistics Director, gives her some information about Lyreco.

eight-week internship NOT eight-week̶ internship

Jan   Good morning. You must be Ms Murphy. Nice to meet you. My name is Jan Baumgarten. I'm the Logistics Director of this branch of Lyreco.
Merlene Good morning. Pleased to meet you.
Jan   I'm glad to see you got here all right. Is this the first time you've been to Germany?
Merlene No, I was in Berlin on a school trip a few years ago, but it's my first time in Barsinghausen. It's a bit different, but I like it here.
Jan   I'm pleased to hear that. Right. Shall we get started? First of all, I'll tell you a bit about logistics in general and then I'll move on to what we do here. Oh, would you like a cup of tea or coffee?
Merlene No, thank you. I'm fine for the moment, thanks.

Jan	Right. Well, I think any definition of logistics must include three things: information, communication and therefore, of course, people. People are necessary for the transport of goods, but if they don't have all the information they need to organize things, they will make mistakes and things will go wrong. My professor at university always liked to quote an example from the Crimean War. The chief quartermaster for the army – we would now call him the Logistics Director, like me – decided to divide up and send the army supplies with different ships, so if one ship sank, not everything would be lost.

goods is always in the plural

Merlene	That sounds sensible enough to me.
Jan	Yes, but nobody told the clerks – the account operatives – the reason for the change. So, no communication. So they told the 'producers' to split the consignments into separate deliveries and the 'warehouse workers' to load these deliveries onto different ships.
Merlene	Ahh, I can see what's coming!
Jan	Exactly. When the soldiers unloaded the supplies they found the boxes of warm winter boots contained only boots for the right foot. The boots for the left foot were on another ship! It was a complete disaster! So that's why people and communication are so important for logistics. I'll take you round after lunch to meet some of the important people here at Lyreco.
Merlene	Great. So what does Lyreco do specifically?
Jan	Well, Lyreco specializes in stationery, and here in the logistics centre, we're responsible for the storage, packing and delivery of the products. We have a mixture of clients – in both the commercial and public sectors.
Merlene	So you're not a freight forwarder in the classic sense?
Jan	I'm sorry, I don't know what you mean by 'classic sense'.
Merlene	I mean, you don't store and forward goods for other people, do you?
Jan	No.
Merlene	Do you use all forms of transport to deliver the goods?
Jan	Well, it depends on what has to be delivered, but because 99.9% of our business is national, i.e. within Germany, we mainly deal with road freight. We've no real need for rail, air or sea freight because we have branches in 29 countries around the world.
Merlene	I see. How many people work here in the Barsinghausen logistics centre?
Jan	At the moment we have 80 employees who deal with basic administration, 135 warehouse staff and 10 drivers. The administrative staff are split up into different departments. In the course of the next eight weeks you'll have the chance to work in each department to get to know them and the people that work there a bit better. And, like I said, I'll give you a tour after lunch.
Merlene	Thanks, Mr Baumgarten. I'm looking forward to it.
Jan	To lunch or to the tour? I wouldn't get too excited about the canteen food!

a **Listen to the CD and say whether the following sentences are true or false. Correct the false sentences.**

1 Jan Baumgarten is the Warehouse Manager.
2 Merlene Murphy has never been to Germany before.
3 Jan says that the three things essential for logistics are information, communication and understanding.
4 Lyreco has branches in 28 other countries.
5 Merlene is on a ten-week internship.

b **Use the cartoon above to explain why communication is so important for logistics.**

c **Find words or phrases from the dialogue which fit the following definitions.**

1 The movement of people or goods from one place to another.
2 A building where goods are stored.
3 To remove things from a vehicle or ship.
4 People who work in an office and deal with customer records.
5 A section of a large business.

d **Make nouns from the verbs below. They are all in the dialogue. Then use the nouns in a sentence.**

communicate • consign • deliver • inform • pack • store • transport

KMK **e** **Complete the following chart with information from the dialogue. Then make a similar information chart for your company.**

Lyreco Deutschland GmbH	
Services	*storage, …*
Customers	…
National / International business	…% …%
Forms of transport	…
Employees	…

4 Organization of the company

After lunch Jan Baumgarten shows Merlene around the different departments.

a Listen to the CD and say what is wrong with the plan of the building.

3

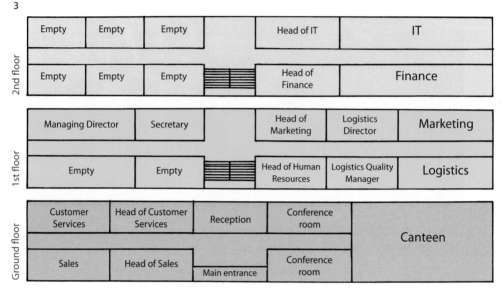

Empty	Empty	Empty		Head of IT	IT

2nd floor

Empty	Empty	Empty		Head of Finance	Finance

Managing Director	Secretary		Head of Marketing	Logistics Director	Marketing

1st floor

Empty	Empty		Head of Human Resources	Logistics Quality Manager	Logistics

Customer Services	Head of Customer Services	Reception	Conference room	Canteen

Ground floor

Sales	Head of Sales	Main entrance	Conference room

b Listen again. Then copy and complete the following organizational chart of Lyreco Deutschland GmbH.

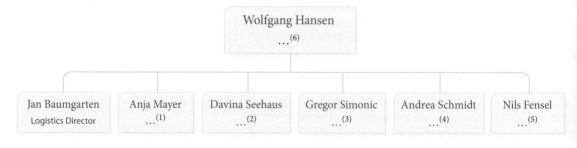

Wolfgang Hansen
…(6)

Jan Baumgarten	Anja Mayer	Davina Seehaus	Gregor Simonic	Andrea Schmidt	Nils Fensel
Logistics Director	…(1)	…(2)	…(3)	…(4)	…(5)

c Which two departments mentioned in the dialogue are missing from the chart?

d Sketch a simple organizational chart of your company.

e PRESENTATION: Use your chart to explain the organization of your company. Say which departments you have already worked in and what you were responsible for.

5 | Introducing yourself

When you meet somebody for the first time, it is important to introduce yourself properly if you want to make a good impression.

USEFUL TERMS AND PHRASES   **Introducing yourself**

Introducing yourself	**Responding to introductions**
Good morning/afternoon/evening.	Nice/Good/Pleased to meet you (too).
Hi/Hello.	It's a pleasure to meet you (too).
My name is / I'm …	Hello. I think we've met before. /
I work in the … department.	Haven't we met before?
Where do you work? / What do you do?	

a **Work with a partner and act out the dialogue. Look at the useful terms and phrases box for help.**

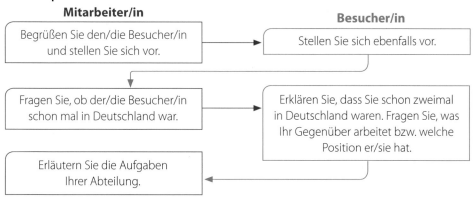

        Mitarbeiter/in   **Besucher/in**

- Begrüßen Sie den/die Besucher/in und stellen Sie sich vor.
- Stellen Sie sich ebenfalls vor.
- Fragen Sie, ob der/die Besucher/in schon mal in Deutschland war.
- Erklären Sie, dass Sie schon zweimal in Deutschland waren. Fragen Sie, was Ihr Gegenüber arbeitet bzw. welche Position er/sie hat.
- Erläutern Sie die Aufgaben Ihrer Abteilung.

b **Read the culture box below. Then put the following words in the order you think they belong in the colour spectrum – from 'very safe' to 'unsafe' topics.**

family • money • politics • sport • travel • work

CULTURE   **Small talk**

very safe topics						**unsafe topics**
weather	…¹ …²	…³	…⁴	…⁵	…⁶	religion

Do: • use short forms; long forms sound much too formal.
           • use your partner's name now and again – it makes things more personal.

Don't: • be bossy! Always be polite.

        ~~We'll sit here.~~ ✗   Would you like to sit here? ✓
        ~~Don't order the steak.~~ ✗   I wouldn't order the steak if I were you. ✓

c **Work with a partner and role-play the dialogue again with small-talk ideas of your own. Remember to avoid the 'unsafe' small-talk topics!**

6 Jobs at Lyreco

Andrea Schmidt gives Merlene a copy of the company newsletter. In it, there are interviews with two employees from overseas branches of Lyreco.

a Complete the interviews with either the correct simple present or present progressive form of the verbs in brackets.

REMEMBER **The present progressive**

1. I **am talking** to some of our drivers; they **are** all **loading** their lorries.
2. I'**m not working** in that department today because the conveyor belts **aren't operating** properly at the moment.
3. **Am** I **speaking** to Ms Moore's assistant?
4. **Is** Mr Jones **dealing with** this order?
5. We'**re giving** a presentation at the meeting *next Thursday.* (future plan + time)

LyroNews | **INTERNATIONAL** | Issue 46

Alex Davidson Lyreco, Australia

Q: What ...[1] *(you / do)* **in your Job?**

A: My colleagues and I ...[2] *(be)* responsible for maintaining customer records. I often ...[3] *(take)* telephone and written orders from customers and then ...[4] *(send)* the consignment note to the warehouse. Sometimes my colleague ...[5] *(do)* this while I ...[6] *(deal with)* customers' queries and complaints by phone, fax or online. That's what I ...[7] *(do)* today – I ...[8] *(handle)* complaints. Most of the time customers ...[9] *(wait for)* a delivery which is delayed or sometimes they ...[10] *(receive)* the wrong item. So today my colleague and I ...[11] *(track and trace)* all the delayed deliveries to find out when they'll arrive.

Amanda Reid Lyreco, Canada

Q: What ...[12] *(your job / involve)*?

A: First of all, I ...[13] *(read)* the packing list to know what to put in the box. Our packing machine then ...[14] *(sort)* the bigger items into boxes. It ...[15] *(be)* a nightmare when the machine ...[16] *(not work)*. We ...[17] *(pack)* smaller items by hand.

Right now these machines ...[18] *(do)* different things. This one ...[19] *(measure)* the amount of empty space between the products so that the boxes can be cut to the optimal size to fit the products. The big black machine ...[20] *(seal)* the full boxes and the smaller machine over there ...[21] *(label)* them so that it ...[22] *(be)* clear what they ...[23] *(contain)*.

b What are the jobs described in the newsletter?

 c Work with a partner. Describe Alex and Amanda's jobs to one another.

d Put these words in the correct order to make sentences about other jobs in a logistics company.

1 arrange / will / vehicles / Transport clerks / be used / which / the / drivers / and / possible / plan / and / cheapest / route.
2 existing / look after / and / customers / new / Sales advisers / acquire / ones.
3 sends out / the / The / bookkeeping. / Finance Department / and / does / invoices

e Interview three of your colleagues about the jobs they do.

f **PRESENTATION: Now put together all the information you have gathered in this unit (site plan, key figures, information chart, organizational chart and information about your colleagues). Then give a presentation on your company. Remember to introduce yourself properly.**

7 The supply chain

There are often many links in the supply chain from the production to the delivery of a consignment, involving many different people, forms of transport and documentation.

Use the flow chart below to describe the roles of the different people and companies involved in the supply chain.

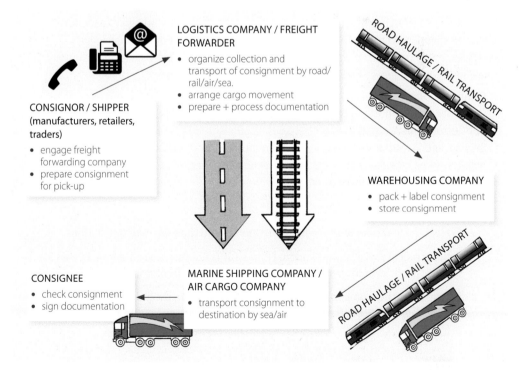

LOGISTICS COMPANY / FREIGHT FORWARDER
• organize collection and transport of consignment by road/rail/air/sea.
• arrange cargo movement
• prepare + process documentation

ROAD HAULAGE / RAIL TRANSPORT

CONSIGNOR / SHIPPER (manufacturers, retailers, traders)
• engage freight forwarding company
• prepare consignment for pick-up

WAREHOUSING COMPANY
• pack + label consignment
• store consignment

CONSIGNEE
• check consignment
• sign documentation

MARINE SHIPPING COMPANY / AIR CARGO COMPANY
• transport consignment to destination by sea/air

ROAD HAULAGE / RAIL TRANSPORT

8 Training and qualifications

Lyreco also offers both on-the-job and off-the-job training courses to make sure that all its staff have the best qualifications.

HOME | SERVICE | KEY FIGURES | PRODUCTS | SITEMAP | TRAINING | CALLBACK

↘ Training and qualifications

Development routes

As part of their development, people receive off-the-job training, the length of which depends on their job. For example, our drivers have three days and our corporate account sales managers have 19 days extending over 16 weeks. Each of the main operational areas has a dedicated trainer from within the training team who is CIPD (Chartered Institute of Personnel and Development) qualified. As part of off-the-job training, many people use e-learning for their development.

5

10

Back in the workplace, people receive on-the-job training. In the sectors Warehouse, Distribution and Marketing this is done formally as people work their way through their key task-training plans. We also have a Personal Development Programme. This is for non-people managers and it covers a range of short courses and distance-learning courses. If we think somebody could become a future leader, we offer them modules from our Leadership Development Programme. This covers key people-management modules such as recruitment, motivation, coaching, performance appraisal and team building. It all helps to ensure we have talented leaders building high-performance teams.

15

Qualifications

20

People have the opportunity to study for qualifications relevant to their area of expertise. Our Customer Service people complete qualifications through the Institute of Customer Service, and Lyreco is also a registered centre for ICS (International Correspondence Schools) qualifications. In Finance, Personnel and Logistics, employees study for professional qualifications sponsored by the company.

a **Explain the meaning of the highlighted terms. Find their German translations.**

 b **Ihr Chef möchte wissen, was andere Firmen für Trainingskurse anbieten. Fassen Sie die wichtigsten Informationen von der Website für ihn auf Deutsch zusammen.**

c **Do you know any companies which offer similar training programmes and qualifications? Write a 'Training and Qualifications' page in English for their website.**

Transport within Europe

1 | Getting to know Europe

A large majority of consignments transported from Germany by road or rail have European destinations. It is therefore important to know the names of the European countries and where they are.

USEFUL VOCABULARY   **Some European countries**

Austria	Denmark	Ireland	Poland	Switzerland
Belarus	Estonia	Italy	Romania	The Netherlands
Belgium	Finland	Latvia	Russia	Turkey
Croatia	Greece	Lithuania	Slovakia	UK
	Hungary	Norway	Spain	Ukraine

▼ See appendix, p.150, for a full list of European countries.

~~The~~ Turkey
~~The~~ Switzerland

 a Ask and answer questions about the map of Europe. Look at the speech bubbles and useful vocabulary box for help.

> Where's …?

> It's beside / between …

> It's north / south / east / west of …

> What are …'s neighbours?

b Name the member states of the EU.

c Identify these international vehicle signs.

2   Road freight vehicles

Ted Nugent is the Freight Manager of a road haulage company in Sunderland, in the north of England. He shows Brian Hadley, a new apprentice, photos of the vehicles that they use.

a   Listen to the CD and put the photos in the order that they are described.

4

b   Copy this table into your exercise book. Then listen to the CD again and complete the table. Look at the useful vocabulary box below for help.

Vehicle	Description
A ...	...
B ...	...

USEFUL VOCABULARY   **Vehicles and equipment**

articulated lorry • bulk loader • container • curtain-sided trailer / tautliner • delivery van • low loader • side loader • tarpaulin

⚠

c   Add a third column to your table: 'Freight'. With a partner, decide which vehicle(s) you could use to transport the following cargoes.

cargo – cargoes

books • construction machinery • gravel • plastic drainage pipes • sand • scrap metal • steel pipes • timber • a tractor

3 | Rail freight vehicles

For long distances, it is often more convenient and quicker to transport freight by rail. The photos below show different types of rail freight vehicles that can be used depending on the size, weight and nature of the freight.

a **Match the names below (1–6) to the photos of the rail rolling stock above (A–F).**

1 bulk wagon	3 flat car	5 (live)stock car
2 car transporter	4 hopper wagon	6 tank wagon

b **Find out about each type of rail rolling stock and its freight. Then write a short text about them. Look at the useful vocabulary box for help.**

USEFUL VOCABULARY   **Types of freight**

bulldozers • cement • coal • electrical equipment • livestock • milk • petrol • railway sleepers • scrap metal • timber • wind turbines • wire cable

Examples: *You can use a tank wagon to transport …*
A bulk wagon can be used to transport … or …

c **PRESENTATION: Which of the road and rail freight vehicles does your company use? Present them to the class either in a PowerPoint presentation or on a poster.**

4 Dealing with an order

Rick Fenton, Customer Services Manager of Mitre Woodcrafts Ltd in England, receives an order from Davina Seehaus, Head of Sales at Lyreco Deutschland GmbH. She wants to include the items in Lyreco's next catalogue. Rick has to attend a conference, so he leaves a note on his colleague Nicola Watson's desk.

Could you please arrange shipment of the above items of furniture to our logistics centre in Barsinghausen? Our guarantee of a 24-hour delivery service means that the products must be available when our new catalogue goes online on 20 May, so I would appreciate it if you could have the consignment delivered by 10.00 a.m. on Friday, 17 May at the latest.

Best regards,
Davina Seehaus

LYRECO | Head of Sales
Lyreco-Straße 4 – 30890 Barsinghausen
Tel: +49 (0) 546 789 098
Fax: +49 (0) 546 789 099
Email: davina–seehaus@lyreco.de

Nicola,
Can you deal with this order for me, please? I think Fast Freight Haulage has delivered to Lyreco before and they're very reliable, so you could try them first. Contact Sheena Hunt for a quote; you'll find her phone number in the system.
Thanks, Rick

a What is the most important information given in Davina's email?

b Why does Rick want Nicola to contact Fast Freight Haulage first?

LANGUAGE   Referring to firms and companies

As you can see from Rick's note above, when we refer to a company, we often use the singular. When we refer to the people in the company and what they do, we often use the plural.

*Fast Freight Haulage **has** delivered to Lyreco before. **They're** very reliable.*
*Lyreco **promises** delivery within 24 hours. **We are** customer-orientated.*

c **Complete the information about Fast Freight Haulage using the words below.**

> consignments • division • equipment • haulage • identifies • needs •
> online • packaging • paperwork • priority • services • track

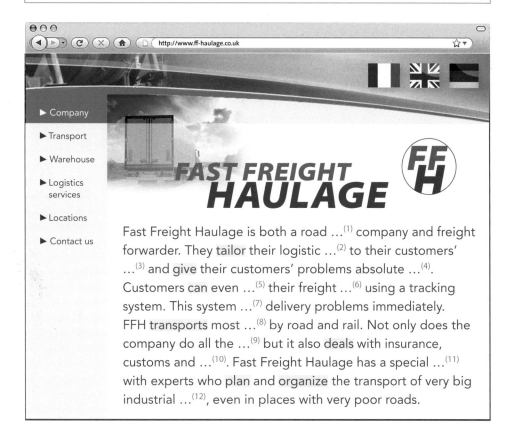

Fast Freight Haulage is both a road ...[1] company and freight forwarder. They tailor their logistic ...[2] to their customers' ...[3] and give their customers' problems absolute ...[4]. Customers can even ...[5] their freight ...[6] using a tracking system. This system ...[7] delivery problems immediately. FFH transports most ...[8] by road and rail. Not only does the company do all the ...[9] but it also deals with insurance, customs and ...[10]. Fast Freight Haulage has a special ...[11] with experts who plan and organize the transport of very big industrial ...[12], even in places with very poor roads.

Navigation on the website:
► Company
► Transport
► Warehouse
► Logistics services
► Locations
► Contact us

d **Explain the difference between a haulage company and a freight forwarding company.**

REMEMBER	Active and passive forms in the simple present

Active	Passive
1. People **say** the firm is reliable.	The firm **is said** to be reliable.
2. The consignee **pays** the insurance.	The insurance **is paid** by the consignee.
3. FFH **handles** our consignments.	Our consignments **are handled** by FFH.
4. **Does** the system **track** all cargo?	**Is** all cargo **tracked** (by the system)?

e **Change the highlighted (active) verbs in part c into passive verbs. Write full sentences.**

Example: *Fast Freight Haulage's logistics services **are tailored** to its customers' needs.*

5 Getting a quote

Nicola calls Sheena Hunt at Fast Freight Haulage, gives her the details of the freight and asks for a quote.

a Listen to the CD and say whether the following statements are true or false. Correct the false sentences.

1 Nicola phones Fast Freight Haulage in the afternoon.
2 Sheena Hunt answers the phone.
3 Sheena knows Rick Fenton.
4 The consignment includes thirty conference chairs.
5 The total weight does not include packaging.

b Sheena takes notes during the phone call. Listen again and complete her notes in your exercise book.

...(1):	100 items of furniture altogether
Total volume:	...(2)
...(3):	6.4 tonnes
Pick-up point:	...(4)
Delivery date + time:	...(5)
...(6):	Lyreco-Straße 4, 30890 Barsinghausen
Freight term:	...(7)
Email:	...(8)

> ⚠ items of furniture NOT furnitures ✗

> See appendix, p. 98, for the Incoterms® rules 2010.

c What does the freight term 'DDP' mean?

d Work with a partner. Practise spelling your email addresses and contact details. Look at the language box below for help.

LANGUAGE   **Names, phone numbers and symbols**

Spelling names:
- The first time you spell your name over the phone, spell it as you normally would: B-R-A-D-L-E-Y.
- If something needs clarifying, you can use the international alphabet: *That's Bravo, Romeo, Alpha, …*
- However, people quite often avoid using the international alphabet and instead use any word beginning with the letter in question: *That's 'B for ball', 'R for rabbit', 'A for apple', …*

Reading out phone numbers:
- Read out phone numbers as individual digits and not as numbers: 051778 = oh (zero/nought), five, one, seven, seven (double seven), eight.

Saying symbols in email addresses:
- For these symbols in email addresses you say: / = forward slash, @ = at, - = hyphen, . = dot, _ = underscore

> See the **language** box on p. 40 for the full international alphabet.

USEFUL TERMS AND PHRASES   Telephoning

Making a phone call
Hello, this is … / it's … from (company) here.
Could I speak to … / the head of the … department, please?
Could you put me through to the … department, please?

When the person is not available
I'm sorry I missed him/her. Could you give him/her a message, please?
Would you mind asking him/her to call me back, please?

Receiving a phone call
Hello. This is … speaking. How may I help you?
Please hold the line and I'll put you through.
I'm afraid … isn't available at the moment. Can I take a message?
Can you give me your name and number, please? I'll ask … to call you back as soon as he/she returns.
I'm sorry. I didn't understand that. Could you repeat that, please?

 e Nicola asks you to call John Shanks at Thompson's Haulage to get a quote for comparison. Use your notes from part **b** to role-play the phone call with a partner. Use the language box and the useful terms and phrases box above for help.

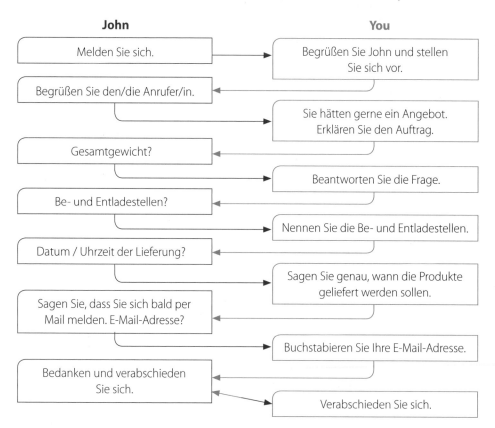

John	You
Melden Sie sich.	Begrüßen Sie John und stellen Sie sich vor.
Begrüßen Sie den/die Anrufer/in.	Sie hätten gerne ein Angebot. Erklären Sie den Auftrag.
Gesamtgewicht?	Beantworten Sie die Frage.
Be- und Entladestellen?	Nennen Sie die Be- und Entladestellen.
Datum / Uhrzeit der Lieferung?	Sagen Sie genau, wann die Produkte geliefert werden sollen.
Sagen Sie, dass Sie sich bald per Mail melden. E-Mail-Adresse?	Buchstabieren Sie Ihre E-Mail-Adresse.
Bedanken und verabschieden Sie sich.	Verabschieden Sie sich.

6 Making an offer

Nicola receives this email from Sheena.

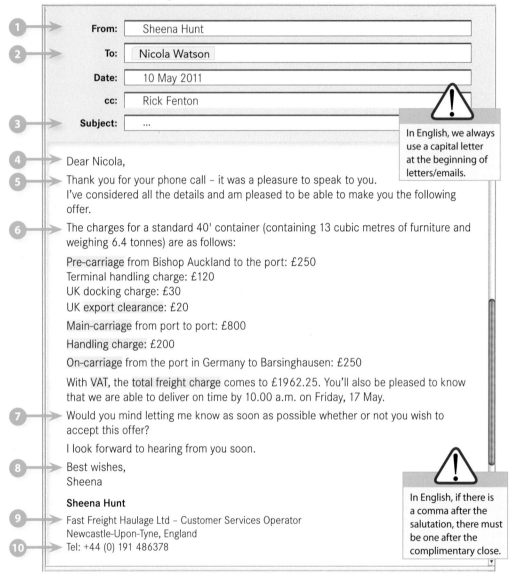

From: Sheena Hunt

To: Nicola Watson

Date: 10 May 2011

cc: Rick Fenton

Subject: ...

⚠️ In English, we always use a capital letter at the beginning of letters/emails.

Dear Nicola,

Thank you for your phone call – it was a pleasure to speak to you. I've considered all the details and am pleased to be able to make you the following offer.

The charges for a standard 40' container (containing 13 cubic metres of furniture and weighing 6.4 tonnes) are as follows:

Pre-carriage from Bishop Auckland to the port: £250
Terminal handling charge: £120
UK docking charge: £30
UK export clearance: £20

Main-carriage from port to port: £800

Handling charge: £200

On-carriage from the port in Germany to Barsinghausen: £250

With VAT, the total freight charge comes to £1962.25. You'll also be pleased to know that we are able to deliver on time by 10.00 a.m. on Friday, 17 May.

Would you mind letting me know as soon as possible whether or not you wish to accept this offer?

I look forward to hearing from you soon.

Best wishes,
Sheena

Sheena Hunt

Fast Freight Haulage Ltd – Customer Services Operator
Newcastle-Upon-Tyne, England
Tel: +44 (0) 191 486378

⚠️ In English, if there is a comma after the salutation, there must be one after the complimentary close.

a Identify the following parts of the email.

> closing paragraph • complimentary close • contact details of sender •
> salutation • introduction • main body of mail • name of sender • name of
> sender's firm and position • subject line • recipient

b Think of a suitable subject line for Sheena's mail.

c Explain the highlighted terms.

CULTURE **Corporate politeness**

- In British and US firms, the use of first names among colleagues – including those higher in rank – is normal, even if you've never met before.
- The British regard orders as rude. They prefer polite requests:
  Could you place that order today, please?
  Would you mind sending me the details?
- And when they can't do something, they start with:
  I'm extremely sorry, but I'm afraid I won't be able to …

d Find the polite language in Sheena's email to Nicola.

e Thompson's Haulage cannot deliver on time, so Nicola accepts Sheena's offer. Write an email to Sheena a) confirming the order and b) asking her about the route she plans to use. Look at the culture and useful terms and phrases box for help.

USEFUL TERMS AND PHRASES **Giving confirmation**

Thank you for your offer/email/fax/call/… dated (date).
I would like / I am pleased to accept …
This is to confirm that I accept … under the conditions mentioned.

7 Planning the route

a **PRESENTATION:** What factors and possible problems should you consider when planning a route? With a partner, draw a mind map. Then present your findings to the class.

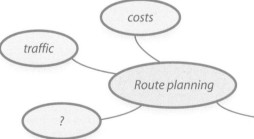

costs

traffic

Route planning

?

b Work in a group and organize the transport of the shipment. The following tasks will help you to structure your project.

1 Find a map showing Gent Road in Bishop Auckland.
2 Work out the most direct route from Gent Road to the nearest port.
3 Choose a ferry route to continental Europe.
4 Look at a map of Germany and choose a route from the port of discharge to Lyreco Deutschland GmbH in Barsinghausen.

c You find out that the ferry staff at your chosen port in the UK are currently on strike. Plan an alternative route for the consignment.

8 Delivering the consignment

On arrival in Barsinghausen the driver gives the consignee a copy of this document.

SENDER (Name and address)		**FAST FREIGHT HAULAGE LTD**		**CMR**
(1)		256 York Lane South Shieldfield Newcastle-Upon-Tyne NE2 A91 **FFH**		**TRIP NO.** 6734 **REF NO.** CB91648
CONSIGNEE (Name and address) (2)		CARRIER (IF DIFFERENT)		
DELIVERY ADDRESS (3)		CARRIER'S REMARKS DELIVERY BY 17 MAY AT 10.00 a.m.		
TRANSPORT MODE	PORT OF LOADING (4)	PORT OF DISCHARGE (5)		
VESSEL	SHIPMENT DATE (6)	SERVICE ROUTE NORTH GERMANY		
DESCRIPTION OF GOODS (7)		WEIGHT (KGS) 8,900.00	VOLUME (CU. FT) (8)	VALUE (£)
TOTALS				
CARRIAGE PAYMENT DETAILS prepaid		Goods Taken Over By Carrier (Sign and date)		
C.O.D. COLLECTION DETAILS		Goods received in Good Condition by Consignee (Sign and date) *Kartla*		

a What is this document called and what is it used for?

b Use the case study on pages 20–25 and the ports you chose in your project (exercise 7b) to complete the document (1–8).

c Which piece of information already given is incorrect?

9 │ Rail transport

KMK **First read the article from the Kuehne + Nagel magazine and then summarize it for a German colleague.**

When rails travel by rail

Railway lines have to be transported to the place where they are laid. For long distances there is only one way of doing this: by rail.

A round-trip time of only two weeks is the service that Kuehne + Nagel offered ThyssenKrupp Verkehr GmbH for the transport of the 120-metre-long rails from the German production plant in Oberhausen to the construction site in Finland and back. The rails were for the Kerava-Lahti line in Finland, where they were laid directly on the sleepers without intermediate storage.

24 six-wagon units, each containing 36 rails, were transported to Finland between June and September. Placed end to end, this corresponds to a track length of roughly 55 km. But before the first rail could be fixed in place, extensive and detailed logistical preparations were needed.

The wagon groups (roughly 140 metres long) were loaded at the steelworks in Oberhausen. Care had to be taken to place the rails in the correct position so the train could be unloaded at the construction site along the new section of track. [...] A maximum of 2.5 days was planned to unload the train, meaning that an average of 1.5 rails were laid per hour. [...]

From the production plant in Oberhausen, the railway wagons were taken to the ferry port of Lübeck-Skandinavienkai. Here the indivisible wagon group was shunted onto a special railway ferry and shipped to the Finnish port of Turku/Pansio. On arrival at the ferry port of Turku, the wagon

combination was moved onto the Finnish rail gauge on a state-of-the-art axle-changing facility within an hour, which meant that the freight itself didn't have to be unloaded and then reloaded back onto the wagons. Overnight the rails then travelled to their destination, where they were shifted off the wagons at the construction site using a so-called ESKO rail pusher. The empty wagon combination then returned to Germany by the fastest route in order to pick up more rails and return in accordance with the schedule.

(Adapted from: *World Magazine* No. 2/2005 © Kuehne + Nagel)

Maritime transport

1 | Global sea ports and shipping routes

The map below shows the world's shipping routes mapped out over the period of one year using GPS.

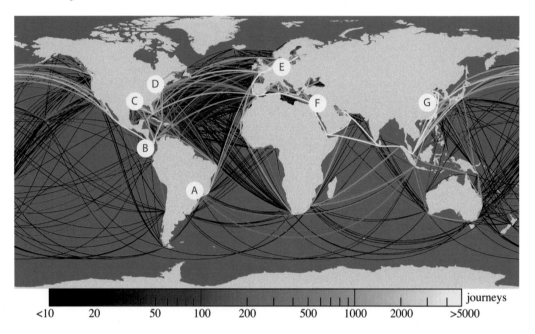

									journeys
<10	20	50	100	200	500	1000	2000	>5000	

a Identify the seven sea ports and shipping routes on the map (A–G) using the names in the box.

> Hamburg • Houston • New York • Panama Canal • Santos • Shanghai • Suez Canal

b Does your company offer sea freight? If so, which ports do you use most often?

c What percentage of world trade is transported by sea: 50%, 70%, 90%?

d List the advantages and disadvantages of transporting consignments by sea.

Advantages	Disadvantages
...	...
...	...

2 | Ships and cargoes

Although the amount of air freight has increased over the past 30 years, transporting goods by sea is often still the cheapest method of transport.

a Match the photos (A–F) with the explanations (1–6) below.

1 Roll-on/roll-off ships are specially designed to transport cars and lorries and are loaded via a stern ramp.

2 Container ships have big, flat decks so that they can hold large numbers of containers.

3 General cargo ships (tramps) carry freight that cannot be carried in a container. Most of this is stored in holds below the deck.

4 Heavy-lift ships have deck cranes for loading and unloading very heavy freight.

5 Bulk carriers are used to transport grains, coal, ore and cement.

6 Sea-going barges can transport very large, heavy objects, like other ships, which are either floated onto the low, flat deck or are lifted aboard using large cranes.

b Work with a partner. Which of the ships above would you choose to transport the following cargoes? Explain why.

sacks of peanuts · wheat · textile machines in crates ·
olive oil in drums · a windmill · a yacht · waste paper · fertilizer ·
scotch whisky in barrels · double-decker buses

3 Containerization

Containerization has changed the face of freight forwarding. In the past, freight consignments were loaded individually in a variety of different forms of packaging, whereas today, most freight is shipped in containers.

 a **Work with a partner and rearrange the following 11 sentences (A–K) to make a text about containerization. The first sentence has been done for you.**

An intermodal container is a strong metal box used for the transport of freight by ship, road and rail. The system which bears its name,

A   container ships, which are designed to carry as many containers as possible.

B   the containerization system, was developed from the 8-foot metal transport cubes used by the US army during World War II. Following on from this,

C   Today about 90% of international freight is transported in containers and as a result

D   the height can vary – the most common is 8.6 feet. A typical

E   measurements are set by the International Standards Organization (ISO) and their capacity is measured in TEU (Twenty-foot Equivalent Unit) which is

F   there are now about 20 million containers in use worldwide. Their

G   The most common standard lengths in feet for international containers are 20', 40' and, in the USA, 30', but while the length is standardized,

H   container is made from corrugated steel with double doors at one end. They are sealed for complete security, offering greater protection against damage and loss and are transported on

I   the space taken up by a standard intermodal container 20 feet long and 8 feet wide.

J   1951 that the first specialized container ships were built.

K   in 1946, many surplus oil tankers were converted into container ships but it wasn't until

LANGUAGE   Measurements and weights

Imperial measurements are often still used alongside metric measurements in English-speaking countries:
one inch = 2.54 cm
one foot (1 ft / 1') = twelve inches (12 ins / 12'') = 30.48 cm

Length, width and height:
- A twenty-foot container is twenty feet long, eight feet wide and eight feet six inches high. – It's 20' by 8' by 8' 6''.
- A forty-foot container is forty feet long, eight feet wide and eight feet six inches high. – It's 40' by 8' by 8' 6''.

Area is usually measured in square metres (sqm/m²): *The warehouse is 500 m².*
Capacity is usually measured in cubic metres (cbm/m³):
The container has a capacity of 50 m³.

tare weight	= *Taragewicht*	gross weight	= *Bruttogewicht*
payload	= *Ladegewicht*	net weight	= *Nettogewicht*

b Why do you think it is important to have ISO standards?

c Write a short text discussing the advantages of containerization. Consider the following.

> delivery time • freight costs • insurance • protection • reliability •
> security • theft • (un)loading

d Identify the different types of container in these photos using the names in the box.

> bulk container • flat rack container • reefer •
> standard container • tank container

e **Answer these questions about the container below. Use the language box on page 31 for help.**

1   What are its external measurements?
2   What are its internal measurements?
3   What is its tare weight?
4   If the goods weigh 29,000 kg, what will its gross weight be?
5   Which size of container would be required for an industrial machine with the measurements 2.4m x 2.5m x 10m.

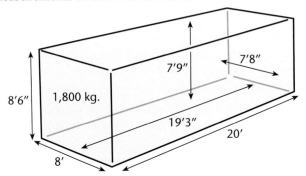

f   **PRESENTATION: Research the characteristics and dimensions of each of the containers in part d and state what types of freight they can be used for. Then add this information to your text from part c and present the topic 'containerization' to the class.**

4 | LCL and FCL

The advantages of shipping consignments by container are reduced when the consignment doesn't make a Full Container Load (FCL). Costs increase significantly when there is a Less than Container Load (LCL). This article explains how LCL consignments can be made more economical.

Our Multi Country Consolidation (MCC) services in the LCL sector have proven very successful. Consignments from different consignors are delivered to a central distribution station (a 'hub'), where they are sorted according to their destinations. The freight is then stuffed into groupage containers and shipped to the port of destination.

After on-carriage to an inland receiving station, the forwarder strips the groupage container and breaks bulk. The goods are then delivered to their respective consignees. This system has reduced the number of times the individual consignments are transloaded and has minimized the risk of damage. With the help of this system, we have shortened transit times and have cut costs significantly.

a   **Explain the highlighted terms.**

b   **Find words and phrases in the text with similar meanings to the words below.**

area • shipment • to load • to unload • danger • breakage • considerably

c Read the text again and explain in your own words how MCC services work. The following diagram and the vocabulary in part b may help you.

Transport by freight forwarder

HUB

GROUPED CARGO (ON-CARRIAGE)

INLAND RECEIVING STATION

Delivery to final destination / consignee

Consignment stuffed

Break bulk

REMEMBER   **The present perfect**

1. I**'ve called** five times since yesterday.
2. The shipper **has given** us a list.
3. **Have** you **sent** them a reminder yet?
4. What **has happened** to the cargo?
5. They **haven't made** any progress for about a year.

I've been in Berlin ~~since~~ *for* 3 weeks.

d Use the table below to make sentences in the present perfect. You may or may not need the signal words in the fourth column.

I	read	profitable for insurance companies	already
you	write	the volume of sea freight	already?
business	not be	ferry services a lot	before
everybody	increase	dramatically	over the last few years
this transport system	fill in	a bill of lading	recently
severe storms	interrupt	in popularity	since 2000
pirate attacks on this sea route	not affect	the email to the forwarder	yet
cheaper airfreight rates	fall	the details of the insurance contract	yet?

5 A very big contract

The German forwarding agency WWLog, which has branches worldwide, won a contract for the shipment of five evaporators for a paper mill from Portland in the USA to Santa Cruz de la Sierra in Bolivia. Leon Jagger, the Project Manager in Santiago travelled to Portland months in advance to inspect the facilities at the production site and the shipping possibilities from there to Santa Cruz de la Sierra.

6

a **Leon Jagger and Paul Becker, Head of WWLog's Global Projects Division in Berlin, set up a video conference. Listen to their conversation and then answer the questions below.**

1 What do you think Paul is showing Leon?
2 Copy and complete this table.

	Dimensions (m); (l x w x h)	Weight (tonnes)
Large evaporators	…	…
Small evaporators	…	…

b Now listen to the rest of the conversation and answer the following questions.

7

1 How does the team plan to transport the evaporators from the factory to the Portland docks?
2 Why will Leon Jagger need a heavy-lift ship at the Portland docks?
3 Say what the remaining problem is and how it can be solved.

c Write an email from Paul Becker to Mr Moore, Chief Executive Officer (CEO) of the American construction firm, asking him for an exact shipment date.

d Complete the text about the next part of the journey to Arica using the words below.

> barges · cranes · docks · flatbed trailers · ocean vessel ·
> paper mill · voyage

Everything went according to plan. The factory completed the second batch of the … (1) evaporators in the last week of May. Just one week later, all five evaporators together with their components were loaded onto …(2) and tugged down the river to the …(3) in Portland. The …(4) MS Adventure had arrived the day before and was waiting at the dockside. It was equipped with two heavy-duty dock …(5) for lifting the cargo. The total weight of the cargo including extra equipment was more than 300 tonnes. The …(6) to Arica in Chile was smooth and uneventful. The five evaporators were lifted onto five …(7) – three with eighteen axles and the other two with twenty-four axles.

6 A hold-up

As soon as Leon Jagger arrives at the docks in Arica, he gets a call from Santiago.

 a Use the sentences (a–f) opposite to complete Leon's part in the conversation.

Leon   …
Martina Hello, Mr Jagger. I'm Martina Silva, Operations Manager here at Borges Road Haulage in Santiago. I'm afraid I have some bad news, Mr Jagger. As you will no doubt have heard, there's been a horrific landslide in southern Peru between Arica and Tacna, along the route we were planning to take.
Leon   …
Martina Unfortunately I am sure. Large parts of the area have been badly damaged and the road is covered in debris. Officials have suggested that the road will take at least a week to clear but that even after that, heavy goods vehicles will not be allowed along the route because several sections are likely to need substantial rebuilding before they can support anything heavier than a car.
Leon   …
Martina That was actually the only good-sized road from Arica into Peru, and even if there was another route the roads would be too small to cope with the weight that we're going to be bringing through.

Leon   …

Martina   Yes of course. Hold on and I'll put you through.

Diego   Hi Leon, not good news is it?

Leon   …

Diego   I know, I understand, but listen: my team here is working on another solution right now. It will involve extra costs, and a lot of extra distance. It also means going through a different country to the one planned, but it's looking feasible so far.

Leon   …

a   Not good news?! That's certainly an understatement! This is a catastrophe! I'm sitting here at a port with five enormous evaporators and nowhere to take them!

b   OK, tell me about it, Diego.

c   Hello, Leon Jagger here.

d   Oh you've got to be joking! Are there any other roads around there that we could use instead?

e   This is not good at all. Thanks anyway. Can you put me through to Diego please?

f   Yes, Martina, I had seen it on the news but wasn't able to ring you from the boat to talk about it. Are you sure that there's no way we could find a way along the road?

 b Now listen to the CD and check your answers.

8

REMEMBER   The simple past

1. I **asked** for a quote two weeks ago.
2. The shipper **wasn't able to** deliver on time.
3. They **didn't send** an invoice.
4. Who **checked** the tyres?
5. **Did** you **pick up** the consignment? No, I **didn't**.

f̶o̶r̶ two weeks *ago*

c **Put the verbs in brackets into the simple past.**

Borges Road Haulage …¹ *(plan)* the route from Arica to Santa Cruz de la Sierra long before the MS Adventure …² *(leave)* the docks in Portland. The haulage firm …³ *(inform)* the authorities in southern Peru of their intentions but this …⁴ *(not help)* because they …⁵ *(not be able)* to go through Peru anyway. Just before the ship arrived in Arica, the haulage firm …⁶ *(find out)* from the news that there had been a landslide in the region north of Arica and that the route into Peru …⁷ *(be)* now blocked. Leon Jagger …⁸ *(not be)* happy when he …⁹ *(hear)* the news, but there was nothing they could do about it, so he …¹⁰ *(ring)* Diego González to discuss a new route. It …¹¹ *(not end up)* as a disaster because the alternative route, although longer and more difficult, …¹² *(do)* the job.

7 | An alternative route

 a Work in a group. Download a map which shows Arica in Chile and Santa Cruz de la Sierra in Bolivia and work out how the evaporators could reach the plant in Santa Cruz de la Sierra if all the possible routes to Peru were blocked. Present your findings to the class.

 b Listen to Leon Jagger talking to the *WWLog* magazine about the alternative route that they took. Then put these difficulties into the order they occurred en route to Santa Cruz de la Sierra.

9

> engine trouble • road works • power cables removed and replaced • not enough clearance • 15% gradient in road

KMK **c** Machen Sie sich Notizen anhand der folgenden Stichpunkte, damit Sie das Problem einem deutschen Kollegen erklären können.

- *alle Firmen, die am Transport des Verdampfers beteiligt waren und ihre jeweiligen Aufgaben*
- *die Kosten*
- *wie die Schwierigkeiten überwunden wurden*

8 | Shipping documents

A consignment not only has to be delivered on time, but it also has to have the correct documentation such as a **sea waybill** *or a* **bill of lading** *if it is sent by sea.*

a Read the information in texts A and B and then answer the questions opposite.

A

> This shipping document is issued by the carrier (i.e. a shipping line) to the shipper of the freight (consignor) and contains the details of the contract of carriage between these two parties. It provides detailed information about the carrier, the shipper and the freight that is being carried (e.g. descriptions, identifying marks and numbers, weights and measurements, value, insurance number, destination, name of consignee, etc.). This document is:
>
> - documentary evidence of the contract of carriage between shipper and carrier.
> - a receipt signed by the carrier which confirms that the goods described have been received in good condition and are on board the ship. If the person who signs this document is satisfied that the consignment is in good condition, the bill is said to be 'clean'. If, however, the consignment is damaged, it must be noted in a clause on the bill that it is 'foul' or 'unclean'.
> - a negotiable document of title. This means that the bill represents the consignment itself and can be passed on to another person or a bank (for payment by letter of credit, for example).

B

> This document contains the same information as document A and is also evidence of a contract as well as a receipt for the goods it describes. But, unlike document A, it is non-negotiable and is not a document of title. This document is often used in the container trade when:
>
> - the consignment is one of a series of loads to the same consignee.
> - the consignor and the consignee are the same person or company.

1 Identify documents A and B and explain the most important difference between them.
2 What must the person signing the bill of lading do if he/she notices that part of a consignment is damaged?
3 Which shipping document would a consignor in Spain use for a weekly consignment of fresh tomatoes to Sweden?
4 Which document would a road haulier need to pick up a container from a port and deliver it to the consignee?
5 **PRESENTATION:** There are different types of bills of lading, for example, Received for Shipment bill, Shipped on Board bill, Combined Transport bill, Port to Port bill, House bill, 'clean' bill and 'foul' bill. Find out the differences between them and then present your results to the class.

b **Look at the standard bill of lading below. Then find expressions which mean the same as the following.**

1 The place where the carrier receives the consignment.
2 The place where the consignment is taken on board the ship.
3 The place where the ship is unloaded.
4 The place where the consignment is handed over to the consignee.
5 The field for the name of the ship which carries the consignment.

c **Work with a partner and complete the bill of lading below (1–8) for the evaporator case study. All the information you need can be found on pages 33–36.**

Shipper/Exporter (Name and address) MILWAUKIE INDUSTRIAL	**ORIGINAL**	Bill of Lading no. 4573214
	Export references	
Consignee (Name and address) Da Silva Construcción, Avenue de Arica 16, Zona Equipetrop, Santa Cruz de La Sierra, Bolivia	Forwarding agent and references WWLog	
	Country of origin of goods ①	
Notify address (Name and address)	Domestic routing / Export instructions	
Place of receipt Portland	Place of delivery	
Vessel / Voyage no. ②	Port of loading ③	Onward/Inland routing
Port of discharge ④	For transhipment to	

Marks and numbers	No. of pkgs.	Description of packages and goods	Gross weight	Measurements
	⑤	⑥	⑦	⑧

9 Radical innovations

Ship of the future

The last few years have seen some interesting marine innovations, mainly motivated by the rising price of oil.

In the next five to ten years, the shipping company Wallenius Wilhelmsen intends to build a cargo ship which will make full use of modern technologies and which will also look radically different.

The E/S Orcelle will have five hulls: a long, slender main hull and four support hulls to provide stability at sea. Because of this stability and the new propulsion systems the ship will not need ballast water. Present-day cargo ships have to take on and release ballast water to adjust their stability, and this is a harmful pollutant when released into the sea. The ship will get its energy from renewable sources, such as the sun, wind and waves. These will be used in combination with a fuel cell system powered by hydrogen. Some of the hydrogen for the fuel cells will be produced on board by solar, wind and wave energy. The only by-products of electricity production from fuel cells are water and heat.

a What do you think the abbreviation E/S stands for? Give reasons.

   a) electronically safe ship • b) externally stable ship • c) environmentally sound ship

b Match the highlighted terms in the text to their German equivalents below.

   1. Nebenprodukt   4. erneuerbare Energiequellen   7. Rumpf
   2. Brennstoffzelle   5. Schadstoff   8. Wasserstoff
   3. Antriebssystem   6. Ballastwasser   9. Brennstoffzellensystem

 c Erklären Sie einem deutschen Kollegen die Unterschiede zwischen heutigen Fracht-schiffen und dem E/S Orcelle.

 d PRESENTATION: Work in a small group and present the effects one of the following topics could have on the logistics world: fuel cells, wave energy, marine propulsion systems, cargo ships of the future.

Unit 4

International air freight

1 | Cargo planes

Most passenger planes can, and usually do, also transport freight. But goods which are heavy, bulky or dangerous must be transported in special cargo planes.

a Identify the parts of a cargo plane in the diagram below.

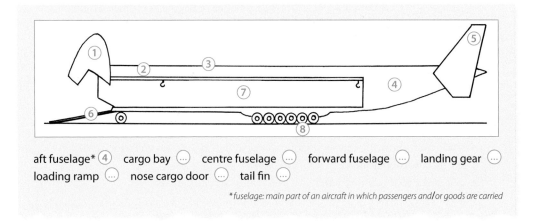

aft fuselage* (4)   cargo bay (...)   centre fuselage (...)   forward fuselage (...)   landing gear (...)
loading ramp (...)   nose cargo door (...)   tail fin (...)

* fuselage: main part of an aircraft in which passengers and/or goods are carried

b Work with a partner. Would you send the following airfreight consignments on a passenger or on a cargo plane? Give reasons.

1   75 tonnes of food, water and medical aid for a refugee camp in Darfur. C = schwer
2   150 boxes of computer components for a factory in Shanghai. = P
3   350 cartons of bananas for a fruit wholesaler in Amsterdam. = P
4   80 drums of diesel oil, 8 drums of grease, 50 boxes of explosives and 20 air compressors for a construction site in Tunisia. = C (gefährlich)
5   Lungs, liver and heart for a transplant clinic near Paris. = P

c Work in a group. Discuss the advantages and disadvantages of air freight compared to sea freight. Look at the useful terms and phrases box for help.

USEFUL TERMS AND PHRASES   **Air freight vs. sea freight**

> See the **Remember** box on p. 45.

Sending consignments by air/sea is faster/slower // more/less reliable (than by ...).
There is a smaller/greater payload when you ...
There are higher/lower freight charges / additional costs / environmental costs on air freight / sea freight.
It is (often) easier / more difficult to load/unload ...
There is greater security when goods are sent by air/sea because ...

39

2 The International Air Transport Association

The IATA is an international trade body, created by a group of airlines to represent, lead and serve the airline industry.

 a Read the text and answer the questions below with a partner.

The IATA represents 93% of scheduled international air traffic. It works closely with its members in the air transport industry to promote safe, reliable and economical air travel. Its activities include the development of containerization programs, freight handling techniques and uniform rates and rules.

IATA codes (combinations of letters that make locations, equipment, companies and times easy to identify) are intended to improve air travel for both passengers and freight forwarders by standardizing international flight operations. Filling in traffic documents using IATA codes avoids the need for lengthy descriptions and reduces the potential for making mistakes. These codes are also fundamental to the smooth running of hundreds of electronic applications which have been built around these coding systems for passenger and cargo traffic purposes.

All codes within each group follow a pattern:

• IATA *airport* codes use three letters, for example: VLC (Valencia Aeroporto, Spain), SXF (Berlin Schönefeld).

• IATA *airline* codes use two letters, for example: 9K (Nantucket Airlines), MX (Mexicana Aero).

KMK

1   What services does the IATA provide?

2   Explain the function of the IATA codes to a German colleague.

 b Take turns to read the following IATA airport codes to your partner and see if he/she can identify them. Use the language box for help pronouncing the letters.

1. ACY • 2. BSL • 3. THF • 4. BOM • 5. DEN • 6. DUB • 7. HKG • 8. IBZ • 9. LHR • 10. LGW • 11. LGA • 12. ORY • 13. CDG

LANGUAGE   **The international alphabet**

Normally, the international alphabet is only used in more formal/official situations to avoid or clarify misunderstandings.

A: Alfa	E: Echo	I: India	M: Mike	Q: Quebec	U: Uniform	Y: Yankee
B: Bravo	F: Foxtrot	J: Juliet	N: November	R: Romeo	V: Victor	Z: Zulu
C: Charlie	G: Golf	K: Kilo	O: Oscar	S: Sierra	W: Whisky	
D: Delta	H: Hotel	L: Lima	P: Papa	T: Tango	X: X-ray	

c Match the following international airlines to the IATA codes in the box.

1. Air Canada, 2. Air China, 3. Air Pacific,
4. Alitalia, 5. El Al Israel Airlines, 6. Emirates,
7. LOT Polish Airlines, 8. Lufthansa,
9. Qantas Airways, 10. Qatar Airways

QR • LO • CA • AZ • LH • QF •
EK • LY • FJ • AC

REMEMBER   **Adjectives and adverbs**

Noun + adjective	1. Some **cargoes** are too **bulky** for passenger aircraft. 2. They must be transported in **special cargo planes**. 3. **Business** isn't very **good** at the moment, I'm afraid.
Verb + adverb	4. They **checked** the documentation **quickly** and **carefully**. 5. The airline **is doing** really **well** at the moment. 6. If you **work hard** and **fast**, we **can finish early**.
Spelling rules	terrible – terri**bly**; careful – careful**ly**; easy – eas**ily**

⚠️
good – well
hard – hard

d Copy and complete the table with the highlighted adjectives in the IATA text on page 40 and their forms as adverbs.

Adjective	Adverb
safe	*safely*

e Complete the sentences with either the adjective in brackets or its form as an adverb.

1 The ground crew made sure that the heavy load was tied down …[1], but just to make sure, the pilot checked that the cargo was …[2] before the plane took off. *(secure)*

2 Security procedures at most airports are usually quite …[3]. Most passengers value the work of the security staff …[4]. *(high)*

3 The ground crew were glad to finish loading the …[5] ULDs onto the plane before it started to rain …[6]. *(heavy)*

4 It was …[7] to land in such stormy weather, but the flight attendants worked …[8] to keep the passengers happy. *(hard)*

5 The air industry and the IATA have always worked …[9] together; the IATA has a very …[10] reputation. *(good)*

3 | The Air Cargo Tariff

IATA TACT contains information regarding air cargo rules, regulations, rates and charges.

a Complete the information about TACT by choosing the most suitable highlighted word or phrase.

The Air Cargo Tariff and Rules (TACT)

Adaptability for a changing cargo environment

IATA TACT (The Air Cargo Tariff) contains comprehensive information/informations [1] regarding air cargo rules, regulations, rates and charges.

The TACT solution

More as/than [2] 100 airlines contribute to TACT, making it the reliablest / most reliable [3] and comprehensive source on the market. It is also the definitive source for general industry rules and regulations — including country and carrier regulations. Some 70,000 professionals from the cargo industry consult it on a regular base/basis [4]. TACT has the world's/worlds [5] best coverage, with more than 3.3 million/3,3 million [6] rates and charges.

Designed for: airlines, general sales agents, cargo agents, forwarders, airports, customs/customer [7] authorities

Stay actual / up to date [8]

The IATA TACT is adapting to meet the needs of an industry in an environment that never stays the same. With the last/latest [9] edition of TACT, cargo professionals can obtain valuable insight into the rates and rules governing the industry.
TACT offers all the information needed to make day-to-day air cargo transactions more simple and more quick / simpler and quicker [10] as well as updated features specially adapted to a changing cargo landscape.

For more information
see: www.iata.org

b Are the following sentences true or false? Correct the false sentences.

1 TACT is not a reliable source for carrier regulations.
2 TACT is designed for road haulage companies only.
3 The air cargo industry is constantly changing.
4 Cargo professionals should consult the most recent edition of TACT for rates and rules.
5 You can find all the information you need for daily cargo transactions using TACT.

4 | Cargo Account Settlement Systems

CASS simplifies the billing and settling of accounts between airlines and freight forwarders. It operates through CASSlink, an online e-billing solution.

For more information
see: www.iata.org

Listen to the CD and answer the following questions as fully as possible.

10   1   How does CASS replace paper-based invoices from an airline?
  2   What are the advantages of online e-invoices?

5 | The airfreight process

a Complete the text with the missing words from the box below.

> customs • date • destination • details • dimensions • flight • forwarder •
> ground • handling • pallet • security • transportation

A consignor contracts a freight …[1] who checks that the consignment complies with all …[2] regulations and other applicable laws. The freight forwarder will book a …[3] with an airline suitable for the route, …[4] of shipment and type of freight. The forwarder provides the airline with …[5] of the freight, i.e. what it is, the number of pieces, and the weight and …[6]. The freight forwarder will arrange …[7] and delivery between the shipper and the cargo depot of the airline. The forwarder must also check that the consignment is packed to withstand normal …[8] and is correctly labelled. At the airport, the cargo is checked by …[9] staff and customs officials. The airline …[10] crew then load the cargo either into a container or onto a …[11] and this is then sealed and loaded onto the aircraft. The airline flies the consignment to its …[12] airport where it is unloaded and cleared through import customs before being delivered to and signed for by the consignee.

b Using the information from the text, copy and complete the table below to show the role that each party plays in the airfreight process.

Party	Role
Consignor	a …
Freight forwarder	b *checks that the consignment complies with regulations*
	c …
	d …
	e …
	f …
Customs officials	g …
Ground crew	h *load the cargo into a container*
	i …
Airline	j …
Import customs officials	k …
Consignee	l …

6 Loading cargo onto a plane

A Unit Load Device (ULD) is a type of airfreight container used to load luggage, freight and mail onto wide-body and narrow-body aircraft. ULDs come in two basic forms: closed containers and open pallets.

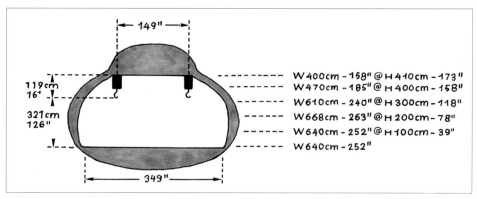

W 400cm – 158" @ H 410cm – 173"
W 470cm – 185" @ H 400cm – 158"
W 610cm – 240" @ H 300cm – 118"
W 668cm – 263" @ H 200cm – 78"
W 640cm – 252" @ H 100cm – 39"
W 640cm – 252"

a **What types of freight do you think closed containers and open pallets are used for?**

b **Look at the cross-section of an aircraft fuselage in the diagram above. How does it explain why ULDs come in so many different shapes and sizes?**

c **Read the text and answer the questions below.**

ULDs

Putting a large quantity of cargo into a single ULD is the best way to save ground crews time and effort. Each ULD has its own packing list (or manifest) – this is the easiest method of tracking its contents. IATA uses three-letter codes to describe key characteristics of ULDs in the shortest and most direct way possible. For freight forwarders, the first and second letters are the most important as they identify the type of container and its size. The third letter provides structural and technical information.

1 Why does each ULD have a separate packing list?
2 What does each of the letters in the IATA code identify?
3 Who might find the third letter of the ULD code important?

CULTURE **ULD codes in the USA**

In the USA, air freight and air transport are regulated by the ATA (**A**ir **T**ransport **A**ssociation) which has its own system of codes for ULDs. Most airlines include both the IATA code and the equivalent ATA code, if there is one.

For example: **IATA** **ATA**
                      AMA   M1

Although the United Kingdom and other English-speaking countries now officially use the metric system, the 'Imperial' system is still the official standard in the USA, and IATA freight information uses both systems.

d **Find out the ATA equivalents of these IATA ULD codes.**   AAP • AKE • AMF

e **PRESENTATION: Work in a group and discuss the advantages of ULDs. Then present them to the class. Consider the following aspects.**

> convenience • costs • easy to load/unload •
> effect on environment • flexibility • optimal use of space available •
> reliability • safety and security of goods

REMEMBER **Comparative and superlative forms of adjectives**

1. Freight transport by road and rail is **fast**, but not **as fast as** by air, although it is much **faster than** transport by ship or ferry. Actually, air freight is often **the fastest** form of transport over long distances.
2. The problem with air freight is that it is **expensive** – **more expensive than** road or rail freight. In fact, it is probably **the most expensive** way of transporting goods.
3. Packing items separately can sometimes be a **good** way to transport goods, but often, packing a few items together is **better**. However, putting large quantities of cargo into a single ULD is **the best** way to save time and effort.

Spelling rules: thin – thin**ner**; heavy – heav**ier**

bad – worse – worst
little – less – least

f **Copy and complete the table using the adjectives in the box.**

> angry • bulky • careful • cheap • competitive • dangerous •
> economical • efficient • essential • fat • high • important • large •
> quick • reliable • safe • secure • slow

Adjective	Comparative	Superlative
angry	angrier	angriest

7 Organizing air freight to China

Uwe Strück works in the Logistics Department of Hämer Spedition GmbH in Flensburg. He receives a phone call from Mette Hansen, a client in Denmark.

a Listen to the CD. Then answer the questions below.

11

1   What information does Uwe need before he can advise on the most suitable mode of transport?
2   When should the consignment be delivered by?
3   Uwe says Mette's client needs the shipment 'ASAP'. What does this mean?
4   Which mode of transport does Uwe suggest? Explain his reasons.
5   Which route would the consignment take from Hamburg?
6   Write down what other information Uwe needs in order to give a comprehensive quote.

b Find out the IATA codes of the three airports mentioned in the conversation.

c Uwe leaves you this note. He wants you to speak to Ms Hansen when she calls back with the missing information.
Role-play the call with a partner using the information on the package below.

Sendung nach Shanghai
Folgende Informationen fehlen:
1 Stückzahl
2 Maße
3 Gewicht
4 Name und Adresse des Absenders
5 Name und Lieferadresse des Empfängers

Sender:
Plastitape Ltd
Hammerichsgade 29
Copenhagen
Denmark

100 KG

Shengwen Trading Co.
Kangquiao West Road
Building 6, No. 1276
Pudong District 201319

Shanghai
People's Republic of China

0.72 m

0.8 m

1.20 m

d **You find this 'contact us' form on the Cathay Pacific Cargo website and use the information on the previous page to ask for a quote. Write the email to the airline in your exercise book. Look at the language box below for help.**

CATHAY PACIFIC
CARGO

Contact us

Please use this form to contact the Cathay Pacific Cargo office for assistance. For office contacts, please refer to Network. For charter enquiries, please refer to Cargo Charter Services.

Title	Last Name	First Name	Email Address
...(1)	...(2)	...(3)	...(4)

Station

If you have the air waybill, please select the departure station of your shipment. Otherwise, select the station to which you want your email to be sent.

Subject
...(5)

Comment
...(6)

LANGUAGE **'Contact us' email forms**

In an email, if you don't know the name of the person you are writing to, you can start with: *Dear Sir or Madam*. When filling in a 'contact us' email form, there is no need for any salutation. Just state your request in as few words as possible (in the field usually called 'Comment') and provide all the necessary information, for example:

I would like a quote for the following ...
Please give me a quote for ...

KMK **e** You receive the following freight quote from the airline. Send the information in German to Uwe either as a text message or an email.

> **Weight of consignment:** 100 kg **Tare weight of ULD:** 15.5 kg
> **Chargeable weight:** 115.5 kg **Freight rate:** 4.44 EUR per kg
> **Total:** 512.82 EUR
>
> **Charges:** Fuel: 55.00 EUR; Security: 17.00 EUR

8 Time zones

Work with a partner and answer the questions below.

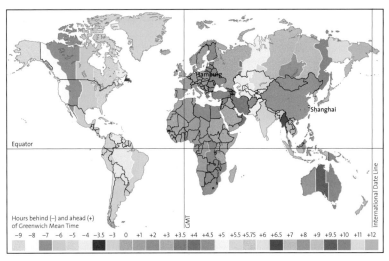

1 What does the abbreviation GMT stand for?
2 What is the International Date Line (IDL)?
3 Work out the local time of arrival taking the following points into consideration and say whether the consignment will reach the consignee on time with this flight.
   • Departure: Hamburg, 7 March at 1.00 p.m.
   • Flight duration: 16.5 hrs
   • Stopover in Hong Kong: 4 hrs

9 Filling in an air waybill

Once the consignment has been booked, the airline issues an air waybill (AWB).

With a partner, fill in the marked fields (1–15) of the air waybill opposite using the information you were given about the consignment in exercise 7.

Shipper's Name and Address	Shipper's Account Number	Not negotiable **Air Waybill** Issued by: Cathay Pacific Swire House, 9 Connaught Road C, Hong Kong PH 5 – 8425000 / TLX: 82345	CATHAY PACIFIC CARGO
(1)			

Consignee's Name and Address	Consignee's Account Number 60293	Copies 1, 2 and 3 of this Air Waybill are originals and have the same validity.
(2)		

Issuing Carrier's Agent Name and City **(3)**	It is agreed that the goods described herein are accepted in apparent good order and condition (except as noted) for carriage SUBJECT TO THE CONDITIONS OF CONTRACT ON THE REVERSE HEREOF. ALL GOODS MAY BE CARRIED BY ANY OTHER MEANS INCLUDING ROAD OR ANY OTHER CARRIER UNLESS SPECIFIC CONTRARY INSTRUCTIONS ARE GIVEN HEREON BY THE SHIPPER; AND SHIPPER AGREES THAT THE SHIPMENT MAY BE CARRIED VIA INTERMEDIATE STOPPING PLACES WHICH THE CARRIER DEEMS APPROPRIATE. THE SHIPPER'S ATTENTION IS DRAWN TO THE NOTICE CONCERNING CARRIER'S LIMITATION OF LIABILITY: Shipper may increase such limitation of liability by declaring a higher value for carriage and paying supplemental charge if required.

Agent's IATA Code 24-5-8196-2034	Account No	

Accounting information

L/C
Reference: LD97522

Airport of Departure (Addr. of First Carrier) and Requested Routing **(4)**	Optional Shipping information

Reference Number
1011-110-02

Routing and Destination			Currency		PPD	Declared Value for Carriage	Declared value for customs
To **(5)**	By First Carrier **(6)**	To	EUR		P	NVD	NCV

Airport of Destination **(7)**	Requested Flight/Date		Amount of insurance
	CX296/10	CX 360/8	NIL

No of Pieces **(8)**	Gross Weight **(9)**	Chargeable Weight **(10)**	Rate/Charge **(11)**	Total **(12)**	Nature and Quantity of Goods (incl. Dimensions or Volume) **(13)**

Weight Charge		Other Charges **(14)**
Prepaid	Collect	

Total Other Charges Due Carrier **(15)**	I hereby certify that the particulars on the face hereof are correct and that insofar as any part of the consignment contains dangerous goods, I hereby verify that the contents of this consignment are fully and accurately described above by proper shipping name and are classified, packaged, marked and labelled and in proper condition for carriage by air according to applicable national governmental regulations.
	Signature of Shipper Agent

Total prepaid	FOR ABOVE NAMED CARRIER: CATHAY PACIFIC CARGO
	8/03/10
	Expected on (date) at (place) Signature of Issuing Carrier or its Agent

10 Understanding an AWB

Johan Edmonson is a Danish trainee doing a two-week placement at Hämer Spedition. He asks Uwe about AWBs.

Listen to the CD and complete Johan's notes in your exercise book.

12

> ### AWB:
>
> * receipt for ...$^{(1)}$ and evidence of ...$^{(2)}$
> * NOT a document of ...$^{(3)}$ / non-...$^{(4)}$
> * Most secure way of paying:
>   - Consign shipment to ...$^{(5)}$
>   - Arrange payment on ...$^{(6)}$ basis
> * COD = ...$^{(7)}$: goods handed over only ...$^{(8)}$ payment has been made
> * If freight forwarder is involved, the consignor provides a ...$^{(9)}$
>   - This gives the forwarder the right to ...$^{(10)}$ the AWB on behalf of ...$^{(11)}$
> * AWB must have signature either from a) ...$^{(12)}$ or b) ...$^{(13)}$
> * Tracking number good for checking ...$^{(14)}$
> * Copies:
>   - 1st copy: ...$^{(15)}$; 2nd copy: ...$^{(16)}$; 3rd copy: ...$^{(17)}$

11 Letter of credit

Plastitape is paying for the consignment by letter of credit. Letters of credit (L/C) are often used in international trade for consignments with a high value and when the supplier of the goods is in one country and the customer is in another. The bank pays the beneficiary an agreed sum when he or she hands the specified transit documents over to the bank. One of these is usually either an air waybill or a sea waybill.

Work with a partner and put this explanation of a letter of credit in the correct order.

A   The buyer receives the consignment and the shipping documents
    (i.e. a commercial invoice, an air waybill or a bill of lading).
B   The shipping documents are then sent to the bank.
C   The buyer asks a/his/her bank to issue a letter of credit in favour of the seller.
D   The bank pays the seller.
E   This is a document which guarantees payment to the seller.
F   The bank informs the buyer and seller that an L/C has been issued.
G   These documents show that the consignment has been delivered.

12 When natural disaster strikes

Drug manufacturers in "desperate" situation

JOANNA RIPARD AND ANTHONY MANDUCA

Pharmaceutical manufacturers are among the worst hit by the ash cloud crisis, as they faced a "desperate" situation and risked losing business to non-EU competition, the Malta Chamber of Commerce, Enterprise and Industry told *The Times Business*. The closure of European airspace has had a far-reaching effect on the business community, although the Chamber said it was premature to quantify the financial consequences. Chamber members whose business relies on just-in-time exports or their physical presence abroad have been especially hit. Many businesses have suffered the inconvenience of having key team members stranded overseas.

"In terms of imports and exports, many sectors depend more heavily on maritime and road transport, which has not been affected," the Chamber said. "Unfortunately, those companies which depend on air transport and couriers, including some large manufacturers and pharmaceutical companies, have been at the mercy of this unfortunate crisis. Members from pharma companies have informed the Malta Chamber that this problem is currently their greatest difficulty, as pharmaceuticals are always transported by air since they have a tight expiry date. The airspace closure has created great havoc among product delivery with delays of weeks. The situation is a desperate one in this sector and the risk of losing clients to non-EU competitors is high."

The Chamber pointed out the best alternative solution [...] was to deploy goods to Italy by ship and then by truck to the client. This solution, however, drastically prolonged times of delivery as the bottlenecks caused by traffic being diverted towards these routes lengthened the delays.

Adapted from: *www.timesofmalta.com, 22 April 2010*

a **Find the German equivalents of the highlighted terms in the text.**

1 ausgedehnt
2 ausgeliefert sein
3 fertigungssynchrone Exporte
4 betroffen
5 gestrandet
6 weitreichende Auswirkung
7 etwas verschicken
8 Verwüstung anrichten
9 sich verlassen auf

b **Read the text and then answer the questions below.**

1 Why were pharmaceutical manufacturers facing a "desperate" situation?
2 Which industries suffered most from the airspace closure?
3 Why do pharmaceuticals depend on air freight?
4 Explain the problem with the alternative solution.

c **PRESENTATION: Work in a group and discuss what effects natural disasters can have on logistics and the economy. Then present your results to the class.**

Unit 5

Insurance and risk

1 | Accidents always happen

No matter how careful we are, accidents always happen. Sometimes they can lead to financial difficulties if risks are taken.

a Describe what has happened in the photos. Look at the **useful terms and phrases** box for help.

USEFUL TERMS AND PHRASES		Describing accidents
The container ship		been damaged.
The crew		been derailed.
The equipment		been hurt/injured.
The goods	has	capsized.
The livestock	have	come off the tracks.
The lorry		crashed.
The plane		made a crash landing.
The rolling stock		turned over.

 b Work with a partner and brainstorm how to minimize the financial risks of accidents. Consider the words in the box below.

damage • fire • injury • insurance • loss • theft

> A pilot should be insured in case he/she gets injured in a crash.

> Ships should have marine insurance.

2 An insurance nightmare

When the MSC Napoli was beached, a lot of people involved had the right to an insurance claim.

a **Read the information below and then match the headings in the box (a–f) to the texts (1–6).**

a Environmental pollution
b MSC Napoli beached
c Marine accident investigation report
d Cargo insurers
e Ship details
f Rescue service

... (1)

Registered owner: Metvale Ltd
(British Virgin Islands)
Port of registry: London
Flag: United Kingdom
Registered operator:
Zodiac Maritime Agencies Ltd
Under charter to: Mediterranean
Shipping Company

... (2)

The hull of the Napoli had been weakened in a previous accident and the ship was overloaded.

... (3)

The crew was rescued by two helicopters. There were no injuries.

... (4)

41,777 tonnes of cargo in 103 containers was washed off the deck into the sea by huge waves.

... (5)

On 18 January 2007 a violent storm damaged the hull of the MSC Napoli and the container ship began to sink. The captain made a distress call at 1.25 a.m. and then he and the crew of 26 abandoned the ship. The Napoli was in British Territorial Water.

Although there were closer ports in England and France, the MRCC (the **M**aritime **R**escue **C**o-ordination **C**entre) instructed CROSS Corsen to tow the Napoli to Portland Harbour, a distance of 140 miles.

On 19 January strong winds and rough seas threatened to sink the Napoli. So the MRCC beached the wreck in Lyme Bay on a beach near Sidmouth.

Vessel insurer
Constructive total loss.

Polluted beaches
These are owned by the National Trust and Sidmouth County Council.

... (6)

The cargo contained 1,684 tonnes of products classified as dangerous. 8km of beach, including a bird sanctuary was contaminated by fuel oil.

Contract salvage

This was organized by the MRCC in Falmouth, UK. The salvor (person or company that saves goods from damage or loss) was CROSS Corsen. Two tugs took the Napoli in tow.

 b **Class discussion. Say who you think could claim what from whom. Give reasons.**

> The registered owner could claim damages.

> There should be a finder's fee.

> The bird sanctuary could claim a percentage of the recompense.

c **Copy and complete this table based on the results of the discussion.**

Name of claimant	Claim for	Claim from
Metvale Ltd (registered owner)	damages	...

| REMEMBER | Active and passive forms in the simple past |

Active	Passive
1. The carrier **paid** the insurance.	The insurance **was paid** by the carrier.
2. People **said** the firm **was** shaky.	The firm **was said to be** shaky.
3. **Did** you **make** a claim?	**Was** a claim **made**?
4. We **had to notify** the consignee.	The consignee **had to be notified**.

d **Read the information on page 53 again and then do the following tasks.**

1 Rewrite all the sentences with the yellow highlighted verbs in the passive.
2 Rewrite all the sentences with the blue highlighted verbs in the active.

e **PRESENTATION: Find out about one of the following types of marine insurance policy. Then give a presentation to the class.**

- A standard policy (e.g. Lloyd's Open Form)
- A floating policy
- A voyage policy for exports

3 | Whose property?

In the case of salvaged property, it is often unclear who, by law, owns the goods. This information brochure explains the possibilities.

■ **Contract salvage** is the term used when, in a contract, the owner of the property and the salvor agree on a fixed fee for the salvaged property.

■ **Flotsam** is marine debris (e.g. cargo) from a shipwreck. It remains the property of the owner, but a salvor who has officially registered the salvaged goods can claim 10% of the value.

■ **Jetsam** is marine debris that has been deliberately thrown overboard (jettisoned) by the crew. It becomes the property of the finder.

■ **Pure salvage** is the term used when ship and cargo become the property of the salvor in the absence of a previous agreement with the owners. By tradition, an abandoned ship and its cargo are 'derelict'.

a **Complete this information about the MSC Napoli shipwreck with a suitable word from the information brochure above.**

If you save shipwrecked ...[1], from further damage, you are the ...[2]. If you have officially ...[3] the goods, you can ...[4] ten per cent of the value. The goods on the beach are the result of a ...[5], so they are ...[6]. But not everybody agrees with this. They say that the beached ship was deliberately ...[7] during a storm, so both the ship and its cargo are now ...[8] and, the cargo becomes the ...[9] of anyone who finds it.

b **Now read this article and answer the questions below.**

CAN YOU KEEP SHIPWRECKED GOODS?

Unwanted items such as bibles in Zulu lie scattered on the beach. But can people keep the things they find?
So far, the police have not closed off the beach to stop them coming.

Hundreds of people are out on Branscombe beach in Devon, where cargo is washing up from the beached ship MSC Napoli. Lucky treasure hunters have found BMW motorbikes, wine casks, electrical goods, perfume, sport shoes and babies' nappies.

1 Describe what is happening in the photo.
2 How would you answer the question in the title of the article? Give reasons.

4 | Bad news

Mrs Anna Mertens moved to Lisbon to work for a bank and was looking forward to the MSC Napoli delivering a crate with some of her favourite things. The day after the shipwreck, however, Carol Oates from the London branch of WWLog, the forwarding company responsible for transporting her goods, calls Mrs Mertens to tell her the bad news.

a **Listen to their call and choose the correct endings to the following statements.**

1 Mrs Mertens …
   a heard about the shipwreck on the radio.
   b read about the shipwreck in the newspaper.
   c found out about the shipwreck while watching the news.

2 Carol Oates is waiting for …
   a a letter from the insurance company.
   b a phone call from the police.
   c the marine surveyor's report.

3 Carol says that the police took so long to react because …
   a they were on their tea break.
   b they weren't sure whether the damaged containers were flotsam or jetsam.
   c they had better things to do with their time.

4 Mrs Mertens lost …
   a her grandfather's painting and her daughter's Rosenthal dinner service.
   b her grandmother's painting and her parents' Rosenthal dinner service.
   c her grandfather's painting and her parents' Rosenthal dinner service.

b Listen to the CD again. Which of the phrases from the **useful terms and phrases** box below does Carol Oates use during the conversation?

USEFUL TERMS AND PHRASES   Apologizing

Breaking the news
I'm afraid I have some bad news.
I'm sorry / I regret to inform you that there has been …
… a fire/flood/shipwreck / serious delay / …

Giving a reason
It was due to / caused by / the result of …
… a violent storm / bad road conditions / a mechanical breakdown / circumstances beyond our control.

Showing understanding
I can understand your anger / that you are angry/upset.
We'll do our best to solve the problem / reach an agreement / find an alternative (route/delivery date/…) / keep you informed of any new developments / minimize the delay/costs/inconvenience.

Saying sorry
On behalf of …
I/We'd like to say how sorry we are for the delay.
I/We'd like to apologize for any inconvenience.
I/We regret any inconvenience this will cause.
Please accept my/our apologies for the damage.

Reassuring people
We'll do everything we can to ensure that this doesn't happen again.
We hope that we'll continue to enjoy your trust.

c Do you think that Carol deals with the situation well? Give reasons.

 d Read the **culture** box and then explain the illustration to your partner.

CULTURE   Politeness

The British are renowned for standing in orderly queues and being polite and apologetic – sometimes too apologetic. They often apologize for things that are not even their fault!

I'm terribly sorry, but would you mind stepping off my foot?!

REMEMBER   **Question forms**

1. **Does** he **have** insurance?
2. **How do** you **fill in** an insurance proposal form?
3. **Where did** the ship **sink?**
4. **Were** you shocked after the accident?
5. **Will** you **read** the surveyor's report?

e **A journalist calls to interview Mrs Mertens about the shipwreck. Write the journalist's questions to Mrs Mertens' answers below.**

1 I was watching the news and saw the shipwreck – that's how I found out about my things being stolen!
2 Yes, I can describe what I saw. I saw a man and a woman carrying a large oil painting like mine.
3 I realized it was mine when the camera showed a close-up of the painting because it is ripped at the corner.
4 Next they started putting something familiar into a large bag.
5 It was my Rosenthal dinner service!
6 Yes, of course! I was extremely annoyed! I was furious!
7 The British police made me angry.
8 Well, because they just stood there and let people steal all my lovely things.

5 | Assessing the damages

As soon as the accident happened, Carol phoned WWLog's insurance company but, because it was a Saturday, nobody was in the office. So she called an independent marine surveyor to assess the damages.

 Work with a partner and role-play the conversation using these cards.

Carol Oates

Phone the firm of surveyors and loss adjusters, Quayside Marine Surveyors. Ask them to send someone to the scene of the accident to conduct a survey. Use the information in exercise 2 on page 53 to give the necessary details.

Surveyor

You work for Quayside Marine Surveyors. Take the call from WWLog and find out the details you need to conduct a survey at the scene of the accident. Ask questions beginning *what, where, when, how,* etc.

6 | The marine surveyor's report

The MSC Napoli was also carrying barrels of wine for Wingerstock Distillery. A few days later Quayside Marine Surveyors delivered their survey report to Sun Maritime Insurance on behalf of WWLog.

Find the English equivalents of these words and phrases in the report on page 58.

1 Versicherungsnehmer/in
2 Verlust
3 Begutachtung
4 Seesachverständige/r
5 ernannt durch
6 Verpackung
7 Beteiligte
8 vermutlich
9 Verunreinigung
10 Totalschaden
11 Unterzeichner
12 entsprechend/gemäß
13 laut/zufolge
14 Handelsrechnung
15 Wertverlust
16 Bergungskosten

Quayside Marine Surveyors Ltd
PO Box 2394
Sidmouth, Devon
EX10 0NY
Tel: (+44) (0) 13692 57104
Fax: (+44) (0) 13692 57105
Email: contact@quaysidems.co.uk

Quayside Marine
Surveyors Ltd

Sun Maritime Insurance
Your policy holder: WWLog
Subject: Loss of Allier wine barrels for maturing spirits

28 January 2007

Your ref: 39876/07
Our ref: 76 P 9806

Survey report	Name of marine surveyor:	James C. Preston
	Employed by:	Quayside Marine Surveyors Ltd
	Appointed by:	Sun Maritime Insurance Company
	On behalf of:	WWLog
	Date of survey:	25 January 2007
	Place of survey:	Branscombe Beach (near Sidmouth), Devon, UK
	Vessel:	MSC Napoli
	Description of goods:	135 empty Allier wine barrels for maturing spirits
	Packaging:	5 x FCL; 2 x LCL (deck freight)

Involved parties	Freight forwarder:	WWLog, Hamburg
	Carrier:	Mediterranean Shipping Company S.A., Antwerp
	Shipper:	Delfino Vinhas S.A., Porto
	Consignee:	Wingerstock Distillery, Bloemfontein

Surveyor's examination

a) Condition of packaging

Three containers were found intact and undamaged on the deck of the MSC Napoli. Two containers were on the beach. They had been damaged and the doors were open. Two containers could not be found. They had presumably sunk after being washed from the deck.

b) Condition of goods

60 barrels recovered intact and undamaged. 40 barrels lost or destroyed. 35 barrels recovered with no structural damage, but minimal to moderate contamination by sea water, oil and dirt.

Cause of damage

Four containers containing wine barrels were washed off the deck of the Napoli as the vessel was beached during a violent storm on 19 January 2007. Two containers containing 40 barrels sank and cannot be located. Even if located and salvaged, contamination with sea water will have reduced their value drastically. These 40 barrels are considered a write-off by the undersigned.

Amount of damages

The 40 barrels that sank are considered to be a total write-off. In accordance with the shipper's representative, the 35 barrels with no structural damage but with minimal to moderate contamination by sea water were salvaged by H. M. Coastguard and sold at a public auction for the amount of (US) $6,300. The market value in US dollars of the 75 barrels according to the commercial invoice (No. 70952 dated 12 January 2007) was $41,250 of which $6,300 was recovered at auction.

The amount of damages is therefore determined as follows:

Loss of value	$34, 950.00
Salvage costs payable to CROSS Corsen	$2,062.50
Salvage costs payable to MRCC	$2,062.50
Total	**$39,075.00**

Report issued without prejudice and to whom it may concern.

28 January 2007

James C. Preston

7 Contacting the involved parties by letter

Carol Oates had to contact the parties involved in the insurance claim.
She wrote to the CEO of Wingerstock Distillery.

a Complete Carol's letter with words from the surveyor's report on page 58.

WWLog

Customer Services Department, WWLog, 56 Florence Way,
Rockingham Road, London, UB9 5JK

Mr Jan de Vere
CEO Wingerstock Distillery
Nelson Mandela Avenue 9
South Africa

Your ref:
Our ref: CO/co

Date: 28 January 2007

Dear Mr de Vere

Loss of wine barrels for maturing

We are very sorry to inform you that the ship which was transporting your wine barrels for ...[1] spirits was seriously ...[2] in a storm and ...[3] on the south-east coast of England. Please find enclosed a copy of the marine surveyor's report from the ...[4] company.

The main points of the report are:
- 40 barrels cannot be ...[5] and are therefore a total ...[6].
- 35 barrels were ...[7]. Although undamaged, they were ...[8] by sea water, oil and ...[9]. They were sold at public ...[10] for $6,300. This will be credited to your account.

We deeply regret the delay and inconvenience this accident has undoubtedly caused you, but it was the result of circumstances beyond our control. We will do our best to give you the transport details of the undamaged barrels as soon as we can.

If you require any further information, please do not hesitate to contact us. We look forward to doing business with you again.

Yours sincerely

Carol Oates

Carol Oates
Customer Services Department
Enclosure

Dear Mr/Mrs/Ms ...
► Yours sincerely
Dear Sir or Madam
► Yours faithfully

---

b Translate the highlighted sentences or phrases in Carol's letter into German.

KMK **c** Write the main points in Carol's letter as an email to a German colleague who works for WWLog in Hamburg.

> See appendix pp. 96–97 for more information on business letters.

USEFUL TERMS AND PHRASES **Business letters**

Introduction to an enquiry
I am / We are writing in connection with / to enquire about …
I am / We are interested in …

Introduction to a reply
Thank you for your letter/fax/email/enquiry of (date) concerning …
I was / We were pleased to receive …

Polite closing remarks
I/We look forward to receiving … / hearing from you.
I/We hope to do business with you again.
If you require any further information, please do not hesitate to contact me/us.

KMK **d** Herr de Vere fragt nach dem Schadenersatz. Verfassen Sie ein Rückschreiben in englischer Sprache und machen Sie Angaben zu den folgenden Punkten.

- Bedanken Sie sich für seinen Brief und entschuldigen Sie sich dafür, dass Sie den Schadenersatz in Ihrem ersten Brief nicht erwähnt haben.
- Erklären Sie, dass die Versicherungsfirma den verbleibenden Wertverlust ($34.950) sowie die Bergungskosten ($4.125) zurückerstatten wird.
- Versichern Sie ihm, dass WWLog eine zuverlässige Firma ist.
- Beenden Sie Ihren Brief auf eine höfliche Art und Weise.

8 Contacting the parties involved by phone

Carol called Manuel Perez, the manager of Delfino Vinhas, to explain the situation.

Work with a partner and role-play the phone call. Look at the **useful terms and phrases** box on page 56 for help.

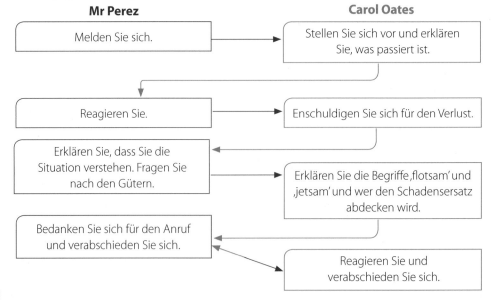

Mr Perez	Carol Oates
Melden Sie sich.	Stellen Sie sich vor und erklären Sie, was passiert ist.
Reagieren Sie.	Enschuldigen Sie sich für den Verlust.
Erklären Sie, dass Sie die Situation verstehen. Fragen Sie nach den Gütern.	Erklären Sie die Begriffe ‚flotsam' und ‚jetsam' und wer den Schadensersatz abdecken wird.
Bedanken Sie sich für den Anruf und verabschieden Sie sich.	Reagieren Sie und verabschieden Sie sich.

9 Insurance is a risky business

Everyone in logistics has heard the name of Lloyd's, especially in the field of marine insurance. Many people think it is an insurance company, but it is really the world's biggest insurance market, which started in 1687 when Edward Lloyd opened a coffee house in London.

At that time there were no insurance companies. If a ship was lost at sea, the owners of the ship and its cargo lost all the money they had invested. Edward Lloyd noticed that many of his customers were using his coffee house as a place to meet and do business. Ship owners and merchants would offer investors a small share of the potential profits from a voyage if they would 'underwrite' (share) some of the risk. At first, Edward Lloyd was only interested in attracting customers to his coffee house and keeping them there. He offered them free paper and pens and he printed a daily newspaper called *Lloyd's News* which contained business information and details of ships and their cargoes. He was a good businessman and soon realized that he could make more money in the new business of providing marine insurance than by selling coffee. He became an insurance 'underwriter' and established rules of conduct and insurance conditions for all the other underwriters who did business in his coffee house. Only ten years later, the main business of his coffee house was 'selling' marine insurance policies.

Marine insurance remained the most important form of insurance for over 125 years. The first car insurance was sold in 1901, and the underwriter simply assumed that a car was a ship on dry land and wrote a normal marine policy. Since then things have changed — today almost anything can be insured, and Lloyd's has become famous for insuring some very bizarre things. Recently a grain of rice with a picture of Queen Elizabeth II and the Duke of Edinburgh on it was insured for $20,000. The Cutty Sark Whisky Company has offered a £1 million prize to anyone who can capture the Loch Ness monster alive, protecting themselves from a claim with a Lloyd's insurance policy. Professional footballers have insured their legs, singers their voices and other celebrities other bits of their anatomy! The strangest of all though must be that over 25,000 Americans have an insurance policy with Lloyd's that will pay them or their relatives $1.5 million if they are kidnapped by aliens!

Read the text and do the tasks below.

1 Think of a title for the whole text and headings for each paragraph.
2 Explain the function of an 'underwriter'.
3 Find words in the text with the following meanings:
   a the goods carried by a ship
   b people who buy consumer items
   c people who buy goods and sell them at a profit somewhere else
   d with no additional cost or charge
   e the way people behave in a particular place or situation
   f something very strange and unusual
   g a request for the money promised in an insurance policy

Unit 6

Warehousing and packing

1 | Basic functions of a warehouse

Over the years, warehousing has become a very important part of logistics. It continues to develop with advancements in technology, but its basic functions remain the same.

a Explain what a warehouse is.

b Put these processes in the order you think they occur when a product is delivered to a warehouse.

checking goods against order form • moving products out of storage • packing • putting products into storage • receiving deliveries • shipping • sorting

c Copy and complete the mind map below with words from the lists.

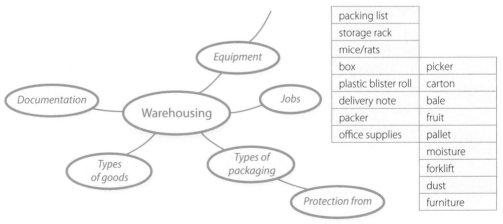

packing list	
storage rack	
mice/rats	
box	picker
plastic blister roll	carton
delivery note	bale
packer	fruit
office supplies	pallet
	moisture
	forklift
	dust
	furniture

d Work with a partner. Using the information from parts **b** and **c**, talk about a warehouse that you have been to / worked in.

2 Delivering goods to the warehouse

Most truckers call and inform the warehouse in advance of a delivery. If they have problems finding the way, they ask for directions – usually in English if they are from Scandinavia or Eastern Europe.

a Listen to the dialogue between a warehouse scheduler and a trucker whose SatNav system has broken down. Then complete these sentences with words from the dialogue.

1 Which … are you facing?
2 The road is too …
3 There's a … about 150 metres ahead.
4 How … is the next turn-off?
5 You … be able to see a large brick building.
6 Which … of the road is it on?
7 You can't … it.

b Listen to the dialogue again. Follow the directions on the map on page 91 and say where the warehouse is.

c Now work with a partner and role-play the dialogue below. Use the map and the useful terms and phrases box on page 64 for help.

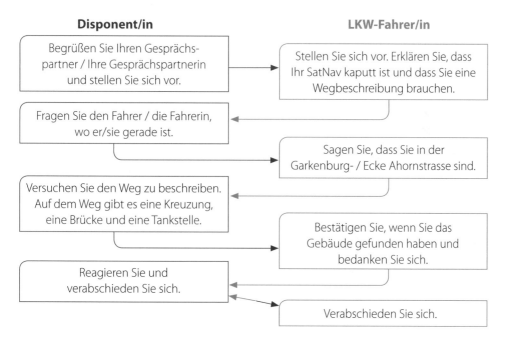

Disponent/in	LKW-Fahrer/in
Begrüßen Sie Ihren Gesprächs-partner / Ihre Gesprächspartnerin und stellen Sie sich vor.	Stellen Sie sich vor. Erklären Sie, dass Ihr SatNav kaputt ist und dass Sie eine Wegbeschreibung brauchen.
Fragen Sie den Fahrer / die Fahrerin, wo er/sie gerade ist.	Sagen Sie, dass Sie in der Garkenburg- / Ecke Ahornstrasse sind.
Versuchen Sie den Weg zu beschreiben. Auf dem Weg gibt es eine Kreuzung, eine Brücke und eine Tankstelle.	Bestätigen Sie, wenn Sie das Gebäude gefunden haben und bedanken Sie sich.
Reagieren Sie und verabschieden Sie sich.	Verabschieden Sie sich.

d Look up a map of your town and describe the way to your company/warehouse.

USEFUL TERMS AND PHRASES   **Asking for and giving directions**

Asking for directions
Can you give me directions / tell me how to get to …, please?

Saying where you are / what you are doing
I'm parked in a street/road called … *(without an article, e.g. Europaallee)*
I'm facing north/south/east/west.
I'm now turning (left/right) into / driving along … / turning around.
I'm coming up to / I can see a crossroads/T-junction/bridge/sign / petrol station.
There's a … (about … metres) ahead / (straight) in front of me / on the left/right.
I can/can't see it.

Asking where someone is
Where are you now? / What's the name of the street/road?

Giving directions
You're facing/going the right way. Just drive straight ahead.
You're facing/going the wrong way. You'll have to turn around.
Drive north/south / straight ahead / under/over the bridge.
Turn left/right into …
There's a / You should see a / You'll come to a … / Turn left/right at the …
Can you see a … (straight) ahead of you / on your left/right?

e **Complete the sentences with the correct form of the verbs in brackets. Look at the remember box below for help.**

1 If the SatNav is broken, the driver usually … *(ring)* to ask for directions.
2 If you don't arrive before 5.00 p.m., we … *(assume)* that you have got lost.
3 If Jenny hadn't noticed the hole in the box, the goods … *(might fall out)*.
4 We … *(pay)* the costs of the damaged goods immediately if you had sent us the insurance adjuster's report.
5 If you introduced new technology to your warehousing operations, you … *(reduce)* the operating costs.
6 Perhaps they … *(think of)* a more efficient way of packing the goods if they all sit down together and discuss the matter.
7 If you can see a bridge up ahead, you … *(be)* on the right road.
8 She wouldn't have missed the turn if he … *(give)* her clearer directions.

REMEMBER   **If-sentences**

Type 0:	simple present, simple present
	If they have problems, they ask for directions.
Type 1:	simple present, modal verb *(will/can/must)* + infinitive
	If you take the ring road, it'll be quicker.
Type 2:	simple past, *would/could/should/might* + infinitive
	If I were you, I'd try to turn round.
Type 3:	past perfect, *would/could/should/might* + have + past participle
	If you had called us, we would have given you directions.

3 | Tracking and tracing

Once the driver has unloaded the goods at the receiving station, they are electronically 'marked' to make them easier to trace. Throughout the years, the method of marking products has changed, and continues to change as technology advances.

a Complete the text below with the words from the box.

> 1974 • barcodes • Identification • label • paper • reliable • shipment •
> stocktaking • store • updated

Electronic record keeping

It is important to keep accurate records of the goods moving through each sector of a warehouse – from receipt, storage, packing and …[1]. These records used to be kept on …[2] until Uniform Product Codes, or …[3] were introduced in …[4].

These are simply parallel lines printed on a …[5]. Every product has its own code – like a fingerprint. These codes can be tracked, and the data can be stored in a computer.

These labels, which can be read by machines, were first used at supermarket checkouts because they were much faster and more …[6] than human cashiers. Other advantages were that …[7] and re-ordering supplies could be computerized and made more efficient. From supermarkets, the use of UPC barcodes quickly spread to warehouses.

The next big innovation was RFID (Radio Frequency …[8]). RFID tags are labels which contain a transponder. The information stored on this circuit can be read, changed and added to when it is activated by a radio signal with exactly the same frequency. RFID tags can …[9] much more information than a barcode. This information can be constantly …[10]. They have other advantages for warehousing too. Any RFID tag on a box or carton can be activated and read from a central point and tracked throughout the warehousing process. RFID tags can be read whether inside or outside the package and they are unaffected by dirt.

KMK | **b Fassen Sie die wesentlichen Inhalte dieses Textes auf Deutsch in dieser Tabelle zusammen.**

Vor 1974:	...
1974:	...
Beschreibung eines UPCs:	...
Erster Einsatz des UPCs:	...
Grund:	...
Weitere Vorteile des UPCs:	...
Beschreibung eines RFID-Tags:	...
Fünf Vorteile des RFID-Tags:	...

4　Around the warehouse

Nicolas Dupont recently moved to Germany. He used to work in the Sales Department of a Belgian logistics company, but decided he'd like to try something different and so has applied for a position in warehousing at THM Storage in Hanover.
He finds this page on their website, where different people describe their jobs.

Jens Hillermann

I'm in charge of ten operatives at the receiving station where the truckers deliver their goods. I guide the trucks to a delivery bay and secure the rear wheels with wedges, so the trucks can't move while they are being unloaded. Almost all the freight is marked with RFID tags. If everything is correct, I sign the delivery note on the driver's handheld. If the goods are on pallets, we can either use a forklift truck or a pallet truck to unload them, but packages have to be unloaded using a hand pallet jack or a mobile cart.

Uwe Kronkamp

I drive a pallet truck and deliver goods to storage, which is divided into two parts — the mezzanine area with shelves for goods on pallets and the mixed area for bales and outsize items, for example, carpets. The mixed area is the only place where people still decide where something should go. It's a big empty space, and the floor is divided into numbered areas. We're test-driving the new vertical order picker at the moment, which should make things easier.

Bianca Hernandezis

I work on one of three picking stations for small items that haven't been computerized yet. We still need real people to pick and pack these items.

Hans-Dieter Elvers

I work in the maintenance department. My job is to keep everything working. The conveyor system is very reliable, so my main task is servicing the various machines in the packaging sector.

a Use the information given in the job descriptions to find out the names of the different areas of a warehouse (1–7) on the diagram below .

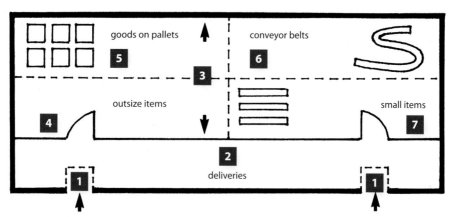

b Put these letters in order to make words from the text. Then write a sentence to say what they are or what they are used for. Look at the **useful terms and phrases** box for help.

> wdeegs • dlvieery ntoe • floikrft tcruk • meoibl crat • plleat tucrk • platels • svlhees • cvenooyr styesm • hlnahedd

Warehouse equipment

The … is used for	moving heavy pallets around the warehouse quickly.
	loading and unloading lorries and delivery vans.
	transporting small boxes and cartons.
	lifting pallets on and off the racks.
	moving palletized goods around the warehouse.
	storing delivery data.

15

c When he comes to see the warehouse, Nicolas asks Rita Wolinsky about her job. Listen to their conversation and then do the following tasks.

1 Choose the correct answer.
   a Rita drives a (forklift / vertical order picker / delivery van).
   b The spaces between racks are called (floors/aisles/corridors).
   c When the computer sends instructions, it also gives the driver an acoustic (signal/alarm/warning).
   d The warehouse computer sends instructions to the driver's (screen/terminal/monitor).
   e In an emergency, the driver can stop the picker by pressing the (red/yellow/green) button.
   f The goods are on (trays/shelves/boards).

2 In what way is the new order picker better than the older models?
3 Why isn't Rita enthusiastic about the new pickers?

5 Packing and packaging

The shipper is responsible for packing the goods so that they reach their destination in good condition. The packaging must protect the goods from damage by moisture, dust and dirt, and the stresses of transport like impact, vibration and pressure.

a Match these German words (1–10) with their English equivalents (A–J).

1	Schienennetz	A	shipping label
2	Güterzug	B	palletizer
3	Verpackungsbereich	C	free space
4	Kartonaufrichter	D	shipping area
5	Freiraum	E	plastic strap
6	Versandetikett	F	railway network
7	Kunststoff-Folie	G	packaging area
8	Palettierer	H	freight train
9	Kunstoffbänder	I	case erector
10	Versandbereich	J	plastic film

pack ► verb
packaging ► noun

b Put this description of the packing process (A–H) into the correct order.

A The package then goes to the sorting area. All the packages for the same destination go through the palletizer.

B Another machine shrink wraps the package with a plastic film to protect it from moisture.

C After the items in the consignment have been selected, the carton goes to a box cutter where a sensor measures how full the package is and cuts it down to an optimal size for the contents. If there is too much free space in a package, the contents could roll around and get damaged.

D The package then goes to a machine which tapes it and from there to another machine which prints a shipping label and sticks it on the package.

E The conveyor system is like a railway network, and each package for shipment is a like a freight train travelling from station to station and picking up goods. The biggest and most expensive machines are in the packaging area. The case erector selects a carton which best fits the size of the consignment.

F The wrapped and palletized packages go to the shipping area.

G The palletized load then goes to a machine which covers it in stretch wrap plastic film. This secures and protects the packages.

H This machine places the packages onto a pallet and secures them with plastic straps.

c Work with a partner and match the Illustrations of different types of external packaging (A–F) with the descriptions (1–6) below.

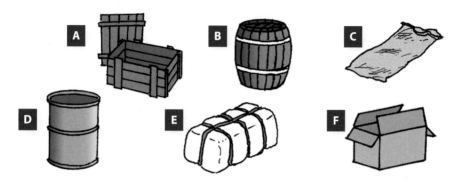

1 **bale:** bulky goods, wrapped in plastic or sacking and secured with plastic straps

2 **drum:** a round plastic or metal container for transporting liquids and dry chemicals

3 **barrel:** a container made of wood for transporting wines and spirits

4 **carton:** the most widespread form of packaging

5 **sack:** used to transport grains and small, loose goods

6 **crate:** a robust 'closed' wooden box or a wooden 'skeleton' framework

d Explain which type of external packaging would be suitable for these goods.

bananas • carpets • flowers • laptops • light bulbs • petrol • tea leaves

 e PRESENTATION: Work in a group and give a presentation on the types of internal packaging below. Include the following:
- a description of the packaging
- the function and special features of the packaging
- what type of product it might be used for.

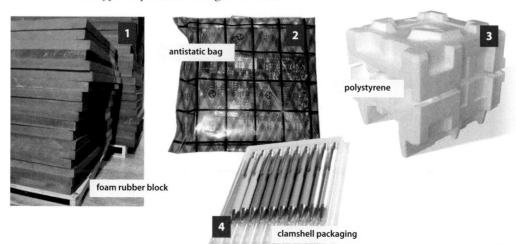

antistatic bag

polystyrene

foam rubber block

clamshell packaging

f Look at the illustration and explain how the wheel rim is packed and the function of the packaging. Use the **useful terms and phrases** box for help.

USEFUL TERMS AND PHRASES   Packing and packaging

Description

The … fits inside / on top of / into the …
The … slots into the …
The … is filled up with …
The … is covered by / with a / the …
The … is closed/sealed …

Function of packaging

The … protects the … from impact / dirt / …
The … keeps the … secure / dry /…
The … stops the … moving around.
The … is designed to absorb vibrations/moisture/shock/…
Packaging prevents damage from handling /…

corrugated cardboard

plastic bag   *wheel rim*

double box

6 Labelling

Without proper and adequate labelling, products may be handled wrongly and could therefore get damaged in transit.

Match the instructions in the box with the markings below (1–7) and explain how goods marked with these labels should be handled.

> This way up • Keep away from direct sunlight •
> Fix sling or chain as indicated • Fragile • Don't use hand hooks • Centre of gravity
> • Keep dry and away from water

7 Dangerous goods

There are separate symbols and handling regulations for dangerous goods and hazardous materials. Dangerous goods must also be accompanied by a Dangerous Goods Note.

Match the symbols for hazardous goods (1–7) with the dangers mentioned in the box.

> corrosive • environmentally hazardous • explosive • flammable •
> harmful/irritant • oxidizing • toxic

8 A big packaging problem

The quadriga on top of the Brandenburg Gate may be Germany's most famous monument, but the quadriga in front of the Guelph Palace in Brunswick was generally considered to be not only the most beautiful equestrian monument in Germany, but also the biggest in Europe. The original was destroyed by a fire in 1865 and replaced with a half-size copper replica, which was stolen by metal thieves in the late 1940s.

In 2003 Brunswick city council decided to reconstruct the original monument exactly as it was created by Ernst Rietschel in 1836. The four horses in front of the chariot are almost five metres high, and the chariot wheels are three metres in diameter. The monument was cast in bronze at a specialist foundry in Poland, and the total weight was 26 tonnes. The casting process took two years!

The first attempt to transport the monument in 2007 was a failure. Several parts of the sculpture were damaged during transport and had to be recast. After that, a specialist logistics team from Kuehne + Nagel was brought in to examine the problem. They discovered that the damage had been caused by vibration during transport, and that even low levels of vibration could damage the bronze castings.

They realized that the solution to the problem was the packaging. Securing the parts of the monument in wooden crates just wasn't sufficient.

a Erklären Sie einem deutschen Kollegen sinngemäß, wie die Quadriga während der Fahrt von Polen nach Braunschweig beschädigt wurde.

b Role-play a meeting of the Kuehne + Nagel logistics experts discussing possible solutions to the problem.

c Have you ever had a packaging problem in your company? Explain what happened.

d Go through the unit again and add as much vocabulary as you can to the mind map in exercise 1c – *Basic functions of a warehouse*.

Unit 7

International freight forwarding

AEROFLUX MODEL CO.
1927 Duesenberg Roadster

1 A complex chain

Aeroflux Models in Kolding, Denmark specializes in construction kits of classical automobiles. They sent an order for 756 cartons of plastic mouldings to Lin Chi Han Industrial, a toy company in Hong Kong, which buys the parts cheaply from its partner firm, Nanshan Hanliang Industry in Shenzhen, China.

 a Work in a group. Look up the places on a map and work out possible routes and forms of transport for the delivery of the consignment.

b Listen to the CD and take notes on the consignment. Then complete the mind map using the words in the box.

16

> Combi Spedition • consignee • consignor • first haulier •
> Fitzgerald & Brown Freight Ltd • Nanshan Hanliang Industry • second freight
> forwarder • shipping company • warehousing company

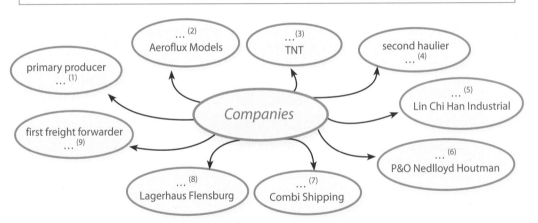

primary producer
... (1)

... (2)
Aeroflux Models

(3)
...
TNT

second haulier
... (4)

first freight forwarder
... (9)

Companies

... (5)
Lin Chi Han Industrial

... (6)
P&O Nedlloyd Houtman

... (8)
Lagerhaus Flensburg

(7)
...
Combi Shipping

 c Work with a partner. Put the companies in chronological order from the primary producer in China (1) to the consignee in Denmark (10).

KMK **d** Listen again and take notes to help you answer the following questions.

1. How are the 'frames' packed for transport to Hong Kong?
2. Where is the shipment packed into a container?
3. How does the consignment get to Hamburg?
4. Describe the route from the container terminal in Hamburg to the final destination.

e What documents do you think are needed for this shipment?

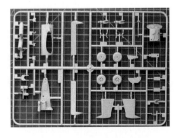

2 Arranging an export

Janet Wu works for Fitzgerald & Brown Freight Ltd. She organized the transport of the container from Hong Kong to the CTA Terminal in Hamburg. One of her first jobs was to compare online freight quotes and then choose a shipping line.

CULTURE   Chinese names

In traditional Chinese names, the family name comes first. So 'Gao Chang' is 'Mr Gao' and **not** 'Mr Chang'. However, Chinese emigrants to western countries as well as many Chinese business people and citizens of Hong Kong and Singapore often use a 'Western' first name and put their family name last, e.g. Edward Gao, Betty Wan, etc.

a **Work with a partner. Look through the shipping documents on pages 76–80 and find the information Janet needed for the online freight calculator.**

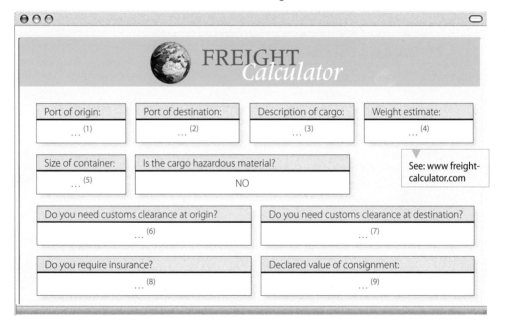

b **What information does the freight forwarder TNT need to collect the container in Hamburg?**

c **Use an online calculator to get a quote for the transport of the container from:**
  - Hamburg to Flensburg
  - Flensburg to Kolding in Denmark

d **Share and compare your results with the class.**

3 Writing an advice of dispatch

The day before the shipment leaves Hong Kong, Janet Wu writes an advice of dispatch to Bettina Renner at TNT to tell her that the goods are on their way.

> An **advice of dispatch** gives details of the transport, the date of dispatch and the estimated date of arrival at the port of discharge or the customer's premises. Nowadays, an advice of dispatch is usually sent as an email.

a Complete Janet's email with information from the shipping documents on pages 76–80.

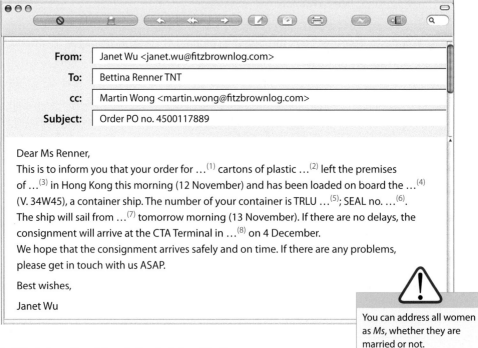

From: Janet Wu <janet.wu@fitzbrownlog.com>

To: Bettina Renner TNT

cc: Martin Wong <martin.wong@fitzbrownlog.com>

Subject: Order PO no. 4500117889

Dear Ms Renner,

This is to inform you that your order for …⁽¹⁾ cartons of plastic …⁽²⁾ left the premises of …⁽³⁾ in Hong Kong this morning (12 November) and has been loaded on board the …⁽⁴⁾ (V. 34W45), a container ship. The number of your container is TRLU …⁽⁵⁾; SEAL no. …⁽⁶⁾. The ship will sail from …⁽⁷⁾ tomorrow morning (13 November). If there are no delays, the consignment will arrive at the CTA Terminal in …⁽⁸⁾ on 4 December.

We hope that the consignment arrives safely and on time. If there are any problems, please get in touch with us ASAP.

Best wishes,

Janet Wu

> ⚠ You can address all women as *Ms*, whether they are married or not.

b What does the abbreviation 'cc' stand for?

c Who could Janet also have copied into the email as 'cc'?

LANGUAGE   Formal and informal writing

> Start formal emails with 'Dear Mr / Mrs / Ms …,' and use long forms:
> *I am writing to tell you … There is a problem. We will inform you as soon as possible*, etc.

> Start informal emails with 'Dear Tom / Susan / …,' and use short forms:
> *I'm writing to tell you … There's a problem. We'll inform you ASAP*, etc.

REMEMBER   **Future tenses – The *going to*-future and the *will*-future**

*Bei einfachen Aussagen über die Zukunft können meistens beide Futurformen verwendet werden, d.h. **going to** und **will**.*

Our company **is going to open** another branch in Hamburg next year.
Our company **will open** another branch in Hamburg next year.
They **are going to investigate** the delay once they have all the details.
They **will investigate** the delay once they have all the details.

*Das **will future** wird in der Regel für spontane Absichtserklärungen oder Versprechen genommen oder dann, wenn etwas als unzweifelhaft oder unvermeidbar angesehen wird.*

The consignment **won't be cleared** at customs without the necessary documentation.
I can't access my system at the moment, so **I'll give** you the details later.

d **Complete the dialogue by filling in the gaps with either the *will*-future or the *going-to* future form of the verbs in brackets.**

Lucy: When …[1] *(the lorry / leave)* for the docks?
Sam: At 9.00 a.m. tomorrow morning, I think.
Lucy: And …[2] *(it / go)* directly there?
Sam: If there aren't any difficulties, the driver …[3] *(drive)* straight there.
Lucy: Has she got all the documentation?
Sam: No, not yet. The internet is down right now, but I …[4] *(send)* it to her as soon as it is emailed to me.
Lucy: Do you think any difficulties …[5] *(come up)*?
Sam: There …[6] *(be)* some delays on the road to the docks because of an accident that has caused some structural damage to a bridge. If the bridge collapses, we …[7] *(not make)* it on time.

e **Work with a partner. Use the shipping documents and Bettina's notes below to write the advice of dispatch from the freight forwarder TNT to Aeroflux Models.**
Provide the following information:

- Description of the consignment
- Identification numbers for the container
- Pick-up point and route
- Delivery address, date and time

– Abholort: Containerterminal in Hamburg
  • Lagerhaus Flensburg
  • Aeroflux Models, Kolding
– Lieferdatum und -zeit: 5. Dezember um 16.00 Uhr (wenn alles gut läuft)

4 | Filling in a pro forma invoice

Nowadays most documentation is processed in a paperless environment. Nevertheless, the information contained in the documents remains the same. Before shipping the consignment, Lin Chi Han Industrial sends Aeroflux Models a pro forma invoice.

Complete the missing information (1–8) in the pro forma invoice with the information in the box below.

> A **pro forma invoice** is a short form of an invoice sent by a seller to a buyer in advance of the shipment of goods. It notes the kind and quantity of goods, their value, weight and transportation charges. Pro forma invoices are commonly used as preliminary invoices with a quotation, or for customs purposes in importation.

Ausstellungsdatum:	12. November 20..
Rechnungsnr.:	KI 5680089
Rechnung an:	Aeroflux Models, Albuen 41, 6000 Kolding, Dänemark
Artikelnr.:	4212281
Insgesamt:	756 Kartons
Schiff:	P+O NEDLLOYD HOUTMAN V.34W45
Verschiffungshafen:	Hongkong
Bestimmungshafen:	Hamburg, Deutschland

Lin Chi Han Industrial Ltd

7/F Block 2, Hang Kwong Building · Tit Shu Street, Tai Kok Tsui, HONG KONG
Tel: 4481 8004 · Fax: 44820 9872

INVOICE

BILL TO:

Invoice No.: (2) Date: (3)

PAYMENT TERM: 30 DAYS BY TT
BANKER: THE HONG KONG & SHANGHAI BANKING CORPORATION LTD,
SAN PO OFFICE, 54 HONG KEUNG ST., KOWLOON, HONG KONG.
A/C NO. 006-12345-005

Item No.:	Description:	Quantity:	Unit Price:	Amount:
(4)	Plastic mouldings PO No. 4500117889 POS No. 10 8378 Duesenberg Roadster M36	3,024 PCS	FCA HK PCS	HKD: 338,256.32
	Total: (5)			

SAY: HONG KONG DOLLARS THREE HUNDRED THIRTY-EIGHT THOUSAND TWO HUNDRED FIFTY-SIX & 32/100 ONLY

FROM: (6)

TO: (7)

SHIPPED BY: (8)

MARKS: 4 PCS, PER MASTER CARTON

For and on behalf of
LIN CHI HAN INDUSTRIAL LIMITED

Director/Authorized Signatory

5 | Departing from Hong Kong

The shipment requires a certificate of origin to be released from the port in Hong Kong.

 a **Use the internet to find out who usually issues the certificate of origin and what functions it has in international trade.**

1. Goods consigned from (Exporter's business name, address, country): NANSHAN HANLIANG INDUSTRY LTD, CHINA	Reference No.: ZC1905/09/1175 GENERALIZED SYSTEM OF PREFERENCES CERTIFICATE OF ORIGIN
2. Goods consigned to (Consignee's name, address, country): AEROFLUX MODELS Albuen 41, 6000 Kolding, Denmark	(Combined declaration and certificate) FORM A Issued in THE PEOPLE'S REPUBLIC OF CHINA - (country) See notes overleaf
3. Means of transport: FROM SHENZHEN, CHINA TO HONG KONG BY TRUCK ON/AFTER 10 NOV., THENCE TRANSHIPPED TO HAMBURG, GERMANY BY SEA	4. For official use:

5. Item number:	6. Marks and numbers of packages:	7. Number and kind of packages; description of goods:	8. Origin criterion (see notes overleaf):	9. Gross weight or other quantity:	10. Number and date of invoices:
1	Plastic mouldings 756 cartons; 3,024 PCS 4 PCS, PER MASTER CARTON	Model parts PO NO. 4500117889 ART NO. 4212281 8378 Duesenberg Roadster M36 **Total:** SEVEN HUNDRED FIFTY-SIX (756) CARTONS ONLY	"W" 95.03	3,024 PCS	0529/05 10 Nov. 20..

11. Certification It is hereby certified, on the basis of control carried out, that the declaration by the exporter is correct. - Place and date, signature of authorized signatory	12. Declaration by the exporter The undersigned hereby declares that the above details and statements are correct; that all the goods were produced in CHINA And that they comply with the origin requirements specified for those goods in the Generalized System or Preferences for goods exported to GERMANY - (importing country) - Place and date, signature of authorized signatory

b **Study the document and answer the following questions.**

1   What do you think "4 PCS" means?
2   Where was this document issued?
3   Why would a certificate of origin be issued in this case?

6 | Arriving in Hamburg

When the goods arrive in Hamburg, they cannot be cleared by customs until they have been presented at the customs office along with the necessary documentation.

a **The certificate of origin is required along with the two documents below. Identify them. Then match the explanations below to each document to say what its function is.**

b **Which other document could have been used instead of the commercial invoice? How does it differ from the commercial invoice?**

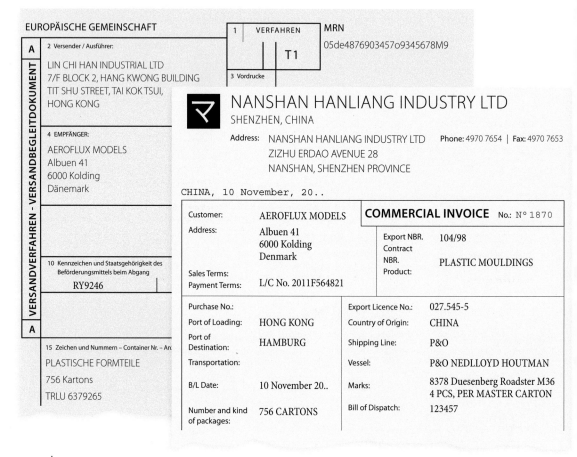

A

This document is used as a customs declaration provided by the person or company that is exporting goods across international borders. It must include specific information such as the parties involved in the shipping transaction, the goods being transported and the country of manufacture. It must also include a statement certifying that the invoice is true, and a signature.

B

The forwarder issues this document and presents it along with other customs documentation in order to have goods cleared that have come from outside the EU. At customs, this document is exchanged for a T2 document, which means that the goods are now free to move anywhere within the EU.

7 | Negotiable bill of lading

The bill of lading is necessary for TNT to take possession of the goods when the ship docks in Hamburg.

> See unit 3, pages 36–37 for more information on bills of lading.

Negotiable bill of lading (B/L)

To be negotiable, a B/L must be written 'To Order' of the consignee and must be clean. If it does not fulfil these two conditions, it is termed non-negotiable.

Read the document and explain the meaning of the highlighted terms and abbreviations.

Consignor: LIN CHI HAN INDUSTRIAL LTD 7/F BLOCK 2, HANG KWONG BUILDING TIT SHU STREET, TAI KOK TSUI, HONG KONG	**NEGOTIABLE FIATA MULTIMODAL TRANSPORT BILL OF LADING** Issued subject to UNCTAD/ICC Rules for Multimodal Transport Documents (ICC Publication 481)

Consigned to order of: AEROFLUX MODELS, Albuen 41, 6000 Kolding Denmark	**FB** **FITZGERALD & BROWN FREIGHT (FAR EAST) LTD** **International Freight Forwarders**
Notify address: SAME AS CONSIGNEE	

Port of loading: HONG KONG	Place of receipt: HONG KONG	Tel: 4908 6664 Fax: 4809 6665 MAILING ADDRESS: PO BOX TST/88491, LAI CHI KOK, HONG KONG LICENCE NO. 001
Ocean vessel: P&O NEDLLOYD HOUTMAN	Voyage number: V.34W45	
Port of discharge: HAMBURG, GERMANY	Place of delivery: Kolding, DENMARK	

Marks and numbers	Number and kind of packages / Description of goods	Gross weight	Measurement
FREIGHT COLLECT TRLU 6379265 1x40' SEAL: HK0599024 Plastic mouldings 3,024 PCS 756 CARTON(S) SHIPPER'S LOAD, COUNT AND SEAL (1x40') (FCL/FCL) CONTAINER S.T.C.	Model parts – FINISHED GOODS PO No. 4500117889 ART.No. 4212281 8378 Duesenberg Roadster M36 Total: SEVEN HUNDRED FIFTY-SIX (756) CARTON(S) ONLY	(KGS) 6312.6	(CEH) 49.792

According to the declaration of the consignor

Declaration of interest of the consignor in timely delivery (clause 6.2.). Declared value for ad valorem rate according to the declaration to the consignor (clauses 7 and 8). The goods and instructions are accepted and dealt with subject to the Standard Conditions printed overleaf. Taken in charge in apparent good order and condition unless otherwise noted herein at the place of receipt for transport and delivery as mentioned above. One of these Multimodal Transport Bills of Lading must be surrendered duly endorsed in exchange for the goods. In Witness whereof the original Multimodal Transport Bills of Lading all of this tenor and date have been signed in the number stated below, one of which being accomplished, the other(s) to be void.

13/11/20..

Freight amount: AS ARRANGED	Freight payable at: ODENSE	Place and date of issue: HONG KONG 13/11/20..
Cargo insurance through the undersigned: [X] not covered covered according to attached policy	Number of original FBLs: THREE	For and on behalf of: FITZGERALD & BROWN FREIGHT (FAR EAST) LTD

8 | Checking the packing list

On arrival in Kolding, the plastic mouldings are carefully checked against the packing list.

Lin Chi Han Industrial Ltd

7/F Block 2, Hang Kwong Building · Tit Shu Street, Tai Kok Tsui, HONG KONG
Tel: 4481 8004 · Fax: 44820 9872

PACKING LIST

Description:	G.W.	N.W.	MEASUREMENT
PO No. 4500117889 POS No. 10 ART NO. 4212281 8378 Duesenberg Roadster M36 CONTAINER No. TRLU 6379265 ~~ORIGINAL~~ 3024 PCS. (756 CTNS.) SEAL No. HK0599024 8.35 7.52 39.4 X 33.3 X 50.2 PACKING: 8 PCS, PER MASTER CARTON TOTAL: SEVEN HUNDRED FIFTY SIX (756) CARTONS PACKED INTO 1X40' CONTAINER ONLY	/ctn.	/ctn.	/ctn.

REMARKS:

1. SHIPPED PER:	P&O NEDLLOYD HOUTMAN V.34W45
2. SAILING ON/ABT:	13 NOV. 20..
3. FROM:	HONG KONG
4. TO:	HAMBURG, GERMANY
5. MARKS:	8378 Duesenberg Roadster M36 8PCS, PER MASTER CARTON

For and on behalf of
LIN CHI HAN INDUSTRIAL LIMITED

Director/Authorized Signatory

a   **What information does this document give the consignee?**

> It tells the consignee that …

> It provides information about …

b   **Which piece of information given in the document is incorrect?**

KMK   **c**   **Your boss asks you to explain all the documents in this unit to a group of new trainees. You can either:**

    a   write notes and give an oral presentation or
    b   give a written report.

9 Rolling works of art

Buses and trucks in Pakistan are more than just vehicles that carry freight or passengers, they are also works of art. Pakistan's roads are moving art galleries – every bus and lorry is painted with bright colours and decorated with metal ornaments, chains of LED lights and reflective tape. On doors and side panels there are paintings of idealized landscapes, and portraits of film stars or cricket idols. Other favourites are the Prophet Mohammed on his horse and Princess Diana. Hammered steel leaves hang from the chassis and crash together loudly whenever the truck drives over a bump in the road, which does happen frequently, even on the best of Pakistan's roads. The cabs of these trucks are treasure chests with LED light chains, decorative ornaments of gold and silver, and seats and doors covered with artificial roses and marigolds made of silk and satin.

Truck art is also big business. In Karachi more than 50,000 skilled workers in small, family businesses work at converting basic lorries fresh from the factory into these extravagant works of art. The transformation can take up to 12 weeks and cost the driver-owner up to $4,000. "It's worth the expense," says truck owner Doda Khan. "More people will hire me if I have a beautifully painted truck."

The first trucks appeared in Pakistan in the late 1940s, and their owners invented colourful logos so that illiterate people (who were then, as now, the majority of Pakistanis) could recognize who owned the trucks. Over time, these logos became bigger and more flamboyant, and spread to fill every possible space on the outside surfaces of the trucks.

a **Read the text and then answer these questions in your own words.**

1 How does 'truck art' help the Pakistani economy?
2 Imagine you are a truck driver in Pakistan. What advantages can you see in paying a lot of money to decorate your truck?

b **PRESENTATION: Work in a group and find photos and information about 'truck art' in Pakistan and other Asian countries. Then give a presentation to the class.**

Unit 8

Applying for a job

1 | The importance of English

English is now so widely spoken that it can be regarded as a global language. By international treaty it is the official language for international air traffic and maritime communications as well as for many international organizations. Therefore, English could be extremely important for your career – whether you work in Germany or abroad.

 a Look at these signs from different countries and discuss with a partner why you think they are not only in the original language but also in English.

 b Fassen Sie die wesentlichen Inhalte des Berichts auf der CD in der folgenden Tabelle auf Deutsch zusammen. Verwenden Sie für die Lösung ein eigenes Blatt.

17

KMK

Englisch: eine globale Sprache	
380 Millionen Menschen:	...
500 Millionen Menschen:	...
1 Milliarde Menschen:	...
89 % aller EU-Bürger:	...
86 % aller Erwachsenen in Skandinavien:	...

 c Work with a partner and discuss situations in which you have to use English and why.

d How important is it to be able to speak good English in your present job?

2 Improving your English

Never before have there been so many ways to learn English and improve your English language skills.

a On a scale of 1 (very poor) to 10 (very good), how would you rate your current conversational ability in English?

 b Work in a group and brainstorm ways of improving your English.

 c Work with a partner. Copy and complete the mind map below with the ideas from the box. Add any further ideas of your own from part **b**.

> a training course • blogs • documentation • DVDs (with subtitles) •
> emails • English language courses • films in the cinema • holiday •
> language trips • letters • newspapers • magazines • evening classes (VHS) •
> novels • podcasts • the radio • school trips • travel books • TV

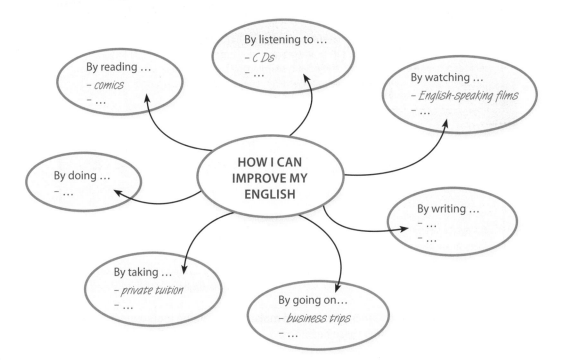

d **PRESENTATION:** Which methods in the mind map have you already tried? Give a short presentation about what works best for you and what you plan to try in the future.

3 | Job hunting

Soon after finishing his training, Martin Spielberg found a job with Pohlmann Logistik GmbH in Coburg, but he is interested in acquiring work experience abroad. He decides to look up a reliable employment website and finds the following.

CAREER TOOLS | JOB-HUNTER LOG-IN | ADVANCED SEARCH | RECRUITER LOG-IN | ADVERTISE

http://www.careersinlogistics.co.uk

Looking for that new job in logistics?
You'll find all the best ones here.

CAREERS IN **LOGISTICS**

Sales Executive

Salary: £25,000–£40,000
Location: Glasgow, Scotland
Experience: Seeking to employ a dynamic and focused Freight Sales Executive who will provide support to trade and industry in domestic exchange of goods, inland transport and in all the associated logistics services. The successful candidate will be responsible for establishing needs and requirements of customers, and suggesting and implementing logistics solutions. Some experience with Microsoft Office and of working in the promotion of freight forwarding services is required. An ability to self-motivate, self-manage and produce results is crucial, as is the ability to communicate effectively at all levels, manage and organize work efforts, achieve sales goals and build relationships with internal and external clients.

Export Clerk

Salary: £20,000–£25,500
Location: Middlesex, England
Experience: At least two years of working within a freight forwarding Export Department. The successful candidate will have the ability to prepare and rate airline air waybills according to TACT rules, complete export customs entries and classify goods using the customs tariffs. Familiarity with Microsoft Office and a good working understanding of Outlook, Excel and Word is essential. Good written skills, a friendly, open nature and good verbal communication skills with clear spoken English are required.

a Read the job advertisements above and make a list of all the requirements for each. Organize your list under these headings:

Work experience	Tasks	Skills	Personal characteristics
...	...	...	...

b Which of the personal characteristics from part **a** do you possess?

c Say which of these jobs you would apply for and why.

d What are your career plans? Can you imagine working abroad?

4 | How to write a CV

Martin decides to apply for one of the jobs, but he isn't sure how to write a British CV (curriculum vitae), so he types "How to write a CV" into a British internet search engine and finds the following website.

⊖ ○ ○   ⬭

| CAREER CHOICES | **RESUMES & CVS** | COVERING LETTERS | INTERVIEWS |

⚠

TIPS ON HOW TO WRITE A CV

| AE ▶ resumé |
| BE ▶ CV |

Over a maximum of two pages, a CV should summarize your abilities, work experience, education and qualifications. Think of it as a sales brochure that focuses on what you can offer and highlights your unique selling points (USPs). It should have a font size that is big enough to read, have a clear and simple layout, and should cover the following features:

Personal details

☐ name   ☐ telephone number(s) (home/mobile)
☐ address   ☐ email address (Make sure it is sensible!)

Personal statement or objective

This should capture the attention of the reader and summarize your skills and experience relevant to the job you are applying for in one paragraph. Never talk about your family or use "I" or "we" in your personal statement. Instead, write in the third person throughout to help to keep your CV more focused and direct, for example: *Motivated import clerk with experience in customs entries*. And remember: be positive, honest and factual.

Work experience

CVs should be in reverse chronological order, with the most recent position listed first.
For each position you should provide:

☐ start and end of employment
☐ employer's name (and address)
☐ job title
☐ main duties, responsibilities and achievements

Education

Briefly describe your qualifications, academic and/or professional. State the grades achieved and give the names of any schools or colleges attended in reverse chronological order.

Skills and achievements

This section should contain information about useful skills gained throughout your education and work experience, such as languages, IT skills or having a full, clean driving licence. These skills are of interest to any employer.

Hobbies and interests

This feature is optional but could provide something more personal to discuss at an interview. Avoid talking about any dangerous hobbies, socializing or political and religious interests.

References

Due to data protection laws, candidates should not provide referees' names, addresses or any other contact details on CVs, but should write: *Details available on request*. Always ask your referees' permission before you give a potential employer their details, and remember to provide referees who will comment on you favourably – and who are easy to contact.

a Read the tips on the website on page 85. Then copy and complete this table by putting the recommendations in the box below under the correct heading in this table.

Do	Don't
...	...

> provide personal details about your referee • keep your CV honest and factual • be positive • write dates in chronological order • use a complicated layout • give dishonest information to get the job • check your spelling and grammar • use a suitable font size • give details of your religion and political interests • focus on what you can offer • include negative aspects • provide detailed information of all the schools you have attended • provide details about your family

b Which of the recommendations in part **a** is not mentioned in the text on page 85? Which heading did you put it under?

CULTURE   **CVs in the UK**

When applying for a job in the UK, you should not include your date of birth or age on your CV. Age discrimination laws mean that this kind of information should not be discussed at any point during the recruitment process, or even during employment itself. Attaching a passport photo to a CV in the UK is also discouraged, unless the job relies on a photo (modelling, acting, etc.) or unless the employer specifically asks for one. If you are asked to attach a photo, make sure that it is a professional head-shot like a passport photo.

5   A draft CV

Martin's Scottish friend, Caroline, checks the first draft of his CV. She points out that he did not follow the tips on the website on page 85 very closely.

a Find the mistakes in Martin's draft on page 87 and correct them in your exercise books.

b Say which of the jobs on page 84 you think Martin is most qualified for. Give reasons.

c Use this timeline and Martin's CV to talk about his academic and professional life so far.

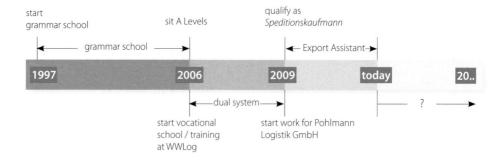

MARTIN SPIELBERG

Regenstr. 56, 96439 Coburg, Germany • Tel: (+49) 9561 440371
Email: martin.spielberg@usernet.com

OBJECTIVE

I am a highly-motivated, team-orientated Export Assistant with experience in a German freight forwarding Export Department. I am seeking experience on the British logistics market using my English language skills and I am pursuing a career in logistics because my father also worked in a logistics company.

WORK EXPERIENCE

2006–2009	WWLog, Nuremberg Training as *Speditionskaufmann*, certified by the Chamber of Commerce, Nuremberg
2009–2010	Pohlmann Logistik GmbH, Coburg Export Assistant, taking care of Europe-wide customer base, arranging transport and processing documentation

EDUCATION

2006–2009	Staatliche Berufsschule II Coburg – part-time vocational school (dual system)
1997–2006	Gymnasium Ernestinum Coburg Abitur (final exams similar to A Levels) Main subjects: Maths and English

SKILLS	Excellent IT-Skills (MS Office) Familiar with TACT rules Used to working under pressure; team-orientated; friendly Fluent Spanish; very good English (oral and written); conversational French Driving licence for cars
REFERENCES	Mrs Stefanie Pohlmann Export Manager – Pohlmann Logistik GmbH Leopoldstrasse 59 96452 Coburg

6 | Writing your own CV

Use the tips from the website and the list of do's and don'ts (pages 85–86) to write your own CV.

7 | A covering letter

a Complete Martin's covering letter below with the following phrases.

> position of • I would like to apply • I have been working • I studied • I look
> forward to • short notice • Please find enclosed • After three years of training •
> My Spanish is fluent • My present job involves • was certified by

KMK   **b Choose one of the jobs in exercise 3 and write your own covering letter.**

MARTIN SPIELBERG

Regenstr. 56, 96439 Coburg, Germany • Tel: (+49) 9561 440371
Email: martin.spielberg@usernet.com

BE ► covering letter
AE ► cover letter

Mr Brendan Mathers
Personnel Manager
Hermes Freight Forwarding Ltd
149 Bath Road
Middlesex UB7 0DU
Great Britain

15 July 20..

Dear Mr Mathers

EXPORT CLERK

…[1] for the position of Export Clerk advertised on the Careers in Logistics website.
…[2], I qualified as a *Speditionskaufmann* last May and …[3] the Chamber of Commerce.
Since then …[4] for Pohlmann Logistik GmbH, Coburg as an Export Assistant. …[5] taking
care of a Europe-wide customer base, arranging transport and processing documentation.
…[6] my CV for the …[7] Export Clerk, a diploma from the Chamber of Commerce, a
diploma from my vocational school and an English language certificate showing my
professional and language qualifications. …[8] English for nine years at grammar school
and Logistics English for a further three years as part of my training at vocational school
which I attended once a week as part of the dual system. …[9] as my father is Spanish, and
I was raised bilingually. Furthermore, I studied French for five years at school.
This position appeals to me both on a personal and career basis. I believe I can add value
to your export team through my experience and my language skills.

I am available for an interview at …[10]. Please do not hesitate to contact me should you
require any further information.

…[11] hearing from you.

Yours sincerely

Martin Spielberg

ENCLS.

8 | Arranging an interview

Brendan Mathers from Hermes Freight Forwarding Ltd is interested in Martin's application, so he calls him to arrange an interview.

18

KMK

a Listen to the CD. Copy and complete this table while you listen.

1	Why does Mr Mathers ring Martin?	…
2	Reason why Mr Mathers is in Nuremberg:	…
3	Martin's journey time to Nuremberg:	…
4	Day and time of appointment:	…
5	Martin's mobile phone number:	…

b Listen again and complete the following sentences from the phone call.

1 When would … you?
2 What … Thursday, 30 July?
3 I'm sorry, I'm … all day on 30 July.
4 Would Friday be … for you?

5 I'm … 5 p.m. is a bit too early for me.
6 Are you still … at 6 p.m.?
7 That's … with me.

USEFUL TERMS AND PHRASES   **Making appointments**

Suggesting a time
- When would suit you?
- Would Thursday be convenient for you?
- Can we fix a meeting for Saturday, 1 August at 6 p.m.?
- Are you free at 3 p.m.?

Replying to a suggestion
- Any time tomorrow morning/afternoon/ evening.
- Yes, that's fine/OK with me.
- I'm sorry. I'm not free / I'm busy then. Could we arrange something else?
- I'm afraid that's too early/late. I'd prefer 8 p.m. / 9 a.m.

---

c Work with a partner. Role-play the conversation again using the information in Brendan Mathers' diary (A) and Martin's notes (B) below.

A

	a.m.	p.m.
Wed 29 Jul	–	Meeting 5–9 (incl. dinner)
Thurs 30 Jul	Meet Jule 11–12	Schmidt 5–6
Fri 31 Jul	–	Business lunch 2–4 Available from 5
Sat 1 Aug	Breakfast interview	Free from 5
Sun 2 Aug	–	–
Mon 3 Aug	Huber 11	Fly home at 7

B

– Mittwoch + Donnerstag: Arbeit 08.00 bis 17.00 (Donn: Fitness 18.00 bis 20.00)
– Freitag: Arbeit 08.00 bis 15.00 (abends frei)
– Samstag: bis 18.00 frei (Abendessen mit Vanessa um 19.00)
– Sonntag: frei (relaxen — lieber zu Hause bleiben)
– Montag: Arbeit 08.00 bis 13.00 (nachmittags: Gleitzeit)

9 Preparing for an interview

Caroline helps Martin prepare for both types of interview by writing down some tips for him.

Useful tips for phone interviews:

- Keep your CV in clear view near the phone.
- Have a pen and paper handy for note taking.
- Make sure you know the name and position of the person interviewing you. Always ask them to spell their name if you don't understand the first time, and use it when answering questions.
- If the time isn't convenient, ask if you could talk at another time. Suggest some alternatives.
- Use a landline if possible. This avoids static on the line.

Useful tips for interviews in restaurants:

- Be careful: food and drink can make an applicant relax and reveal negative characteristics.
- Don't sit down until the interviewer does.
- Order a meal that is slightly less expensive than the interviewer's.
- Don't start eating until he or she does.
- Don't order anything messy or difficult to eat.
- If the interviewer orders a dessert, you can too.

a Read Caroline's tips above and then say whether the following sentences are true or false. Correct the false sentences.

1 You should never ask the interviewer to spell their name again on the phone.
2 You should take advantage of the free meal and order the most expensive meal in a restaurant.
3 You should always order the same as your interviewer.
4 Using a mobile phone is better for a phone interview.
5 You shouldn't order a meal like spaghetti bolognese in a restaurant.

 b Work with a partner. Role-play the job interview between Martin and Brendan Mathers.

Partner A: You are Martin. Read through your CV and covering letter and prepare yourself for Mr Mathers' questions.

Partner B: You are Brendan Mathers. Ask Martin the questions you have written down (below) and any further questions you can think of.

1 Describe yourself in just three sentences.
2 Are you a team player or do you prefer to work alone?
3 What makes you qualified for this position?
4 You wrote in your CV that you studied under the "dual system". Can you explain what that is?
5 Tell me about your strengths and weaknesses.
6 Where do you see yourself in 5—10 years from now?

Street map   (Unit 6, ex. 2b, page 63)

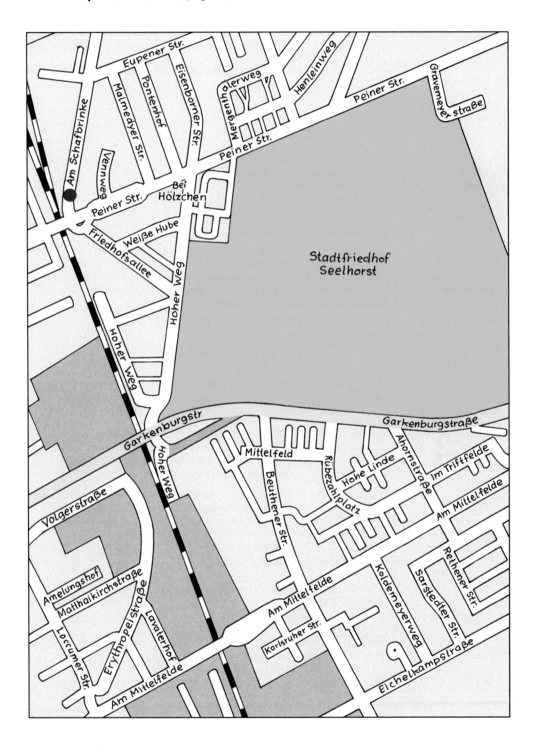

	Form
Das simple present	+ wird aus der Grundform des Verbs gebildet. ! In der dritten Person *(he/she/it)* wird *-(e)s* an das Verb angehängt. − mit *do not / don't / does not / doesn't* gebildet (wenn kein anderes Hilfsverb bzw. Form von *be* vorhanden ist) ? mit *do/does* gebildet (wenn kein anderes Hilfsverb bzw. Form von *be* vorhanden ist) Signalwörter: *usually, normally, regularly, often, every week / day / …*
Das present progressive	+ wird mit *am/is/are* und der *ing*-Form des Vollverbs gebildet. − mit *not/n't* gebildet ? durch Umstellung gebildet Folgende Verben haben keine progressive Form: *believe, hate, know, like, love, mean, notice, see, seem, understand, want, wish* Signalwörter: *just, now, at the moment, while,* eine Zeitangabe (*next week,* usw.) oder ein Fragewort der Zeit (*when* usw.)
Das present perfect	+ wird mit *have/has* + Partizip Perfekt (3. Form) des Vollverbs gebildet. − mit verneinter Form von *have* gebildet ? durch Umstellung gebildet Signalwörter: *for, since*
Das simple past	+ Alle Personen des **simple past** der regelmäßigen Verben enden auf *-ed*. ! Unregelmäßige Verben müssen einfach auswendig gelernt werden. − mit *did not / didn't* gebildet (wenn es kein anderes Hilfsverb im Satz gibt) ? mit *did* gebildet (wenn es kein anderes Hilfsverb im Satz gibt) Signalwörter: *yesterday, the day before yesterday, last week/month/Christmas, two days/years ago, in 1999, when she was young,* usw.
Das will future und going to future	+ Das **will future** wird mit *will* und dem Infinitiv des Vollverbs gebildet. − mit *will not / won't* gebildet ? durch Umstellung gebildet + Das **going to future** wird mit *am/is/are* + *going to* + Infinitiv des Vollverbs gebildet. − mit *not/n't* gebildet ? durch Umstellung gebildet Anmerkung: Die Kurzform von *will not* ist *won't*.

+ positive Form   − negative Form   ? Frage   ! Achtung

Gebrauch	Beispielsätze
• bei regelmäßig wiederkehrenden Handlungen und Vorgängen	+ *Jane **goes** to work every day.* − *No, she **doesn't** go by bus.* ? ***Does** she **go** by bus?*
• für Beschreibung von Dauerzuständen und Tatsachen	+ *I **work** in the warehouse.* − *Danny **doesn't like** the noise there.* ? ***Do** you **have** the same problem?*
• für Beschreibung von Berufsangaben	+ *Lucy and Tom **are** drivers.* − *They **aren't** customer services operators.* ? ***Are** they drivers?*
• für zeitlich begrenzte Vorgänge oder vorübergehende Handlungen	+ *Paul **is fixing** the conveyor belts.* − *They **aren't operating** properly at the moment.* ? *What **are** you **doing** today?*
• für Ereignisse in der nahen Zukunft, die fest geplant oder vereinbart sind	+ *We**'re giving** a presentation at the meeting next Thursday.* − *My manager **isn't** coming to the meeting.* ? ***Are** you **coming**?*
• für nicht abgeschlossene Handlungen, die in der Vergangenheit angefangen haben, aber noch andauern	? ***Have** you **finished** that email yet?*
• *since* wird für einen Zeitpunkt verwendet, an dem etwas begann, das sich bis zum aktuellen Zeitpunkt fortsetzt	+ *I**'ve called** five times since yesterday.*
• *for* wird für einen Zeitraum verwendet	− *They **haven't made** any progress for about a year.*
• schildert abgeschlossene Handlungen in der Vergangenheit	+ *My boss **left** a message on the answering machine yesterday.* − *I **didn't hear** the telephone ring.* ? ***Did** you **call** him back?*
• Bei einfachen Aussagen über die Zukunft können meistens beide Futurformen verwendet werden, d. h. *going to* und *will*.	+ *Our company **is going to** / **will open** another branch in Hamburg next year.* − *They **aren't going to** / **won't open** another branch.* ? *When **are** they **going to** / **will** they **open** another branch?*
• Wenn etwas als unzweifelhaft oder unvermeidbar angesehen wird, nimmt man jedoch in der Regel das **will future**. • Das **will future** wird auch verwendet für spontane Absichtserklärungen oder Versprechen.	+ *The consignment **will be cleared** at customs if the necessary documentation is provided.* − *The consignment **won't be cleared** at customs unless the necessary documentation is provided.* ? ***Will** the consignment **be cleared**?* + *I can't access my system at the moment; I**'ll give** you the details later.*

	Form
Das Passiv	+ wird mit einer Zeitform von *be* und dem Partizip Perfekt des Vollverbs gebildet. − mit verneinter Form von *be* gebildet ? durch Umstellung gebildet
Adjektive	
Adverbien	• werden (meistens) durch das Anhängen von *-ly* an das entsprechende Adjektiv gebildet. ! *hard* und *fast*: dieselbe Form wie das Adjektiv
Die Steigerung von Adjektiven und Adverbien	• Einsilbige Adjektive, zweisilbige Adjektive, die auf *-y* enden, und Adverbien, die dieselbe Form wie das entsprechende Adjektiv haben, werden auf *-er, -est* gesteigert. • Mehrsilbige Adjektive werden mit *more/most* gesteigert.
Fragesätze	• Im **simple present:** Ist kein anderes Hilfsverb bzw. eine Form von *be* vorhanden, dann bilden wir die Fragen mit *do/does* + Infinitiv. • Im **present progressive, present perfect, will** und **going to future:** Fragen werden durch Umstellung gebildet. • Im **simple past:** Gibt es kein anderes Hilfsverb im Satz, bilden wir Fragen mit *did*.
Bedingungssätze	• **Type 0:** Bei grundgelegenden Erkenntnissen, die sich nie ändern, stehen beide Satzteile im **simple present.** • **Type 1:** Der *if*-Nebensatz steht im **simple present** und im Hauptsatz wird das **will future** oder ein Modalverb wie *may, can, must* oder *need* + Infinitiv verwendet. • **Type 2:** Der *if*-Nebensatz steht im **simple past** und im Hauptsatz wird *would/could/might/should* + Infinitiv verwendet. • **Type 3:** Der *if*-Nebensatz steht im **past perfect** und im Hauptsatz wird *would/could/might/should* + *have* + Partizip Perfekt verwendet. Anmerkungen: Steht der *if*-Nebensatz an erster Stelle, wird der Hauptsatz durch ein Komma getrennt.

Gebrauch	Beispielsätze
• bei unbekanntem/zweitrangigem Verursacher einer Handlung ▪ Das Ergebnis des Vorgänges steht eindeutig im Vordergrund.	+ *All cargo **is tracked**.* − *The consignment **isn't being transported** by sea, but by air.* ? ***Have** the contents **been insured** against theft?*
• bei bekanntem Verursacher (+ *by*) ▪ Die Handlung steht auch im Vordergrund.	+ *The insurance **was paid** by the consignee.* − *The bill of lading **won't be signed** by the agent unless it is clean.* ? ***Will** the warehouse **be opened** by Prince William at the end of June?*
Adjektive verwenden wir, um Personen und Sachen – also Substantive – näher zu beschreiben.	
• vor einem Substantiv	*They must be transported in **special planes**.*
• nach einer Form von *be*, *become*, *get* und *seem*	*Some cargoes **are too bulky** for passenger aircraft.*
• nach *feel*, *look*, *taste*, *smell* und *sound*, die ein Gefühl bzw. eine Wahrnehmung ausdrücken	*The cargo doors **look** very **secure**.*
Adverbien verwenden wir, um folgende Wortarten näher zu beschreiben:	
• Verben	*If you **work hard** and **fast**, we can finish early.*
• Adjektive	*We will not accept the consignment unless it is **absolutely satisfactory**.*
• andere Adverbien	*The firm made profits of **well over** 10% last year.*
	*Freight transport by road and rail is **fast** – but not **as fast as** by air, although it is much **faster than** transport by ship or ferry. Actually, air freight is often the **fastest** form of transport over long distances.*
	*Sea freight is **expensive**. Air freight is **more expensive** than road freight. In fact, it is probably the **most expensive** way of transporting goods.*
	*Packing items separately can sometimes be a **good** way to transport goods, but often packing items together is **better**. Putting large quantities of cargo into a single ULD is the **best** way to save time.*
	***Does** he **have** insurance?* ***Have** you **filled in** the proposal form?* ***Will** you **read** the report?* ***Are** they **going to make** a claim?* *Where **did** the ship **sink**?*
• für grundlegende Erkenntnisse	*If they **have** problems, they **ask** for directions.*
• für eine erfüllbare Bedingung	*If you **take** the ring road, it**'ll be** quicker.*
• für eine Bedingung, die eher unwahrscheinlich ist	*If I **were** you, I**'d try** to turn round.*
• für eine Bedingung aus, die nicht mehr erfüllbar ist	*If you **had called** us, we **would have given** you directions.*

95

Business letters

· **GPP** ·

GORDON PATRICK PRINT Ltd

Gordon Patrick Print Ltd
7 Hackfield Way
Cambridgeshire CB25 9RT

Telephone: ++ 44 (0)1207 450726
Facsimile: ++ 44 (0)1207 450727
Email: jenny@gordonpatrickprint.co.uk
Website: www.gordonpatrickprint.co.uk

Sender's address

Inside address (Receiver's address)

Acoustic Colour GmbH
Naturweg 22
20387 Berlin
Germany

Reference line

Our Ref: JP/gl   Your Ref: GLK

Date: 19 June 20..

Date

Attention line

For the attention of Ms Glockenmeier

Salutation

Dear Ms Glockenmeier,

Combi ZH-10023 Photocopier

Subject line

Many thanks for your enquiry concerning your order for four Combi ZH-10023 Photocopier units. We are pleased to inform you that your order is now ready for transportation. Please bear in mind the following information about this product:

1. Each machine has measurements 1.4m x 2.2m x 1.8m.
2. The gross weight of each machine incl. packaging is approx. 350kg.
3. The machines cannot be stacked.

Body of the letter

The consignment will arrive at your depot on Thursday, 26 June 20..

We are very pleased to do business with you. Please do not hesitate to contact me if I can be of any further assistance. I look forward to hearing from you.

Compli-mentary close

Yours sincerely,

Signature

Name & position of writer

pp Graham Lockhead,
Customer Services Operator

Enclosure(s)

Encl.

Letterhead

The letterhead of a company usually gives the following information:
*   Type of company: Ltd – Limited; PLC – Public Limited Company; Inc (US) incorporated; & Co – partnership
*   Address, telephone and extension, fax, email, website address

Inside address

This is the recipient's address. Note that the house number comes before the street name in British addresses and that no commas are used.

Date

In modern business letters you need only write *19 June 20..* (GB) or *June 19, 20..* (US). Don't change formats within a letter.

Attention line

The attention line shows who the letter is for. Alternatively, you can include this information in the inside address:
Ms Glockenmeier
Acoustic Colour GmbH

Reference line

The reference line shows who wrote the letter (in capitals), who typed it (in small letters) and possibly other information such as a date or order number.

Salutation line and complimentary close

You open a letter with	when you	and you close with
Dear Sir or Madam	don't know the person's name	Yours faithfully
Dear Mr/Mrs/Miss ...	know the person	Yours sincerely
Dear Ms ...	know that the person is female but are not sure whether she is Miss or Mrs	Yours sincerely

If the salutation has no comma, then the complimentary close ends without a comma. If a comma is used in the salutation, then the complimentary close also ends with a comma.

Subject line

This is a major difference to German business letters. The subject line (or subject heading) comes after the salutation. It is usually written in bold type or underlined.

Body of the letter

This is the main part of the letter. Be precise, be formal and give it a logical structure with sensible paragraphing. Note that the first word of the body of the letter always starts with a capital letter.

Name and position

To let the receiver know who is writing, the position of the writer should be given.

Enclosures (Enc., Encl., Encs.)

If there are more enclosures than one, list them.

Incoterms® 2010

In international trade the eleven Incoterms® 2010 Rules (international commercial terms) are used in contracts of sale to define the rights and obligations of the buyer and seller as regards risk, transport, insurance, packing, customs duty and documentation. They are terms of delivery.

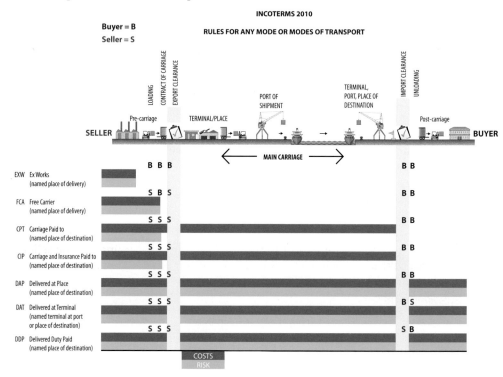

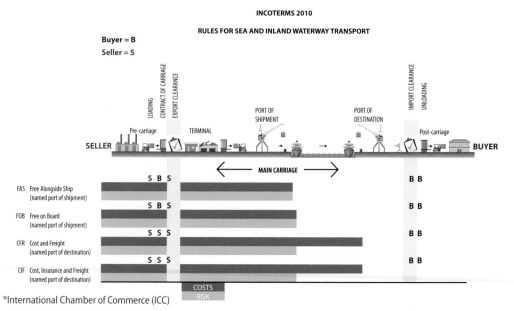

®International Chamber of Commerce (ICC)

Rules for any mode or modes of transport
EXW – EX WORKS (… named place of delivery)

The seller makes the goods available at his premises in the customary packing. The seller assists the buyer in obtaining any documentation needed at the buyer's expense. The buyer is responsible for loading the goods, transporting them to their destination, customs clearance and insurance.

FCA – FREE CARRIER (… named place of delivery)
Multimodal transport

The seller is not responsible for the main carriage of the goods. The seller delivers the goods at his own expense and risk, in the customary packing, cleared for export to the carrier nominated by the buyer. The seller provides the commercial invoice and, if requested, a certificate of origin at the buyer's expense. If the goods are collected at the seller's premises, the seller loads the goods. The seller bears the risks until the goods are in the custody of the first carrier. After that the buyer bears all the costs and risks of transporting the goods to their destination.

CPT – CARRIAGE PAID TO (… named place of destination)
Multimodal transport

The seller pays for the main carriage of the goods. The seller delivers the goods, in the customary packing, cleared for export to the carrier which he nominates. The seller bears the risk until the goods have been delivered into the custody of the first carrier. The seller pays the transport costs for the goods, excluding transport insurance, up to the named destination. The buyer is responsible for insuring the goods for the main carriage and pays all import duties and taxes.

CIP – CARRIAGE AND INSURANCE PAID TO (… named place of destination)
Multimodal transport

The seller pays for the main carriage of the goods. The seller delivers the goods in the customary packing, cleared for export to the carrier which he nominates. The seller bears the risk until the goods have been delivered into the custody of the first carrier. The seller pays the transport costs for the goods, including transport insurance, up to the named destination. The buyer pays all import duties and taxes.

DAP – DELIVERED AT PLACE (… named place of destination)
Multimodal transport

The seller is responsible for the carriage of the goods in the customary packing, cleared for export to the named terminal at the destination by the carrier which he nominates. He bears the risk until the goods have been delivered to the named terminal. The buyer is responsible for unloading the goods at the place of destination and pays all import duties and taxes.

DAT – DELIVERED AT TERMINAL (… named terminal at port or place of destination) Multimodal transport

The seller is responsible for the carriage of the goods in the customary packing, cleared for export to the named terminal at the destination by the carrier which he nominates. He bears the risk until the goods have been delivered to the named terminal. The seller is responsible for unloading the goods at the place of destination. The buyer pays all import duties and taxes.

DDP – DELIVERED DUTY PAID (… named place of destination) Multimodal transport

The seller is responsible for the carriage of the goods in the customary packing, cleared for export to the named terminal at the destination by the carrier which he nominates. He bears the risk until the goods have been delivered to the named destination. The seller pays all import duties and taxes. The buyer is responsible for unloading the goods at the place of destination.

Rules for sea and inland waterway transport

FAS – FREE ALONGSIDE SHIP (… named port of shipment)

The seller is not responsible for the main carriage of the goods. The seller delivers the goods at his own expense and risk, in the customary packing, cleared for export, alongside the vessel selected by the buyer at the named port of shipment. Thereafter, the buyer bears all the costs and risks of transporting the goods to their destination.

FOB – FREE ON BOARD (… named port of shipment)

The seller is not responsible for the main carriage of the goods. The seller delivers the goods at his own expense and risk, in the customary packing, cleared for export, on board the vessel selected by the buyer unless otherwise agreed, at the named port of shipment. Thereafter, the buyer bears all the costs and risks of transporting the goods to their destination.

CFR – COST AND FREIGHT (… named port of destination)

The seller pays for the main carriage of the goods. The seller delivers the goods at his own expense and risk, in the customary packing, cleared for export, on board the vessel selected by the buyer, at the named port of shipment. The seller pays the transport costs for the goods, excluding transport insurance, up to the named port of destination. The buyer is responsible for insuring the goods for the main carriage and pays all import duties and taxes.

CIF – COST INSURANCE FREIGHT (… named port of destination)

The seller pays for the main carriage of the goods. The seller delivers the goods at his own expense and risk, in the customary packing, cleared for export, on board the vessel selected by the buyer, at the named port of shipment. The seller pays the transport costs for the goods, including transport insurance, up to the named port of destination. The buyer pays all import duties and taxes.

Presentations

Preparing a talk

1 Collect information on your topic from the various sources you have already studied.
2 Choose the pictures, texts, diagrams, maps, etc. which will be the most useful for the style of presentation that you have chosen.
3 Organize the information and decide how you can best present it (e.g. as a poster, on an overhead projector, as a wall map, as a PowerPoint presentation, etc.).

> TIP
>
> Make sure that maps, diagrams and pictures are large enough for everyone to see. Using wall maps or overhead projectors is a good, clear way of presenting your information. Pictures and diagrams can be scanned and enlarged and presented on a poster or by using an overhead projector or a light projector. Remember to prepare a short explanation of each of them.

Important tips for giving a talk

- Practise your talk at home to give yourself more confidence on the day you give your presentation.
- Make notes – not full sentences! Use the notes to remind yourself of your main points, but don't read straight from them. Write them clearly so that you can glance at them quickly and easily when you need to.
- Do not rush. A short pause now and then is good for your listeners, and can help you to re-order your thoughts and to speak clearly.
- Do not read out long, complicated texts or lists of numbers that might be difficult to understand.
- If you need to introduce some new vocabulary, make sure to explain it to your audience. To do this, you can write the words up on the overhead projector, or you can prepare a handout with a list of new words and key terms, but remember to keep it short.
- Do not stand in front of the information you are presenting.
- Make eye contact with your audience while you are speaking.

USEFUL TERMS AND PHRASES Giving a presentation

> Today I would like to talk about ... / The topic of my presentation is ...
> Firstly/Secondly/Thirdly ...
> If we take a look at the map/diagram/photo, we can see that ...
> This diagram shows clearly that ...
> If you compare these graphs, you can see ...
> To review this section ...
> I would now like to go on to the next point which concerns ...
> In this photo you can see clearly that ...
> Finally ... / I would like to sum up by saying ... / In conclusion ...

1. Commercial invoice

COMMERCIAL INVOICE		
SELLER/ Shipper (Name, Full Address)	**Invoice Date and Number**	**Customer Order #**
	Other References	
Tax Identification # (EIN)		
CONSIGNEE (Name, Full Address)	**BUYER (If other than Consignee)**	
Origin Airport / Port	**Terms and Conditions of Delivery and Payment**	
Destination Airport / Port **Exporting Carrier**		
Other Transportation Information	**Currency of Sale**	

Marks and Numbers	Total Pieces	Total Gross Weight		Cubic Meters
		lbs.	kgs.	cbm

Complete and Accurate Commodity Description	Quantity/Units	Unit Price	Amount

	Packing Costs	
These comodities, technology, or software were exported from the United States of America in accordance with the Export Administration Regulations. Diversion contrary to U.S. law is prohibited.		
	Freight Costs	
It is hereby certified that this invoice shows the actual price of the goods described, that no other invoice has been or will be issued, and that all particulars are true and correct.	Other Costs	
_____ _____ Signature of Authorized person Date	Insurance Costs	
Page _____ of _____	Total Invoice Value	

2. Bill of lading

Shipper/Exporter (Name and address)	**ORIGINAL**	Bill of Lading No.
	Export References	
Consignee (Name and address)	Forwarding agent and references	
	Country of origin of goods	
Notify address (Name and address)	Domestic routing / Export instructions (additional notify party, etc.)	

Pre-carriage by	Place of receipt	
Vessel / Voyage no.	Port of loading	Onward/Inland routing
Port of discharge	For transhipment to	

Marks and numbers	No. of pkgs.	Description of packages and goods	Gross weight (kg)	Measurements (cbm)

PARTICULARS ABOVE FURNISHED BY THE SHIPPER

According to the declaration of the consignor

Declaration of interest of the consignor in timely delivery (clause 6.2.). Declared value for ad valorem rate according to the declaration to the consignor (clauses 7 and 8). The goods and instructions are accepted and dealt with subject to the Standard Conditions printed overleaf. Taken in charge in apparent good order and condition unless otherwise noted herein at the place of receipt for transport and delivery as mentioned above. One of these Multimodal Transport Bills of Lading must be surrendered duly endorsed in exchange for the goods. In Witness whereof the original Multimodal Transport Bills of Lading all of this tenor and date have been signed in the number stated below, one of which being accomplished, the other(s) to be void.

Freight amount:	Freight payable at:	Place and date of issue:
Cargo insurance through the undersigned:	Number of original FBLs:	For and on behalf of:
☐ not covered ☐ covered according to attached policy		

3. Certificate of origin

Goods consigned from (Exporter's business name, address, country):	Reference No.: ZC1905/09/1175 GENERALIZED SYSTEM OF PREFERENCES CERTIFICATE OF ORIGIN (Combined declaration and certificate) FORM A
Goods consigned to (Consignee's name, address, country):	Issued in - (country of origin) See notes overleaf
Means of transport:	For official use:

Item number:	Marks and numbers of packages:	Number and kind of packages; description of goods:	Origin criterion (see notes overleaf):	Gross weight (kg) or other quantity:	Number and date of invoices:

Certification
It is hereby certified, on the basis of control carried out, that the declaration by the exporter is correct.

Declaration by the exporter
The undersigned hereby declares that the above details and statements are correct; that all the goods were produced in

And that they comply with the origin requirements specified for those goods in the Generalized System or Preferences for goods exported to

----
(importing country)

Place and date, signature of authorized signatory

Place and date, signature of authorized signatory

4. Dangerous goods note / Hazardous goods note

© SITPRO 1999

DANGEROUS GOODS NOTE

Exporter		1	Customs reference/status				2
			Booking number		3	Exporter's reference	4
						Forwarder's reference	5

Consignee	6	DSHA Notification(in accordance with DSHA regulations (as ammended) given by				6A
		Shipper	Cargo Agent	Transport operator	Shipping line	

Freight forwarder	7	International carrier	8
		For use of receiving authority only	

Other UK transport details (e.g. ICD, terminal, vehicle bkg. ref. receiving dates)	9

I hereby declare that the contents of this consignment are fully and accurately described below by proper shipping name, and are classified, packaged, marked and labelled/placarded and are in all respects in proper condition for transport according to the applicable international and national governmental regulations and in accordance with the provisions shown overleaf. **The shipper must complete and sign box 17** `10A`

Vessel	Port of loading	10
Port of Discharge	Destination	11

TO THE RECEIVING AUTHORITY- Please receive for shipment the goods described below subject to your published regulations and conditions (including those as to liability)

Shipping marks SPECIFY: Proper Shipping Name*, Hazard Class, UN No.Additional Information (if applicable) see overleaf For RID/ ADR/ CDG Road requirements see notes overleaf	Number and kind of packages; description of goods	12	Net weight (kg) of goods	13	Gross weight (kg) of goods	13A	Cube (m³) (kg) of goods	14

* Proper Shipping Name - Trade names alone are unacceptable

Total gross weight of goods

Total cube of goods

CONTAINER/VEHICLE PACKING CERTIFICATE
I hereby declare that the goods described above have been packed/ loaded into the container vehicle identified below in accordance with the provisions shown overleaf.

THE DECLARATION MUST BE COMPLETED AND SIGNED FOR ALL CONTAINER/ VEHICLE LOADS BY THE PERSON RESPONSIBLE FOR PACKING/LOADING

Name of Company

Name/ Status of Declarent

Place and date

Signature of Declarent

THIS BOX WOULD BE COMPLETED BY THE COMPANY RESPONSIBLE FOR LOADING THE CONTAINER

Container identification number/ vehicle registration number	16	Seal number(s)	16A	Container/ vehicle size and type	16B	Tare (kg)	16C	Total gross weight (including tare) (kg)	16D

HAULIER DETAILS	**DOCK/TERMINAL RECIEPT**	Name and telephone number of shipper preparing this note	17
	RECEIVING AUTHORITY REMARKS		
Hauliers name	Recieved the above number of packages/containers/trailers in apparent good order and condition unless stated hereon.	Name/status of declarant	
Vehicle reg. no.		Place and date	
Drivers signature	Receiving authority signature and date	Signature of declarant	

630 Non-completion of any boxes is a subject for resolution by the contracting parties

105

1 | Rezeption: Hörverstehen*

Webcode LMU0101

Ein britischer Radiosender informiert junge Leute wöchentlich über verschiedene Berufe. Heute hören Sie Informationen über den Spediteur.

Machen Sie sich Notizen zu folgenden Punkten.

Main job:

What freight forwarders do when contracted:

Three aspects of the shipping process:

Additional offers:

2 | Interaktion

Berichten Sie einem Partner / einer Partnerin über das auf Ihrer Rollenkarte beschriebene Unternehmen. Vergleichen Sie die beiden Unternehmen.

Student A	Student B
Company Channel Logistics	Company North Logistics
History – established 1950 – operates from Portsmouth and Jersey	History – founded 1955 – operates from Flensburg and Rendsburg
Services – twice daily freight service between Portsmouth and Channel Islands – temperature-controlled delivery trailers – purpose-built trailers for distribution services to Channel Islands	Services – specializes in transportation of fresh and frozen meat throughout Germany and Denmark – delivery service within 24–48 hours – headquarters with secure warehousing
Fleet – over 500 trailers	Fleet – 80 trucks
Warehousing – cargo centres: more than 65,000 square feet of secure warehousing	Warehousing – can hold up to 25,000 tonnes of frozen food and 2,000 tonnes of fresh food

* Geben Sie den Webcode im Webcode-Suchfeld auf www.cornelsen.de/matters ein, um den Hörtext anzuhören bzw. herunterzuladen.

1 Rezeption: Hörverstehen

Webcode LMU0201

Sheena Hunt wrote an email to Nicola Watson two days ago, but hasn't yet got an answer from her, so she tries to give her a call on the phone.

Listen to the phone call and find out the following.

How Sheena introduces herself: _____

What information the receptionist gives: _____

The name of the company Sheena works for: _____

How Sheena asks to speak to Nicola again: _____

How the receptionist answers: _____

2 Mediation

Einer Ihrer Fahrer schreibt Ihnen ganz verzweifelt eine SMS und bittet Sie, ihm zu erklären, was er machen soll.

Sie finden dazu folgende Informationen im Internet, deren wesentliche Inhalte Sie Ihrem Fahrer auf Deutsch mitteilen.

Hallo … Ich soll morgen eine Ladung für England mitnehmen und selbstständig einen CMR ausfüllen. Das habe ich bisher nie selbst machen müssen. Können Sie mir eine kurze Info geben, was ich machen soll? …

`+ http://www.shippingdocs.co.uk/cmr`

CMR

The carrier usually completes the CMR (waybill), but the consignor is responsible for the accuracy of the information and must sign the form when the goods are collected. The consignee also signs the form on delivery.

There are four copies of the CMR, each identified by a different colour:

- first copy for sender (red);
- second copy for consignee (blue);
- third copy for carrier (green);
- fourth copy for administration (white with black border).

There is room on the CMR for the consignor or consignee to add any information which might assist the hauler.

Make sure you get the consignee, consignor, and carrier's names and addresses, a description of the load, as well as the value and weight of the goods.

CMR conditions make the carrier responsible for loss of and/or damage to the goods from the time he/she takes possession of them until they are delivered.

1 | Mediation

Sie arbeiten für die Spedition Robert Meier in Hamburg. Ihre Firma transportiert regelmäßig hochwertige Maschinenteile für die Firma Steensen nach England. Eine Lieferung ist fehlerhaft eingetroffen, und der Verkaufsleiter der Firma Steensen, David Müller, schickt Ihnen folgende Reklamation, die ihm der englische Kunde gesendet hat.

Lesen Sie die E-Mail und schreiben Sie ein kurzes Memo auf Deutsch an Ihren Chef, in dem Sie mitteilen, was passiert ist.

From:	Pete.Archibald@machinery_newcastle.uk
To:	DavidMueller@Steensen.de
Subject:	Complaint about damaged consignment (St02112012)

Dear David

I would like to confirm receipt of your consignment as per order no. St02112012 of 3 November 20.. . We are sorry to have to inform you that the contents of two of the six cases was damaged when they arrived. The machine components had obviously been damaged during transit. One of the cases was cracked and two boxes inside this case were broken. On unpacking a second case, which seemed to be unharmed, one of the boxes inside was found to be cracked and the spare parts broken.

This damage has put our firm in a difficult position, as we have to fulfil our commitments to our customers by the end of next month. Please arrange for the components to be replaced at once.

Prompt delivery is all that is needed to settle this matter.

We trust that we will be hearing from you in the very near future.

Kind regards
Pete

2 | Produktion

David Müller setzt sich mit Ihrer Spedition in Verbindung, und nachdem festgestellt wurde, dass der Schaden an der Ware aufgrund eines Transportproblems entstanden ist, teilt die Firma Meier ihrem englischen Kunden mit, dass die Ware schnellstmöglich nach Newcastle gesendet wird.

Verfassen Sie für Herrn Müller eine Antwortmail (*adjustment letter*), in der er Pete Archibald darüber informiert, dass die beiden Kisten mit den Maschinenteilen am Montag um 9:00 Uhr per Luftfracht geliefert werden (*Newcastle airport*) und die Firma die Kosten übernimmt.

Rezeption: Leseverstehen

North Logistics bringt ein Faltblatt heraus und informiert Kunden über die Möglichkeiten der richtigen Transportroute für Sendungen.

Choosing the right transport route for your food

You can choose from our wide range of transport modes and routes. Your choice will depend on how quickly you want to transport your goods and how much you want to spend.

When deciding on the optimum route for your consignments, consider the following questions:

- Do you require more than one mode of transport?
- How quickly do you need to transport your consignments?
- Do your consignments require special packing?

Airfreight
This is the fastest way of transporting your goods, but can be the most expensive depending on the quantity and/or volume of the goods.

Sea
Transporting goods by sea can take longer but can be very cost-effective, especially if you are shipping large volumes.

Consolidation
We often consolidate several consignments with the same destination. This can save you considerable sums of money.

Express courier
If your goods require urgent delivery, our express couriers can provide specialist services.
Take the time to check the route your goods will take. Use our expertise. We have detailed knowledge of the destination countries' infrastructure and may suggest more cost-effective, alternative routes.

Lesen Sie den Text durch und entscheiden Sie, ob nachfolgende Aussagen 1–5 richtig oder falsch sind. Beantworten Sie danach die Verständnisfragen 6–8 in kurzen Stichworten auf Deutsch.

1 North Logistics bietet eine Vielzahl von Transportmöglichkeiten an.
2 Luftfracht ist immer die teuerste Variante des Transports.
3 Es werden grundsätzlich Lieferungen an dieselbe Adresse zusammengefasst, um Geld zu sparen.
4 Expresslieferungen können von Spezialkurieren ausgeliefert werden.
5 North Logistics kennt sich mit der Infrastruktur der Bestimmungsländer aus.

6 Wovon hängt die Wahl des Transportmittels und der gewählten Route ab? (2 Aspekte)
7 Wovon sollte die Entscheidung über die Wahl der Route abhängen? (3 Aspekte)
8 Unter welchen Voraussetzungen sollte man sich für den Transport mit dem Schiff entscheiden? (2 Aspekte)

Mediation

Ihr Unternehmen bietet sowohl Schwer- und Sondertransporte als auch Kurierfahrten an. Während Ihrer Ausbildung sind Sie auch in der Abteilung Kurierfahrten tätig. In der gestrigen Teamsitzung haben Sie über Beschädigungen an gelieferter Ware gesprochen, insbesondere darüber welche Voraussetzungen für eine gute Verpackung gegeben sein müssen und wer für Beschädigungen verantwortlich gemacht werden kann.

In einem Internet-Forum finden Sie eine Frage und einige Kommentare zu dieser Thematik. Fassen Sie die Informationen für Ihr Team zusammen, indem Sie sich Notizen zu folgenden Stichpunkten machen.

1 worum es in diesem Fall geht
2 welche Vertragspartner genannt werden
3 wie die Ware bei Versand verpackt war und in welchem Zustand sie beim Empfänger ankam
4 das Problem, das von Kommentator 1 beschrieben wird
5 was der Versender laut Kommentator 2 bezüglich Verpackung und der Empfänger nach Erhalt der beschädigten Ware beachten müssen
6 welche Information Kommentator 2 dem Empfänger bezüglich des zu erwartenden Schadenersatzes gibt
7 welche ergänzende Bemerkung in Kommentar 3 gegeben wird

Who pays compensation for goods damaged during delivery?

Last Monday I posted a sewing machine in a heavy-duty box, parcelled and wrapped in bubble wrap for protection. When it arrived at the recipient's home on Thursday, it was packed in a blue bag, damaged and unusable.

Who pays the compensation?

The sewing machine was sent via XX courier. There was not a shadow of a doubt that it was in full working order, without any damage and well packaged when it was collected on Monday.

Comments

Comment 1

Obviously XX courier has to pay for the damage – they damaged it and repacked it in a blue bag. Your biggest problem is that you have to provide proof.   *Olli M*

Comment 2

There are some 'buts' here. Goods have to be packed in such a way that they are fully protected, bearing in mind things like sharp edges, uneven weight distribution, etc. The recipient should mark the carrier's delivery receipt note as "Goods damaged in transit". He/She should photograph the goods and keep all packaging for inspection by the carrier at their request. If your customer has not kept all the packaging, you can forget any claim. If he/she has kept all the packaging, the carrier will want to inspect it to assess its suitability for the item it was intended to protect.

If they accept that the packaging was adequate, then you should receive some compensation. If I remember correctly (it's a while since I last used XX courier), their 'standard' compensation is set at £25. If the value of your item is said to be more than that, then you were given the option of full value coverage at an additional charge of £10. If you did not pay for full value compensation, then no matter how expensive your machine was, the most you will get is their 'standard' compensation. Don't expect a quick solution!   *Julie G*

Comment 3

You are responsible for refunding the buyer (including the postage they originally paid, plus any postage to return it to you). You can then claim against the shipper (but obviously you have to prove it was packed well enough).   *Adam K*

1 Produktion

Sie arbeiten in einer international tätigen Spedition, die im Rahmen einer Umstrukturierung Maßnahmen entwickelt hat, ihre Mitarbeiter im Gefahrgutbereich zu schulen.

Erstellen Sie auf der Grundlage folgender Informationen eine Rundmail auf Englisch an alle betroffenen Mitarbeiter.

- Schreiben Sie einen freundlichen Begrüßungssatz.
- Machen Sie darauf aufmerksam, dass die Sicherheit von Mensch und Umwelt im Mittelpunkt steht. Insbesondere bei Gefahrguttransporten muss der sichere Umgang mit gefährlichen Gütern länderübergreifend gewährleistet sein.
- Daher sind geschulte Mitarbeiter eine wichtige Voraussetzung für sicheren und zuverlässigen Umgang mit Gefahrgut.
- Fahrzeugführer benötigen ein spezielles Zertifikat, damit sie alle Gefahrgutklassen befördern dürfen.
- Andere am Gefahrguttransport beteiligte Personen benötigen Schulungen für Ladungssicherung, um Gefahrgut zu Lande, zu Wasser oder in der Luft befördern zu dürfen.
- Am 10. oder 15. des folgenden Monats findet eine Gefahrgutschulung für alle betroffenen Mitarbeiter statt.
- Muntern Sie die Mitarbeiter zur Teilnahme auf, aber machen Sie deutlich, dass eine Anmeldung für einen der beiden Termine erforderlich ist.
- Schreiben Sie einen geeigneten Schlusssatz.

2 Rezeption: Hörverstehen   **Webcode** LMU0601

Ihr Hauptaufgabengebiet soll in nächster Zeit darin bestehen, den Verbleib von Containern herauszufinden. Sie möchten sich mit der Thematik intensiver auseinandersetzen und sind auf einen Podcast gestoßen.

Sie hören den Podcast zweimal. Sie notieren sich für Ihre Unterlagen in Stichpunkten bzw. kurzen Sätzen auf Englisch, was unter *bill of lading tracking* zu verstehen ist.

1 Wozu wird *bill of lading tracking* verwendet? (2)	a … b …
2 Wie können Konnossemente ausfindig gemacht werden? (1)	…
3 Welche Rolle spielt die BL oder Versandnummer? (2)	a … b …

Produktion

In Russland ist der Markt für Hundebekleidung enorm gewachsen. Ihre Spedition transportiert für ein Großhandelsunternehmen, das sich auf Tierbedarf spezialisiert hat, Hundemäntel, -socken und Pfotenschützer von Kiel nach Moskau.

Ein Auftrag über 20 Kartons Hundemäntel (dog coats) der Marke Liberty, 5 Kartons Hundesocken (dog socks) und 5 Kartons Pfotenschützer (protective boots) sind heute von Ihrer Spedition vom Lagerhaus in Kiel abgeholt und zum Flughafen Hamburg gebracht worden. Mit dem Flugzeug wird die Ware am 2. Januar zum Flughafen Moskau-Domodedowo verschickt und dann mit dem LKW zugestellt. So sollte die Ware schnellstmöglich am 3. Januar gegen 10:00 Uhr an die Firma **Dog Clothing** *in Moskau geliefert werden. Dank der Möglichkeiten der Sendungsverfolgung sieht der Kunde jederzeit, wo die Ware zurzeit steckt.*

Schreiben Sie eine Versandanzeige per Mail an die Firma *Dog Clothing* in Moskau.

> Liberty Hundemäntel – 20 Kartons ✓
> Hundesocken – 5 Kartons ✓
> Pfotenschützer – 5 Kartons ✓

Rezeption: Leseverstehen

Nach Ihrer Ausbildung suchen Sie eine Stelle im Ausland. Dabei stoßen Sie auf die unten stehende Anzeige.

◄ ►   [+] www.findajob.co.uk

Job vacancy: Freight forwarder

Location:	London
Salary:	£28,000–£30,000 per annum depending on experience
Job type:	Permanent
Company:	Ocean Trade
Contact:	Kenneth Trade

An exciting opportunity for the right candidate to join one of Europe's leading freight forwarding companies.

We are looking for an experienced freight forwarder who possesses the following SKILLS & PERSONAL QUALITIES

- Excellent knowledge of freight forwarding (experience in air, sea and road freight)
- Strong multilingual skills specifically English, German and French
- Administrative excellence with attention to detail
- Excellent computer literacy; knowledge of all Microsoft packages
- Well-developed numerical and analytical skills
- Ability to commit and grow within this vastly expanding company
- Ability to work well under pressure and use own initiative
- Flexible and co-operative approach to work: willingness to work as a team member in a project-based environment – prepared to work to tight deadlines

Full training provided. The ability to work on your own and as part of a team is crucial.
All applicants must be eligible to work in the EU.

Benefits
Basic salary: £28,000–£30,000 p.a.
Excellent commission
Car, mobile phone and laptop provided

To apply please click on the 'Apply' button below.

Should your application for the position be successful, you will be contacted within 72 hours.

Lesen Sie die Anzeige durch und entscheiden Sie, ob nachfolgende Aussagen 1–4 richtig oder falsch sind. Beantworten Sie danach die Verständnisfragen 5–10 in kurzen Stichworten auf Deutsch.

1 Die Gehaltsangabe bezieht sich auf das Jahresgehalt.
2 Das Stellenangebot ist zeitlich befristet.
3 Die Arbeitszeit bezieht sich auf eine 40-Stunden-Woche.
4 Bewerber müssen die Voraussetzungen erfüllen, in der EU arbeiten zu dürfen.

5 Welche Fachkenntnisse werden erwartet?
6 Wie ausgeprägt sollen die Sprachkenntnisse sein?
7 Was muss der Bewerber an IT-Kenntnissen mitbringen?
8 Welche persönlichen Fähigkeiten *(soft skills)* werden erwartet?
9 Welche Vergünstigungen kann der Bewerber erwarten?
10 Wie soll sich der Interessent auf dieses Jobangebot bewerben?

Schriftliche Prüfung

Zeit:	90 Minuten
Hilfsmittel:	allgemeines zweisprachiges Wörterbuch
Maximale Punktzahl:	100 Punkte

Im Rahmen der schriftlichen Prüfung werden die Aufgabenanteile für die drei Kompetenzbereiche wie folgt gewichtet:

- Rezeption – Hörverstehen 20 %
- Rezeption – Leseverstehen 20 %
- Produktion 30 %
- Mediation 30 %

Im Folgenden werden vier Aufgaben vorgelegt, die Sie bearbeiten sollen. Die erste und die zweite Aufgabe beziehen sich auf Ihre Fähigkeit, englische Texte (gesprochene und geschriebene) zu verstehen = **Rezeption**. Bei der dritten Aufgabe sollen Sie ein Schriftstück erstellen = **Produktion** eines englischen Textes. Bei der vierten Aufgabe wird von Ihnen erwartet, dass Sie Texte von der deutschen oder englischen in die jeweils andere Sprache übertragen = **Mediation**.

Die Prüfung beginnt mit der Hörverstehensaufgabe.
Alle weiteren Aufgaben können in beliebiger Reihenfolge bearbeitet werden.

Rezeption I (Hörverstehen)*　　　　　Erreichbare Punkte: 20

Situation
Sie möchten sich nach der Ausbildung im Ausland bewerben. Bei Recherchen im Internet sind sie auf einen Podcast über den Beruf des Spediteurs (hier: *sales executive – freight forwarding*) gestoßen. Sie hören dem Interview interessiert zu.

Aufgabe
Sie hören den Podcast zweimal. Beantworten Sie folgende Fragen, indem Sie sich Notizen für ihre Unterlagen in Stichpunkten bzw. kurzen Sätzen auf Englisch machen.

1 What kind of company does Pete Deas work for? (3)
2 What is his job title? (1)
3 What are his main duties? (4)
4 How important are language skills in his job? (2)
5 What's his working environment like? (3)
6 Who does he work with? (3)
7 What hours does he work? (1)
8 What special skills does a freight forwarder need? (3)

* Geben Sie den Webcode im Webcode-Suchfeld auf www.cornelsen.de/matters ein, um den Hörtext anzuhören bzw. herunterzuladen.

Rezeption II (Leseverstehen)

Erreichbare Punkte: 20

Situation

Ihre Firma muss gefährliche Güter nach Großbritannien transportieren. Sie wollen als Transportmittel einen LKW benutzen und durch den Eurotunnel fahren.

Aufgabe

In den *Conditions of carriage* auf der Internetseite www.eurotunnel.com finden Sie folgende Informationen.

8. Dangerous Goods

8.1 Eurotunnel will accept the carriage of Dangerous Goods, subject to compliance with the following conditions:

8.1.1 The transport of all goods classified as hazardous under ADR[1] [i.e. European Agreement concerning the International Carriage of Dangerous Goods by Road …] must be declared to *Eurotunnel* prior to carriage specifying the UN number, ADR references (class, number and letter) of all the Dangerous Goods being carried, the official ADR name of substances carried (including volume and weight), details of packaging, the identity and signature of the person making the declaration;

8.1.2 The transport of Dangerous Goods conforms with all statutory rules and other regulations in force (including Eurotunnel's published policy) relating to the transport of such goods.

8.2 Passengers carrying Dangerous Goods on to Shuttles in circumstances contrary to the above, agree to indemnify Eurotunnel against any consequential loss or damage […]

[1] ADR = (Abkürzung ADR, von *Accord européen relatif au transport international des marchandises Dangereuses par Route*)

Source: adapted from http://www.eurotunnel.com/uk/conditions-of-carriage/

a Lesen Sie den Text und entscheiden Sie, ob die folgenden Aussagen richtig oder falsch sind bzw. gar nicht erwähnt werden. Eine falsche Entscheidung führt zu Punktabzug.

Statement	True	False	Not stated
1 *Eurotunnel.com* says that you have to follow certain rules. (1)	…	…	…
2 All goods must be classified as hazardous. (1)	…	…	…
3 All goods have to be packed in special containers. (1)	…	…	…
4 The person who signs the declaration has to provide proof of who he/she is. (1)	…	…	…
5 Whenever you deliver dangerous goods, you have certain rights. (1)	…	…	…

b Beantworten Sie folgende Verständnisfragen in kurzen Stichworten auf Deutsch.

1 Wann müssen gefährliche Güter gemeldet werden? (1)
2 Was bedeutet die ADR-Klassifizierung? (2)
3 Welche Angaben müssen gemacht werden? (10)
4 Welche Folgen ergeben sich, wenn die Vorschriften über gefährliche Waren nicht eingehalten werden? (2)

Produktion   Erreichbare Punkte: 30

Situation

Sie arbeiten für eine Spedition in Norddeutschland. Vor kurzem hat sich die Tochter-firma eines Unternehmens, das Flaschenreinigungsanlagen herstellt (*manufacturer of bottle-cleaning machines*), in Ihrer Nähe niedergelassen. Die Firma hat eine Anlage nach Sword, ca. 15 km nördlich von Dublin, verkauft. Sie organisieren den Versand bis zum Hamburger Hafen und kümmern sich um die Verschiffung nach Dublin.

Aufgabe

Schreiben Sie mit Hilfe folgender Angaben eine Mail an die Partnerspedition *Eire Forwarding* in Dublin. Fragen Sie an, ob sie diese Anlage von Dublin bis Sword befördern kann. Ihr Ansprechpartner ist Mike Roberts.

– Beginnen Sie mit einem höflichen Einleitungssatz.
– Teilen Sie Mike Roberts mit, dass Sie im Internet gelesen haben, dass *Eire Forwarding* u.a. über Erfahrungen mit Sondertransporten verfügt.
– Erklären Sie ihm, dass eine Flaschenreinigungsanlage mit dem LKW nach Hamburg transportiert und dort auf das Containerschiff *Dublin Express II* verladen wird.
– Von Dublin nach Sword ist ein Spezial-LKW notwendig, um die ca. 15 Meter lange und 4 Meter breite Anlage zu transportieren.
– Fragen Sie Mike Roberts, ob er den Versand ab Hafen Dublin nach Sword organisieren kann. Bitten Sie um Kostenangaben. Weitere Auskünfte können auch per Telefon eingeholt werden.
– Schreiben Sie einen höflichen Abschlusssatz.

Mediation

Situation
Ihr Chef möchte gern einen Flyer in englischer Sprache erstellen lassen und benötigt ein paar Vorlagen. Sie finden folgenden Auszug in den Bedingungen des irischen Spediteurs *Eire Forwarding*.

Aufgabe
Lesen Sie folgenden Text und übertragen Sie die wesentlichen Punkte für Ihren Chef ins Deutsche.

With years of experience in helping customers to complete major projects, **Eire Forwarding** is the number one choice for all of your logistic needs.

How do we do it?
We do it by building a project team, led by a project manager, around each specific project's requirements. Transport, warehousing and administration teams also become involved, if and when needed, to ensure success. The project manager co-ordinates Eire Forwarding's involvement and keeps the customer up-to-date with events.

The planning stage is very important. Therefore customers are invited to contact Eire Forwarding as early as possible to take full advantage of all services offered.

We are constantly working to improve our services for our customers and have therefore prepared the following booking form to help organize consignments from receipt right through to delivery. The following fields must be completed:

Consignor	...
Consignee	...
Quantity, gross weight and volume (Number of cartons, packages, pallets, bundles, etc.; gross weight of the whole consignment including packaging and pallets; measurement of the goods in cubic metres)	...
Incoterms • EXW • FOB • DAP	...
Charges payable by (State full name and address of party responsible for payment of our shipping charges. If this is the shipper or consignee please state 'Shipper' or 'Consignee')	...
Customs declaration (Mandatory! You should answer all of the questions with 'Yes' or 'No'.)	...

Once you have completed the requested information, send your booking form to our customer services team by email (EFservices@EF.uk) or by fax to 0123 456 7778.

Mündliche Prüfung

Die Prüfung ist eine Gruppenprüfung, bei der Sie Gespräche persönlichen und fachlichen Inhalts in der Fremdsprache führen sollen. Es wird von Ihnen erwartet, dass Sie der vorgegebenen Situation entsprechend sprachlich agieren und reagieren. Es kommt dabei vor allem darauf an, dass Sie sich spontan äußern, dass Sie versuchen, sich verständlich zu machen und dass Sie gut zuhören.

Die Prüfung besteht aus zwei Teilen (ggf. noch einer dritten Zusatzaufgabe) und dauert insgesamt ca. 20 Minuten. Zur Vorbereitung haben Sie 20 Minuten Zeit.

Im ersten Teil der mündlichen Prüfung werden Sie gebeten, sich zu persönlichen oder beruflichen Themen zu äußern.

Im zweiten Teil sollen Sie zusammen mit einem anderen Kandidaten ein Rollenspiel durchführen. Dazu erhalten Sie vom Prüfer Rollenkarten, auf denen eine Situation beschrieben ist, die Sie vorspielen sollen. Eventuell nehmen Sie in einem dritten Teil zu einer vorgegebenen Situation Stellung.

Hilfsmittel: allgemeines zweisprachiges Wörterbuch.

Mündliche Prüfung Teil II

Situation

Sie möchten sich nach Ihrer Ausbildung auf folgende Anzeige bewerben. Da Sie wissen, dass das Bewerbungsgespräch auf Englisch stattfinden wird, üben Sie mit Ihrem Partner dieses Gespräch (siehe S. 119).

Wir suchen einen Disponenten für Containerverkehr (m/w)

Ihre Aufgaben:

- Organisation der Containertransporte per LKW im In- und Ausland
- Operative Kundenbetreuung und Reklamationsbearbeitung
- Auftragsannahme und -abwicklung
- Frachteinkauf und -verkauf
- Kommunikation mit den Fernfahrern
- Kontrolle und Verwaltung der Beförderungspapiere

Ihre Qualifikationen:

- abgeschlossene Ausbildung im Speditions- oder Logistikbereich
- Selbstständiges und eigenverantwortliches Arbeiten
- Organisationsgeschick
- Gute EDV- Kenntnisse
- Gute Englischkenntnisse

Wir bieten:

- diverse Weiterbildungs- und Qualifizierungsmöglichkeiten
- Bezahlung nach hauseigenem Tarifvertrag
- gute Sozialleistungen, Weihnachts- und Urlaubsgeld
- persönliche Beratung und Betreuung durch einen Disponenten

Für weitere Informationen steht Ihnen unserer Personalberater Herr Stefan Heinrich gerne zur Verfügung.

Bitte senden Sie Ihre Bewerbungsunterlagen unter Angabe Ihrer Einkommensvorstellung mit Anschreiben, Lebenslauf und den relevanten Zeugnissen an: mail@spedition_go.de

Student A

You are the personnel manager at Spedition Go. You are going interview the applicant. Give them enough time to respond and use your imagination to make up possible answers to the applicants questions.

– Introduce yourself and start the conversation with some polite small talk to make the applicant feel at ease
– Find out about the applicant´s reasons for applying to your company
– Find out in which department(s) the applicant has worked during her/his apprenticeship
– Outline the main points in your company´s policy (team work and customer orientation) and ask the applicant if he/she understands the importance of these points
– Ask the applicant about their strengths
– Tell the applicant that the company welcomes motivated employees and usually supports opportunities to further qualifications

Student B

You are an applicant for the job of *Disponent für Containerverkehr* at Spedition Go. You are invited for a job interview. Be prepared to ask and answer questions. Use your imagination to make up possible answers to the interviewer's questions.

Listen to how your partner introduces himself/herself.
– Introduce yourself and continue with polite small talk
– State why you wish to work for Spedition Go
– Give some details about your apprenticeship and the departments you have worked in
– Point out that looking after customers is important to you and give an example from your daily routine
– Describe your strengths
– Ask about *Weiterbildungs- und Qualifizierungsmöglichkeiten* mentioned in the advertisement
– Find out what is expected from employees

Glossary

Bill of lading (B/L) *Konnossement, Seefrachtbrief*
Beleg/Nachweis über den zwischen Befrachter
(Verschiffer) und Verfrachter (im Regelfall die
Reederei) abgeschlossenen Seefrachtvertrag. Es
handelt sich dabei genauer um einen Nachweis
über den Abschluss des Seefrachtvertrags
zwischen Verschiffer und Reederei, den Empfang
der Ware durch die Reederei, die Verpflichtung der
Reederei, die Ware demjenigen auszuhändigen,
der ein Seefrachtbriefexemplar (Konnossement)
vorlegt sowie das Eigentum an der Ware (da es sich
um ein so genannte Inhaberpapier handelt).
Das Konnossement wird bei Schiffsabfahrt vom
Verfrachter (d. h. der Reederei und manchmal der
Spedition) ausgestellt, parallel zur Schifffahrt per
Post verschickt und muss bei Schiffsankunft im
Hafen wieder vorgelegt werden. Es wird in der
Regel in drei Originalexemplaren ausgestellt (so
genannter „voller Satz von Konnossementen").
Die Übersendung der drei Originalkonnossemente
an ihren Empfänger (d. h. den neuen Eigentümer)
sollte zur Sicherheit auf drei verschiedenen
Postwegen erfolgen und ist so vorzunehmen,
dass die Dokumente vor dem Schiff im Zielhafen
eintreffen. Die Reederei muss die Ware (das
Frachtgut) demjenigen aushändigen, der als erster
ein Originalkonnossement vorlegt, d. h. mit der
Vorlage des einen Originals verlieren die restlichen
Originale ihre Wirksamkeit.

Certificate of origin *Ursprungszeugnis*
Weist den Ursprung von Waren nach. Im inter-
nationalen Warenverkehr ist der Nachweis des
Ursprungs häufig erforderlich für:
- die Kontrolle der Warenströme,
- die Durchführung von Antidumping-
  Maßnahmen,
- den Abschluss von Exportkreditversicherungen
  (Hermes-Bürgschaften),
- die Überwachung von Importbeschränkungen
  und Importkontingenten,
- die Überwachung der Einhaltung von Embargos.
In der Regel entscheidet das Zielland über die
Notwendigkeit eines Ursprungszeugnisses.

Commercial invoice *Handelsrechnung*
Dient vor allem der Überprüfung der vertrags-
mäßigen Abwicklung des Warengeschäfts durch
den Empfänger der Ware. Darüber hinaus dient sie
den Behörden zur Ein- und Ausfuhrüberwachung

sowie der zollrechtlichen Abwicklung im Einfuhr-
land. Sie beschreibt durch folgende Informationen
die Ware näher:
- Namen und Anschriften der Vertragspartner
- Warenbezeichnung
- Menge und Preis der Ware
- vereinbarte Liefer- und Zahlungsbedingungen.

Curriculum vitae (CV) *Lebenslauf*
Dies ist die britische Bezeichnung; in den USA ist
resumé üblich.

**Dangerous goods note (DGN) / Hazardous goods
note** *Gefahrgut/-güteranzeige*
Als Gefahrgut (International Dangerous Goods)
bezeichnet man Stoffe, Zubereitungen (Gemische,
Gemenge, Lösungen) und Gegenstände, welche
Stoffe enthalten, von denen aufgrund ihrer Natur,
ihrer physikalischen oder chemischen Eigen-
schaften ihres Zustandes beim Transport
bestimmte Gefahren ausgehen können und die
aufgrund von Rechtsvorschriften als gefährliche
Güter einzustufen sind. Einfach gesagt wird ein
Gefahrstoff, sobald er transportiert wird, ein
Gefahrgut (hazmat – hazardous material). Für die
Beförderung dieser Güter muss eine besondere
Gefahrgutanzeige mitgeführt werden.

**Incorporated / Inc oder Corporation / Corp.
(US)** *Aktiengesellschaft*
Im Gegensatz zu deutschen Aktiengesellschaften
sind Aktiengesellschaften in den USA mit weniger
Eigenkapital zu gründen. Sie ist die von
Ausländern am häufigsten gewählte Rechtsform.

**Letter of credit (L/C) auch Documentary credit
(D/C)** *Dokumentenakkreditiv*
Ein Akkreditiv ist ein abstraktes, bedingtes
Zahlungsversprechen der Bank eines Importeurs,
in dem sie sich gegenüber dem Exporteur einer
Ware verpflichtet, bei Vorlage der entsprechenden
Dokumente Zahlung zu leisten. Somit ist das
Zahlungsversprechen der Bank rechtlich losgelöst
vom Grundgeschäft und steht selbstständig neben
dem Kaufvertrag. Das Akkreditiv ist ein Instrument,
mit dem im Außenhandel die Interessen von
Käufern und Verkäufern von Waren ausgeglichen
werden. Der Käufer erhält durch diese Form der
Abwicklung die Gewissheit, dass er nur zahlen
muss, wenn der Verkäufer geliefert hat, und dies
durch die Vorlage ordnungsgemäßer Dokumente

nachgewiesen hat. Der Verkäufer bekommt die Gewissheit, dass er nach Lieferung und Vorlage ordnungsgemäßer Dokumente seinen Erlös erhält.

Limited company (Ltd) (GB) / **Limited Liability Company (LLC)** (US) *GmbH*
Die Mehrzahl der Unternehmen in Großbritannien wird als Private Limited Company (Ltd) gegründet. Unternehmen dieser Rechtsform dürfen keine Anteile an die Öffentlichkeit abgeben. Es handelt sich hierbei um eine Gesellschaft mit beschränkter Haftung, in etwa mit der deutschen GmbH vergleichbar, aber einfacher, schneller und kostengünstiger zu gründen.

Notify party *Zu benachrichtigende Firma/Stelle*
Damit bezeichnet man die auf dem Seefrachtbrief (bill of lading) aufgeführte Partei, die von der Reederei zu benachrichtigen ist, wenn die Ware im Bestimmungshafen angekommen ist.

Public limited company (plc) (GB) *AG*
Ebenfalls eine Gesellschaft mit beschränkter Haftung, darf aber unter bestimmten Umständen Aktien an die allgemeine Öffentlichkeit abgeben. Unternehmen dieser Rechtsform entsprechen am ehesten der deutschen Aktiengesellschaft (AG).

T1 document *T1-Dokument / Zollversandschein*
Dokumentiert, dass der Ursprung der Ware außerhalb der EU liegt. Europaweit hat es eine maximale Frist von 8 Tagen. Innerhalb dieses

Zeitraumes muss das Zollpapier bei einem Zollamt gestellt werden, wo es dann durch die Verzollung der Ware erledigt wird.

Terms and conditions
Allgemeine Geschäftsbedingungen
In Angeboten werden häufig die AGBs des Kaufes genannt, z. B. Zahlungsbedingungen (Terms of payment) oder Lieferbedingungen (Terms of delivery). Man benutzt also eher den Begriff *terms* als *conditions*. Üblicherweise beginnt man mit *Our terms are as follows: ...*

Trainee *Auszubildender*
Da in angelsächsischen Ländern eine Ausbildung im dualen System nicht bekannt ist, wird eher ein on-the-job training bevorzugt.

Waybill *Frachtbrief*
Ein Beförderungsdokument, das die Güter begleitet. Im § 408 HGB werden die Angaben aufgeführt, die ein Frachtbrief enthalten muss. Der ordnungsgemäß ausgestellte Frachtbrief beweist gem. § 409 HGB Abschluss und Inhalt des Frachtvertrages sowie die Übernahme des Gutes durch den Frachtführer und begründet die Vermutung, dass das Gut und seine Verpackung bei der Übernahme durch den Frachtführer in äußerlich gutem Zustand waren und dass die Anzahl der Frachtstücke und ihre Zeichen und Nummern mit den Angaben im Frachtbrief übereinstimmen. Im nationalen Güterverkehr ist er seit 1998 nicht mehr Pflicht, es können auch andere Warenbegleitpapiere, z. B. Lieferscheine (delivery notes) oder Ladelisten (cargo lists) verwendet werden.

Terms of payment

cash in advance	*Vorauszahlung/Vorkasse*
payment on receipt of invoice / payment on invoice	*Zahlung bei Rechnungserhalt*
cash on delivery (COD)	*gegen Nachnahme*
payment on receipt of goods	*Zahlung bei Erhalt der Waren*
documents against payment (D/P) / cash against documents (CAD)	*Kasse gegen Dokumente*
documents against acceptance (D/A)	*Dokumente gegen Akzept*
payment by irrevocable and confirmed documentary (letter of) credit	*Zahlung durch unwiderrufliches und bestätigtes Dokumentenakkreditiv*

Unit word list

Dieses Wörterverzeichnis enthält alle Wörter in der Reihenfolge ihres Erscheinens.
T = das Wort befindet sich in den Transcripts (Hörverständnisübungen).

Unit 1

p. 7 trainee [treɪ'niː] — Auszubildende/r
internship ['ɪntɜːnʃɪp] — Praktikum
receive [rɪ'siːv] — erhalten, bekommen
site plan ['saɪt plæn] — Lageplan
key [kiː] — *hier:* (Karten-)Legende
entrance ['entrəns] — Eingang
main [meɪn] — Haupt-
warehouse ['weəhaʊs] — Lager(halle)

p. 8 figure ['fɪgə] — Zahl, Ziffer
key figures ['kiː 'fɪgəz] — Kennzahlen
family-owned business [ˌfæməli əʊnd 'bɪznəs] — Familienbetrieb
grow into sth ['grəʊ ɪntə] — sich zu etw entwickeln
major ['meɪdʒə] — bedeutend, wichtig, größer
global ['gləʊbl] — weltweit (*tätig*)
operation [ˌɒpə'reɪʃn] — Betrieb, Geschäft
sale [seɪl] — Vertrieb
delivery [dɪ'lɪvəri] — Lieferung, Zustellung
employee [ɪm'plɔɪiː] — Angestellte/r
alliance [ə'laɪəns] — Bündnis, Allianz
forwarding agency [ˌfɔːwədɪŋ 'eɪdʒənsi] — Spedition
technically ['teknɪkli] — technisch
advanced [əd'vɑːnst] — modern, fortschrittlich
access ['ækses] — Zugriff, Zugang
excellent ['eksələnt] — hervorragend, ausgezeichnet
guarantee [ˌgærən'tiː] — Garantie
efficient [ɪ'fɪʃnt] — effizient
cover ['kʌvə] — sich erstrecken über
area ['eəriə] — Fläche
stocked [stɒkt] — lagernd, gelagert
handle ['hændl] — umschlagen, bearbeiten, erledigen
consignment [kən'saɪnmənt] — Sendung, Lieferung
deliver [dɪ'lɪvə] — liefern, zustellen
van [væn] — Lieferwagen
length [leŋθ] — Länge
conveyor belt [kən'veɪə belt] — Förderband
order ['ɔːdə] — Auftrag, Bestellung
place (an order) [pleɪs] — (*Auftrag*) erteilen, (*Bestellung*) aufgeben
employ [ɪm'plɔɪ] — beschäftigen

p. 9 associated with [ə'səʊʃieɪtɪd wɪð] — verbunden mit
appointment [ə'pɔɪntmənt] — Termin

treat sb [triːt] — jdn behandeln
found [faʊnd] — gründen
package ['pækɪdʒ] — Paket
guarantee [ˌgærən'tiː] — garantieren
introduce sb/sth [ˌɪntrə'djuːs] — jdn/etw vorstellen
director [də'rektə] — Leiter/in
branch (of a company) [brɑːntʃ] — Niederlassung

p. 10 include [ɪn'kluːd] — enthalten
goods [gʊdz] — Güter, Waren
quote [kwəʊt] — zitieren
Crimean War [kraɪˌmiːən 'wɔː] — Krimkrieg (1853–56)
chief quartermaster [ˌtʃiːf 'kwɔːtəmɑːstə] — Oberquartiermeister
divide up [dɪ'vaɪd ʌp] — aufteilen
(army) supplies [ˌɑːmi sə'plaɪz] — Nachschub
sound [saʊnd] — klingen
sensible ['sensəbl] — vernünftig
clerk [klɑːk] — Sachbearbeiter/in
account operative [ə'kaʊnt ɒpərətɪv] — Sachbearbeiter/in
producer [prə'djuːsə] — Hersteller, Produzent
split [splɪt] — aufteilen
warehouse worker ['weəhaʊs wɜːkə] — Lagerarbeiter/in
T load [ləʊd] — laden
unload [ˌʌn'ləʊd] — abladen, ausladen, entladen
contain [kən'teɪn] — enthalten
disaster [dɪ'zɑːstə] — Katastrophe
specifically [spə'sɪfɪkli] — genau, im Einzelnen
specialize in sth ['speʃəlaɪz ɪn] — sich auf etw spezialisieren
stationery ['steɪʃənri] — Schreibwaren, Bürobedarf
responsible for [rɪ'spɒnsəbl] — verantwortlich für, zuständig für
storage ['stɔːrɪdʒ] — Lagerung
packaging ['pækɪdʒɪŋ] — Verpackung
mixture ['mɪkstʃə] — Mischung
client ['klaɪənt] — Kunde/-in
commercial [kə'mɜːʃl] — Wirtschafts-
public ['pʌblɪk] — öffentlich
sense [sens] — Sinn
store [stɔː] — lagern
forward sth ['fɔːwəd] — etw versenden, verschicken
form of transport [ˌfɔːm əv 'trɑːnspɔːt] — Transportart

iː	ɪ	e	æ	ɑː	ɒ	ɔː	ʊ	uː	ʌ	ɜː	ə
see	sit	ten	bad	arm	got	saw	put	too	cut	bird	about

deal with sth	mit etw zu tun haben,	senior management	Betriebsleitung, leitende
['diːl wɪð]	für etw zuständig sein	[ˌsiːniə 'mænɪdʒmənt]	Angestellte, Direktion
depend [dɪ'pend]	davon abhängen	copy ['kɒpi]	abschreiben
freight [freɪt]	Fracht	organizational chart	Organigramm
road freight	Lkw-Ladung, Lkw-	[ɔːgənaɪˌzeɪʃənl 'tʃɑːt]	
['rəʊd freɪt]	Transport, Straßen-	mention ['menʃn]	erwähnen, nennen
	gütertransport	be missing [bi 'mɪsɪŋ]	fehlen
rail [reɪl]	Schiene	sketch [sketʃ]	skizzieren
rail freight ['reɪl freɪt]	Bahnfracht	p. 13 proper(ly) ['prɒpəli]	richtig
air freight ['eə freɪt]	Luftfracht	impression [ɪm'preʃn]	Eindruck
sea freight ['siː freɪt]	Seefracht	respond to sth	auf etw reagieren, auf
basic administration	elementare Verwaltungs-	[rɪ'spɒnd tə]	etw antworten
T [ˌbeɪsɪk ədˌmɪnɪ'streɪʃn]	aufgaben	introductions	Vorstellung
staff [stɑːf]	Angestellte/r, Personal	[ˌɪntrə'dʌkʃnz]	
administrative	Verwaltungs-	pleasure ['pleʒə]	Freude, Vergnügen
[əd'mɪnɪstrətɪv]		order ['ɔːdə]	Reihenfolge
department	Abteilung	belong [bɪ'lɒŋ]	gehören
[dɪ'pɑːtmənt]		colour spectrum	Farbspektrum
course [kɔːs]	Lauf, Verlauf	['kʌlə spektrəm]	
chance [tʃɑːns]	Gelegenheit	unsafe [ˌʌn'seɪf]	gefährlich, nicht sicher
look forward to sth	sich auf etw freuen	avoid [ə'vɔɪd]	vermeiden
[ˌlʊk 'fɔːwəd tə]		p. 14 copy ['kɒpi]	Exemplar
not to get excited about sth		overseas [ˌəʊvə'siːz]	Auslands-, in Übersee
[ˌget ɪk'saɪtɪd əbaʊt]	sich nicht zu viele	operate ['ɒpəreɪt]	funktionieren
	Hoffnungen machen	maintain	(Daten etc.) pflegen,
p. 11 movement ['muːvmənt]	Bewegung, Fortbewegung	[meɪn'teɪn]	verwalten
remove [rɪ'muːv]	entfernen	consignment note	Frachtbrief,
vehicle ['viːəkl]	Fahrzeug	[kən'saɪnmənt nəʊt]	Warenbegleitschein
records ['rekɔːdz]	Unterlagen, Daten	query ['kwɪəri]	Anfrage
customer records	Kundendaten	complaint [kəm'pleɪnt]	Reklamation, Beschwerde
['kʌstəmə rekɔːdz]		delayed [dɪ'leɪd]	verspätet, verzögert
section ['sekʃn]	Teil, Abteilung	item ['aɪtəm]	Artikel
consign sth [kən'saɪn]	etw senden, versenden	track [træk]	(eine Sendung) verfolgen
pack sth ['pæk]	etw verpacken	trace [treɪs]	(eine Sendung) orten
p. 12 ground floor	Erdgeschoss	involve	mit sich bringen,
[ˌgraʊnd 'flɔː]		[ɪn'vɒlv]	beinhalten
head [hed]	Chef/in, Leiter/in	packing list	Packliste, Versandliste
finance ['faɪnæns]	Finanzen, Finanzabteilung	['pækɪŋ lɪst]	
managing director	Geschäftsführer/in	nightmare ['naɪtmeə]	Alptraum
[ˌmænɪdʒɪŋ də'rektə]		measure ['meʒə]	messen
Human Resources	Personal(abteilung)	amount [ə'maʊnt]	Betrag, Menge
[ˌhjuːmən rɪ'sɔːsɪz]		empty space	Leerraum
Customer Services	Kundendienst,	[ˌempti 'speɪs]	
[ˌkʌstəmə 's3ːvɪsɪz]	Kundenbetreuung	cut [kʌt]	zuschneiden
Sales [seɪlz]	Vertrieb(sabteilung)	seal sth [siːl]	etw zukleben
reception [rɪ'sepʃn]	Empfang	label sth ['leɪbl]	etw etikettieren
at first hand	mit eigenen Augen	p. 15 transport clerk	Transportsach-
[ət ˌf3ːst 'hænd]		['trɑːnspɔːt klɑːk]	bearbeiter/in
area ['eəriə]	Bereich	arrange	arrangieren, planen,
enter ['entə]	(Gebäude) betreten	[ə'reɪndʒ]	festlegen
wing [wɪŋ]	Flügel	route [ruːt]	Route, Strecke
T floor [flɔː]	Stockwerk, Etage	sales adviser	Vertriebsberater/in
partly ['pɑːtli]	zum Teil, teilweise	['seɪlz ədvaɪzə]	
pop in [ˌpɒp 'ɪn]	vorbeischauen	acquire [ə'kwaɪə]	akquirieren
carry on	weitergehen,	existing customer	Bestandskunde/-in
[ˌkæri 'ɒn]	weitermachen	[ɪgˌzɪstɪŋ 'kʌstəmə]	
expansion [ɪk'spænʃn]	Erweiterung		

tʃ	dʒ	ʃ	ʒ	θ	ð	ŋ	s	z	v	w	
chips	jet	ship	garage	thing	the	ring	ice	as	very	wet	123

bookkeeping ['bʊkkiːpɪŋ]	Buchhaltung, Buchführung
invoice ['ɪnvɔɪs]	Rechnung
supply chain [sə'plaɪ ˌtʃeɪn]	Lieferkette
consignor [kən'saɪnə]	Versender, Absender, Verlader
shipper ['ʃɪpə]	Versender
manufacturer [ˌmænjuˈfæktʃərə]	Hersteller/in
retailer ['riːteɪlə(r)]	Einzelhändler/in
engage [ɪnˈgeɪdʒ]	beauftragen
freight forwarding agency [freɪt ˌfɔːwədɪŋ 'eɪdʒənsi]	Spedition
pick-up [ˌpɪk ʌp]	Abholung
freight forwarder ['freɪt fɔːwədə]	Spediteur
collection [kəˈlekʃn]	Abholung
cargo movement ['kɑːgəʊ muːvmənt]	Güterbeförderung
process ['prəʊses]	bearbeiten
road haulage [rəʊd 'hɔːlɪdʒ]	Straßentransport
marine shipping company [məˈriːn 'ʃɪpɪŋ 'kʌmpəni]	Schifffahrtsgesellschaft, Reederei
air cargo company ['eə(r) ' kɑːgəʊ 'kʌmpəni]	Luftfrachtgesellschaft
destination [ˌdestɪˈneɪʃn]	Zielort, Bestimmungsort
consignee [ˌkɒnsaɪˈniː]	Empfänger/in, Adressat/in
sign [saɪn]	unterschreiben
p.16 training ['treɪnɪŋ]	Ausbildung
qualification [ˌkwɒlɪfɪˈkeɪʃn]	Abschluss, Qualifikation
on-the-job training [ɒn ðə ˌdʒɒb 'treɪnɪŋ]	innerbetriebliche Ausbildung
off-the-job training [ɒf ðə ˌdʒɒb 'treɪnɪŋ]	schulische Ausbildung, Weiterbildung
development [dɪ'veləpmənt]	Entwicklung, Weiterbildung
depend on sth [dɪ'pend ɒn]	von etw abhängen
corporate account sales manager [ˌkɔːpərət əˌkaʊnt' seɪlz mænɪdʒə]	Geschäftskunden- betreuer/in
extend over [ɪk'stend əʊvə]	sich erstrecken über
operational area [ɒpəˌreɪʃənl 'eəriə]	Geschäftsbereich
dedicated ['dedɪkeɪtɪd]	speziell
trainer ['treɪnə]	Ausbilder/in
chartered ['tʃɑːtəd]	amtlich zugelassen
workplace ['wɜːkpleɪs]	Arbeitsplatz
distribution [ˌdɪstrɪˈbjuːʃn]	Vertrieb, Versand

work one's way through sth [ˌwɜːk wʌnz 'weɪ θruː]	sich durch etw hindurch- arbeiten
cover ['kʌvə]	umfassen
range [reɪndʒ]	Reihe, Auswahl, Bandbreite
distance-learning course [ˌdɪstəns lɜːnɪŋ 'kɔːs]	Fernkurs
leader ['liːdə]	Führungskraft
leadership ['liːdəʃɪp]	Führung, Leitung
people management ['piːpl mænɪdʒmənt]	Personalführung
recruitment [rɪˈkruːtmənt]	Einstellung, Personalbeschaffung
performance [pəˈfɔːməns]	Leistung
appraisal [əˈpreɪzl]	Bewertung, Beurteilung
ensure [ɪnˈʃʊə]	sicherstellen, gewährleisten
opportunity [ˌɒpəˈtjuːnəti]	Gelegenheit, Möglichkeit
relevant to ['reləvənt]	wichtig für
area of expertise [ˌeəriə əv ˌekspɜːˈtiːz]	Fachgebiet
complete [kəmˈpliːt]	(Ausbildung) abschließen
professional [prəˈfeʃənl]	beruflich, Berufs-

Unit 2

p.17 majority [məˈdʒɒrəti]	Mehrheit, Großteil
familiar [fəˈmɪliə]	vertraut
member ['membə]	Mitglied
state [steɪt]	Staat, Land
identify [aɪˈdentɪfaɪ]	bestimmen
p.18 freight manager ['freɪt mænɪdʒə]	Speditionskaufmann/-frau
haulage company ['hɔːlɪdʒ kʌmpəni]	(Straßen-)Spedition(sfirma), Frachtfuhrunternehmen
apprentice [əˈprentɪs]	Auszubildende/r, Lehrling
apprenticeship [əˈprentɪʃɪp]	Ausbildung, Lehre
yard [jɑːd]	Hof
sliding door [ˌslaɪdɪŋ 'dɔː]	Schiebetür
rigid ['rɪdʒɪd]	starr
tilt [tɪlt]	kippen
bulk loader ['bʌlk ləʊdə]	Schüttgutlader
bulk load ['bʌlk ləʊd]	Schüttladung
scrap metal ['skræp metl]	Schrott, Altmetall
wood chips ['wʊd tʃɪps]	Holzspäne
volume ['vɒljuːm]	Menge, Volumen
liquid ['lɪkwɪd]	Flüssigkeit
fuel ['fjuːəl]	Brennstoff, Treibstoff, Benzin
petrol ['petrəl]	Benzin
swing down [ˌswɪŋ 'daʊn]	(sich) herunterklappen (lassen)

iː	ɪ	e	æ	ɑː	ɒ	ɔː	ʊ	uː	ʌ	ɜː	ə
see	sit	ten	bad	arm	got	saw	put	too	cut	bird	about

side loader ['saɪd ləʊdə]	Seitenlader	
timber ['tɪmbə]	(Nutz-)Holz	
pipe [paɪp]	Rohr, Röhre	
trailer ['treɪlə]	Anhänger, Sattelauflieger	
articulated lorry (BE) [ɑːˌtɪkjuleɪtɪd 'lɒri]	Sattelschlepper, Sattelzug	
cover ['kʌvə]	abdecken, bedecken	
heavy-duty [ˌhevi'djuːti]	strapazierfähig	
waterproof ['wɔːtəpruːf]	wasserdicht	
tarpaulin [tɑː'pɔːlɪn]	Plane	
secure sth [sɪ'kjʊə]	etw befestigen	
rope [rəʊp]	Seil	
curtain-sided trailer [ˌkɜːtn saɪdɪd 'treɪlə]	Schiebeplanenauflieger, Gardinenplanen- auflieger	
tautliner ['tɔːtlaɪnə]	Schiebeplanenauflieger, Gardinenplaner- auflieger	
equipment [ɪ'kwɪpmənt]	Gerät(e), Ausrüstung	
sensitive ['sensətɪv]	empfindlich	
cargo ['kɑːgəʊ]	Fracht	
be bound to do sth [bi 'baʊnd tə duː]	etw bestimmt tun	
container trailer [kən'teɪnə treɪlə]	Containerchassis, Containertrailer	
low loader [ˌləʊ 'ləʊdə]	Tieflader	
step frame ['step freɪm]	Tieflader	
construction machinery [kən'strʌkʃn məʃiːnəri]	Baumaschinen	
steel [stiːl]	Stahl	

p.19 convenient [kən'viːniənt] — günstig, praktisch
depending on [dɪ'pendɪŋ ɒn] — je nach
weight [weɪt] — Gewicht
nature ['neɪtʃə] — Art
(rail) rolling stock ['rəʊlɪŋ stɒk] — rollendes Material (Waggons und Loko- motiven)
bulk wagon ['bʌlk wægən] — Schüttgutwagen
car transporter ['kɑː trɑːnspɔːtə] — Autotransportwagen
flat car ['flætkɑː] — Flachwagen
hopper wagon (BE) ['hɒpə wægən] — Schüttgutwagen
(live) stock car ['laɪv stɒk kɑː] — Viehtransportwagen
tank wagon ['tæŋk wægən] — Tankwagen
coal [kəʊl] — Kohle
livestock ['laɪvstɒk] — Vieh
sleeper ['sliːpə] — (Eisenbahn:) Bahnschwelle
wire cable ['waɪə keɪbl] — Drahtkabel

p.20 customer services manager [kʌstəmə sɜːvɪsɪz mætɪdʒə] — Kundenberater/in
attend sth [ə'tend] — an etw teilnehmen
arrange [ə'reɪndʒ] — regeln, arrangieren
shipment ['ʃɪpmənt] — Versand
item of furniture [ˌaɪtəm əv 'fɜːnɪtʃə] — Möbelstück
available [ə'veɪləbl] — verfügbar
appreciate sth [ə'priːʃieɪt] — etw zu schätzen wissen
at the latest [ət ðə 'leɪtɪst] — spätestens
regards [rɪ'gɑːdz] — Grüße
reliable [rɪ'laɪəbl] — zuverlässig
quote [kwəʊt] — Kostenvoranschlag, Angebot
refer to sb/sth [rɪ'fɜː tə] — von jdm/etw sprechen, jdn/etw erwähnen

p.21 division [dɪ'vɪʒn] — Abteilung, Sparte
paperwork ['peɪpəwɜːk] — Formalitäten, Papierkram
priority [praɪ'ɒrəti] — Vorrang, Priorität
tailor ['teɪlə] — (auf etw) zuschneiden
insurance [ɪn'ʃʊərəns] — Versicherung
customs ['kʌstəmz] — Zoll
poor [pɔː] — hier: schlecht

p.22 details ['diːteɪlz] — Einzelheiten, Angaben, Daten
be about [bi ə'baʊt] — da sein
by any chance [baɪ 'eni tʃɑːns] — zufällig
indeed [ɪn'diːd] — in der Tat, tatsächlich
get in touch with sb [get ɪn 'tʌtʃ wɪð] — sich mit jdm in Verbindung setzen
cabinet ['kæbɪnət] — Aktenschrank
wastepaper basket [ˌweɪst'peɪpə bɑːskɪt] — Papierkorb
total ['təʊtl] — Gesamt-
weigh [weɪ] — wiegen
pick up [ˌpɪk 'ʌp] — abholen
precise [prɪ'saɪs] — genau, präzise
short notice [ˌʃɔːt 'nəʊtɪs] — kurzfristig
manage ['mænɪdʒ] — es schaffen
freight term ['freɪt tɜːm] — Frachtklausel
clarify ['klærəfaɪ] — klären, erläutern
digit ['dɪdʒɪt] — Ziffer
(forward) slash [ˌfɔːwəd 'slæʃ] — Schrägstrich
hyphen ['haɪfn] — Bindestrich
underscore [ˌʌndə'skɔː] — Unterstrich

p.23 miss sb/sth [mɪs] — jdn/etw verpassen
mind [maɪnd] — etwas dagegen haben
comparison [kəm'pærɪsn] — Vergleich

tʃ	dʒ	ʃ	ʒ	θ	ð	ŋ	s	z	v	w
ch ips	jet	ship	gara ge	thing	the	ring	ice	as	very	wet

125

p.24 consider [kən'sɪdə]   berücksichtigen
charge [tʃɑːdʒ]   Gebühr, Preis
as follows [əz 'fɒləʊz]   wie folgt
pre-carriage   Vorlauf
[ˌpriː 'kærɪdʒ]
port [pɔːt]   Hafen
handling charge   Rollgebühren
['hændlɪŋ tʃɑːdʒ]
docking charge   Dockgebühren, Löschgeld
['dɒkɪŋ tʃɑːdʒ]
export clearance   Ausfuhrabfertigung
['ekspɔːt klɪərəns]
main-carriage   Hauptlauf
['meɪn kærɪdʒ]
on-carriage ['ɒn kærɪdʒ]   Nachlauf
VAT (value added tax)   Mehrwertsteuer
[ˌviː eɪ 'tiː, ˌvæljuː 'ædɪd tæks]
complimentary close   Schlussformel (Brief)
[ˌkɒmplɪˌmentri 'kləʊz]
closing paragraph   Schlußabsatz
[ˌkləʊzɪŋ 'pærəgrɑːf]
sender ['sendə]   Absender
salutation [ˌsælju'teɪʃn]   Anrede (Brief)
introduction   Einleitung
[ˌɪntrə'dʌkʃn]
main body [ˌmeɪn 'bɒdi]   Haupttext
position [pə'zɪʃn]   Stellung
reference line   Betreffzeile
['refərəns laɪn]
recipient [rɪ'sɪpiənt]   Empfänger
suitable ['suːtəbl]   passend
p.25 politeness [pə'laɪtnəs]   Höflichkeit
rank [ræŋk]   Rang
regard sb/sth as sth   jdn/etw als etw erachten,
[rɪ'gɑːd əz]   jdn/etw für etw halten
order ['ɔːdə]   Befehl
rude [ruːd]   unhöflich, unverschämt
request [rɪ'kwest]   Bitte, Anfrage
I'm afraid [ˌaɪm ə'freɪd]   leider
confirm [kən'fɜːm]   bestätigen
condition [kən'dɪʃn]   Bedingung
findings ['faɪndɪŋz]   Ergebnisse
ferry ['feri]   Fähre
port of discharge   Entladehafen
[ˌpɔːt əv 'dɪstʃɑːdʒ]
currently ['kʌrəntli]   im Moment, aktuell
strike [straɪk]   Streik
p.26 carrier ['kæriə]   Frachtführer, Verfrachter
remark [rɪ'mɑːk]   Bemerkung
transport mode   Beförderungsart
['trɑːnspɔːt məʊd]
port of loading   (Ver)ladehafen
[ˌpɔːt əv 'ləʊdɪŋ]
vessel ['vesl]   Schiff
value ['væljuː]   Wert
carriage ['kærɪdʒ]   Transport
take over [ˌteɪk 'əʊvə]   übernehmen

prepaid [ˌpriː'peɪd]   vorausbezahlt
collection [kə'lekʃn]   Inkasso, Einzug
condition [kən'dɪʃn]   Zustand
p.27 lay [leɪ]   (Gleise) verlegen
round-trip [ˌraʊnd 'trɪp]   Hin- und Rückfahrt
production plant   Produktionsstätte, Fabrik
[prə'dʌkʃn plɑːnt]
construction site   Baustelle
[kən'strʌkʃn saɪt]
intermediate   Zwischen-
[ˌɪntə'miːdiət]
place [pleɪs]   legen, plazieren
correspond to   entsprechen
[ˌkɒrɪ'spɒnd tə]
track [træk]   Gleis
roughly ['rʌfli]   ungefähr
fix [fɪks]   befestigen, anbringen
extensive [ɪk'stensɪv]   umfangreich
preparation   Vorbereitung
[ˌprepə'reɪʃn]
steelworks ['stiːlwɜːks]   Stahlwerk(e)
care [keə]   Sorgfalt
section ['sekʃn]   Abschnitt, Teil(stück)
ferry port ['feri pɔːt]   Fährhafen
indivisible [ˌɪndɪ'vɪzəbl]   unteilbar
shunt [ʃʌnt]   (Eisenbahn:) rangieren
arrival [ə'raɪvl]   Ankunft
rail gauge ['reɪl geɪdʒ]   Spurweite
state-of-the-art   modern, auf dem neuesten
[ˌsteɪt əv ði 'ɑːt]   Stand der Technik
axle ['æksl]   Achse
facility [fə'sɪləti]   Anlage
reload [ˌriː'ləʊd]   wieder/erneut laden
overnight [ˌəʊvə'naɪt]   über Nacht
shift [ʃɪft]   schieben, verschieben
rail pusher ['reɪl pʊʃə]   Schienenschiebe-
vorrichtung
pick up [ˌpɪk 'ʌp]   aufnehmen, aufladen
in accordance with   in Übereinstimmung mit,
[ɪn ə'kɔːdəns wɪð]   nach
schedule ['ʃedjuːl]   Plan, Zeitplan, Terminplan,
Fahrplan

Unit 3

p.28 maritime ['mærɪtaɪm]   See-
sea port ['siː pɔːt]   Seehafen
shipping route   Schifffahrtsweg
['ʃɪpɪŋ ruːt]
map out [ˌmæp 'aʊt]   kartographieren, in eine
Karte eintragen
percentage [pə'sentɪdʒ]   Anteil, Prozentsatz
trade [treɪd]   Handel
advantage [əd'vɑːntɪdʒ]   Vorteil
disadvantage   Nachteil
[ˌdɪsəd'vɑːntɪdʒ]
p.29 increase ['ɪŋkriːs]   zunehmen, steigen

iː	ɪ	e	æ	ɑː	ɒ	ɔː	ʊ	uː	ʌ	ɜː	ə
see	sit	ten	bad	arm	got	saw	put	too	cut	bird	about

specially ['speʃli]	speziell, eigens, für etwas (gedacht)	width [wɪdθ]	Breite
stern [stɜːn]	Heck	tare weight [ˌteə 'weɪt]	Taragewicht
tramp [træmp]	Trampschiff	payload ['peɪləʊd]	Ladegewicht, Nutzlast
crane [kreɪn]	Kran	gross weight [ˌgrəʊs 'weɪt]	Bruttogewicht
heavy-lift ship [ˌhevi lɪft 'ʃɪp]	Schwerlastschiff	net weight ['net weɪt]	Nettogewicht
bulk carrier ['bʌlk kæriə]	Massengutfrachter, Schüttgutfrachter	reliability [rɪˌlaɪə'bɪləti]	Zuverlässigkeit
grain [greɪn]	Getreide	theft [θeft]	Diebstahl
ore [ɔː]	Erz	loading ['ləʊdɪŋ]	Verladung
barge [bɑːdʒ]	Kahn, Lastkahn	unloading [ˌʌn'ləʊdɪŋ]	Entladung
sea-going barge [ˌsiː ˌgəʊɪŋ 'bɑːdʒ]	Hochseebarge, Frachtkahn	bulk container ['bʌlk kənteɪnə]	Schüttgutcontainer
float [fləʊt]	gleiten lassen	flat rack container [ˌflætræk kən'teɪnə]	Flachgestellcontainer, Flat
lift [lɪft]	heben, hieven	reefer ['riːfə]	Kühlcontainer
aboard [ə'bɔːd]	an Bord	p.32 characteristics [ˌkærəktə'rɪstɪks]	Eigenschaften, Merkmale
wheat [wiːt]	Weizen	LCL (less than container load) [ˌel siː 'el]	Teilladung
crate [kreɪt]	Holzkiste	FCL (full container load) [ˌef siː 'el]	volle Containerladung
drum [drʌm]	Fass	economical [ˌiːkə'nɒmɪkl]	wirtschaftlich
tool [tuːl]	Werkzeug	multi-country [ˌmʌlti 'kʌntri]	länderübergreifend
pallet ['pælət]	Palette	consolidation [kənˌsɒlɪ'deɪʃn]	Sammelladung, Zusammenfassung (von Lieferungen)
waste paper [ˌweɪst 'peɪpə]	Altpapier		
fertilizer ['fɜːtəlaɪzə]	Dünger	be around [bi ə'raʊnd]	es geben
barrel ['bærəl]	Fass	prove [pruːv]	sich erweisen als
p.30 intermodal container [ˌɪntəˌməʊdl kənˌteɪnər]	Container für den kombinierten Verkehr	hub [hʌb]	Knotenpunkt
cube [kjuːb]	Würfel	according to [ə'kɔːdɪŋ tə]	gemäß, nach
height [haɪt]	Höhe	stuff [stʌf]	(Container) beladen
vary ['veəri]	schwanken, variieren	inland ['ɪnlænd]	Binnen-
common ['kɒmən]	verbreitet, üblich	receiving station [rɪ'siːvɪŋ steɪʃn]	Empfangsstation, Empfangsbahnhof
measurement ['meʒəmənt]	Maß	groupage container ['gruːpɪdʒ kənteɪnə]	Sammelcontainer
set [set]	festsetzen	strip [strɪp]	(Container) entladen
International Standards Organization (ISO) [ɪntə'næʃnəl 'stændədz ɔːgənaɪzeɪʃn]	Internationale Organisation für Normung	break bulk [ˌbreɪk 'bʌlk]	Sammelladung aufteilen, umpacken
capacity [kə'pæsəti]	Fassungsvermögen, Volumen	contents ['kɒntents]	Inhalt
correspondingly [ˌkɒrɪ'spɒndɪŋli]	dementsprechend	final ['faɪnl]	endgültig
fairly ['feəli]	relativ, ziemlich	transload [trɑːns'ləʊd]	umladen
corrugated ['kɒrəgeɪtɪd]	gewellt, Well-	shorten ['ʃɔːtn]	verkürzen
seal [siːl]	versiegeln, verschließen, abdichten	transit time ['trɑːnzɪt taɪm]	Beförderungszeit, Laufzeit
protection [prə'tekʃn]	Schutz	cut costs [kʌt 'kɒsts]	Kosten senken
damage ['dæmɪdʒ]	Beschädigung	significant(ly) [sɪg'nɪfɪkəntli]	erheblich
loss [lɒs]	Verlust	breakage ['breɪkɪdʒ]	Bruch, Bruchschaden
surplus ['sɜːpləs]	überschüssig, überzählig	considerably [kən'sɪdərəbli]	beträchtlich
convert [kən'vɜːt]	umbauen		
not until [nɒt ən'tɪl]	erst	p.33 reminder [rɪ'maɪndə]	Mahnung, Erinnerung
p.31 alongside [əˌlɒŋ'saɪd]	neben	progress ['prəʊgres]	Fortschritt
inch [ɪntʃ]	Zoll	severe [sɪ'vɪə]	(Unwetter etc.) heftig
length [leŋθ]	Länge, Tiefe		

tʃ	dʒ	ʃ	ʒ	θ	ð	ŋ	s	z	v	w	
chips	jet	ship	garage	thing	the	ring	ice	as	very	wet	127

attack [əˈtæk]	Angriff	flatbed trailer	Flachbettauflieger
rate [reɪt]	Rate, Satz, Preis	[ˌflætbed ˈtreɪlə]	
fill in [ˌfɪl ˈɪn]	ausfüllen	hold-up [ˈhəʊldʌp]	Verzögerung
interrupt [ˌɪntəˈrʌpt]	unterbrechen, stören	operations manager	Einsatzleiter/in
affect [əˈfekt]	sich auswirken auf, beeinflussen	[ˌɒpəˈreɪʃnz mænɪdʒə]	
		landslide [ˈlændslaɪd]	Erdrutsch
ferry service	Fährverbindung,	T debris [ˈdebriː]	Trümmer
[ˈferi sɜːvɪs]	Fährverkehr	cope [kəʊp]	zurechtkommen
bill of lading (B/L)	Konnossement	p. 35 hold (on) [ˌhəʊld ˈɒn]	(Telefon:) dranbleiben
[ˌbɪl əv ˈleɪdɪŋ]		understatement	Untertreibung
popularity	Beliebtheit	[ˌʌndəˈsteɪtmənt]	
[ˌpɒpjuˈlærəti]		involve [ɪnˈvɒlv]	mit sich bringen, nach sich ziehen
contract [ˈkɒntrækt]	Vertrag		
inspect [ɪnˈspekt]	inspizieren	feasible [ˈfiːzəbl]	machbar, durchführbar
facilities [fəˈsɪlətiz]	Anlagen, Einrichtungen	crisis team	Krisenstab
production site	Produktionsstätte,	[ˈkraɪsɪs tiːm]	
[prəˈdʌkʃn saɪt]	Betriebsgelände	p. 36 clearance [ˈklɪərəns]	Durchfahrtsbreite
statistics [stəˈtɪstɪks]	Statistik, statistische Daten	road works	Straßenbauarbeiten
estimation [ˌestɪˈmeɪʃn]	Schätzung	[ˈrəʊd wɜːks]	
do [duː]	hier: ausreichen	demolish [dɪˈmɒlɪʃ]	abreißen
diameter [daɪˈæmɪtə]	Durchmesser	rebuild [ˌriːˈbɪld]	neu bauen
under construction	im Bau	gradient [ˈɡreɪdiənt]	Steigung
T [ˌʌndə kənˈstrʌkʃn]		turn out to be sth	sich als etw erweisen
production manager	Produktionsleiter/in	[ˌtɜːn ˈaʊt]	
[prəˈdʌkʃn mænɪdʒə]		go one's way	klappen
approximately	zirka, ungefähr	[ˌɡəʊ wʌnz ˈweɪ]	
[əˈprɒksɪmətli]		neighbouring	Nachbar-
p. 34 remaining [rɪˈmeɪnɪŋ]	ein/e letzte/r/s	[ˈneɪbərɪŋ]	
tug boat [ˈtʌɡ bəʊt]	Schlepper	undertake [ˌʌndəˈteɪk]	ausführen, vornehmen
tow [təʊ]	schleppen	modification	Veränderung
downriver [ˌdaʊnˈrɪvə]	flussabwärts	[ˌmɒdɪfɪˈkeɪʃn]	
marine surveyor	Seesachverständige/r	involved [ɪnˈvɒlvd]	beteiligt
[məˌriːn səˈveɪə]		representative	Vertreter/in
heavy-lift crane	Schwerlastkran	[ˌreprɪˈzentətɪv]	
[hevi ˌlɪft ˈkreɪn]		road construction	Straßenbaufirma
Chief Executive Officer	Geschäftsführer/in,	company [ˈrəʊd	
(CEO) [ˌtʃiːf ɪɡˈzekjətɪv	Vorstandsvorsitzende/r	kənstrʌkʃn kʌmpəni]	
ɒfɪsə]		specialist [ˈspeʃəlɪst]	Spezial-, spezialisiert
T put pressure on sb	auf jdn Druck ausüben	contractor [kənˈtræktə]	Dienstleister,
[ˌpʊt ˈpreʃə ɒn]		T	Unternehmer/in
plant manager	Betriebsleiter/in	prop sth up [ˌprɒp ˈʌp]	etw aufbauen, aufschlagen
[ˈplɑːnt mænɪdʒə]		clear [klɪə]	räumen
come up with sth	sich etw einfallen lassen,	cover [ˈkʌvə]	decken
[ˌkʌm ˈʌp wɪð]	sich etw ausdenken	incur [ɪnˈkɜː]	(Kosten:) anfallen
reasonable [ˈriːznəbl]	akzeptabel, angemessen	meet [miːt]	(Kosten:) begleichen
safety margin	Sicherheitsspielraum	agreement	Vereinbarung,
[ˈseɪfti mɑːdʒɪn]		[əˈɡriːmənt]	Übereinkunft
finish sth [ˈfɪnɪʃ]	etw fertigstellen	border [ˈbɔːdə]	Grenze
according to plan	nach Plan	border post	Grenzpfahl
[əˌkɔːdɪŋ tə ˈplæn]		[ˈbɔːdə pəʊst]	
component	Bauteil	railing [ˈreɪlɪŋ]	Geländer
[kəmˈpəʊnənt]		power cable	Stromkabel
ocean vessel	Seeschiff	[ˈpaʊə keɪbl]	
[ˈəʊʃn vesl]		replace [rɪˈpleɪs]	wieder aufstellen
equip [ɪˈkwɪp]	ausrüsten, ausstatten	a tight fit [ə ˌtaɪt ˈfɪt]	eine knappe Sache
smooth [smuːð]	reibungslos	manoeuvre [məˈnuːvə]	manövrieren
uneventful [ˌʌnɪˈventfl]	ohne Zwischenfälle		

iː	ɪ	e	æ	ɑː	ɒ	ɔː	ʊ	uː	ʌ	ɜː	ə
see	sit	ten	bad	arm	got	saw	put	too	cut	bird	about

assume [ə'sjuːm]	annehmen, davon ausgehen	gross [grəʊs]	brutto
increase [ɪn'kriːs]	(Zeit) verlängern	p.38 rise [raɪz]	(Preis etc.:) steigen
journey time ['dʒɜːni taɪm]	Fahrzeit	intend [ɪn'tend]	vorhaben
		hull [hʌl]	(Schiffs-)Rumpf
past sth [pɑːst]	an etw vorbei	slender ['slendə]	schlank
T unpleasant [ʌn'pleznt]	unerfreulich, unangenehm	support [sə'pɔːt]	Unterstützung, Stütz-
make it ['meɪk ɪt]	hier: es schaffen	propulsion [prə'pʌlʃn]	Schub, Antrieb
escort ['eskɔːt]	Eskorte	release [rɪ'liːs]	ablassen
notice ['nəʊtɪs]	(es) bemerken	adjust [ə'dʒʌst]	anpassen
plant [plɑːnt]	Fabrik, Betrieb	harmful ['hɑːmfl]	schädlich, gefährlich
dig sth up [,dɪg 'ʌp]	etw aufgraben, (Straße) aufreißen	pollutant [pə'luːtənt]	Schadstoff
		renewable [rɪ'njuːəbl]	erneuerbar
sea waybill [,siː 'weɪbɪl]	Seefrachtbrief	source [sɔːs]	Quelle
contract of carriage [,kɒntrækt əv 'kærɪdʒ]	Frachtvertrag, Beförderungsvertrag	fuel cell ['fjuːəl sel]	Brennstoffzelle
provide [prə'vaɪd]	bieten, zur Verfügung stellen	power ['paʊə]	antreiben, mit Energie versorgen
detailed ['diːteɪld]	genau, detailliert	hydrogen ['haɪdrədʒən]	Wasserstoff
identifying mark [aɪ,dentɪfaɪɪŋ 'mɑːk]	Erkennungszeichen	solar ['səʊlə]	Sonnen-
		by-product ['baɪ prɒdʌkt]	Nebenprodukt
evidence ['evɪdəns]	Nachweis	equivalent [ɪ'kwɪvələnt]	Entsprechung
documentary evidence [dɒkju,mentri 'evɪdəns]	Belege, Nachweis		

Unit 4

receipt [rɪ'siːt]	Empfangsbestätigung, Quittung
clause [klɔːz]	Klausel, Eintrag
foul B/L [faʊl ,bɪl əv 'leɪdɪŋ]	unreines Konnossement
unclean [,ʌn'kliːn]	unrein
negotiable [nɪ'gəʊʃ(i)əbl]	übertragbar, handelbar, begebbar
document of title [,dɒkjumənt əv 'taɪtl]	Inhaberpapier, Besitzurkunde
payment ['peɪmənt]	Zahlung
letter of credit [,letər əv 'kredɪt]	Akkreditiv
non-negotiable [,nɒn nɪ'gəʊʃ(i)əbl]	nicht übertragbar, nicht handelbar
p.37 haulier ['hɔːliə]	(Straßen-)Spediteur
Received for Shipment B/L [rɪ,siːvd fə 'ʃɪpmənt , bɪl əv 'leɪdɪŋ]	Empfangskonnossement
Shipped on Board B/L [ʃɪpt ɒn ,bɔːd bɪl əv 'leɪdɪŋ]	Bordkonnossement
Combined Transport B/L [kəm,baɪnd ,trɑːnspɔːt ,bɪl əv 'leɪdɪŋ]	kombiniertes Transportkonnossement
Port to Port B/L [,pɔːt tə ,pɔːt ,bɪl əv 'leɪdɪŋ]	Port-to-Port Seekonnossement
House B/L [haʊs ,bɪl əv 'leɪdɪŋ]	Spediteurkonnossement
clean B/L [kliːn ,bɪl əv 'leɪdɪŋ]	Konnossement ohne Einschränkung, reines Konnossement
receive [rɪ'siːv]	entgegennehmen

p.39 bulky ['bʌlki]	sperrig
aft [ɑːft]	achtern, Achter-
fuselage ['fjuːzəlɑːʒ]	(Flugzeug-)Rumpf
cargo bay ['kɑːgəʊ beɪ]	Laderaum
landing gear ['lændɪŋ gɪə]	Fahrwerk
loading ramp ['ləʊdɪŋ ræmp]	Laderampe
cargo door ['kɑːgəʊ dɔː]	Ladeluke
tail fin ['teɪl fɪn]	Heckflosse
medical aid [,medɪkl 'eɪd]	medizinische Hilfsgüter
refugee [,refjuˈdʒiː]	Flüchtling
wholesaler ['həʊlseɪlə]	Großhändler, Großhandel
grease [griːs]	Schmierfett
explosive [ɪk'spləʊsɪv]	Sprengstoff
air compressor ['eə kəmpresə]	Druckluftkompressor
liver ['lɪvə]	Leber
transplant ['trɑːnsplɑːnt]	Transplantation
additional [ə'dɪʃənl]	zusätzlich, Zusatz-
environmental [ɪn,vaɪrən'mentl]	Umwelt-
p.40 trade body ['treɪd bɒdi]	Handelsorganisation
serve [sɜːv]	dienen
scheduled ['ʃedjuːld]	planmäßig
air traffic ['eə træfɪk]	Luftverkehr
promote [prə'məʊt]	fördern, voranbringen
freight handling ['freɪt hændlɪŋ]	Frachtumschlag
uniform ['juːnɪfɔːm]	einheitlich
rules [ruːlz]	Bestimmungen

tʃ	dʒ	ʃ	ʒ	θ	ð	ŋ	s	z	v	w
chips	jet	ship	garage	thing	the	ring	ice	as	very	wet

location [ləʊˈkeɪʃn]	Ort, Standort	
intended for [ɪnˈtendɪd fə]	dazu gedacht	
standardize [ˈstændədaɪz]	normen	
operations [ˌɒpəˈreɪʃnz]	Betrieb	
lengthy [ˈleŋθi]	sehr lang	
fundamental to [ˌfʌndəˈmentl tə]	grundlegend für, wesentlich für	
application [ˌæplɪˈkeɪʃn]	Anwendung, *(Computer:)* Programm	
purpose [ˈpɜːpəs]	Zweck	
pattern [ˈpætn]	Muster, Schema	
p.41 crew [kruː]	Mannschaft, Besatzung, Personal	
ground crew [ˈɡraʊnd kruː]	Bodenpersonal	
load [ləʊd]	Ladung	
tie down [ˌtaɪ ˈdaʊn]	(am Boden) festzurren	
procedure [prəˈsiːdʒə]	Maßnahme	
value sth [ˈvæljuː]	etw schätzen	
unit loading device (ULD) [ˈjuːnɪt ləʊdɪŋ dɪˈvaɪs / juː el diː]	Luftfrachtcontainer	
flight attendant [ˌflaɪt əˈtendənt]	Flugbegleiter/in	
reputation [ˌrepjuˈteɪʃn]	Ruf	
p.42 air cargo [ˈeə kaːgəʊ]	Luftfracht	
regulations [ˌreɡjuˈleɪʃnz]	Bestimmungen	
adaptability [əˌdæptəˈbɪləti]	Wandlungsfähigkeit	
environment [ɪnˈvaɪrənmənt]	*hier:* Umfeld	
comprehensive [ˌkɒmprɪˈhensɪv]	umfassend	
regarding [rɪˈɡaːdɪŋ]	bezüglich, betreffend	
definitive [deˈfɪnətɪv]	maßgeblich	
professional [prəˈfeʃənl]	*(in einer bestimmten Branche)* Berufstätige/r	
on a regular basis [ɒn ə ˌreɡjələ ˈbeɪsɪs]	regelmäßig	
coverage [ˈkʌvərɪdʒ]	Deckung	
designed for sb [dɪˈzaɪnd fə]	für jdn gedacht	
general sales agent [ˌdʒenrəl ˈseɪlz eɪdʒənt]	Generalvertreter/in	
cargo agent [ˈkaːɡəʊ eɪdʒənt]	Ladungsagent/in	
authority [ɔːˈθɒrəti]	Behörde	
adapt to sth [əˈdæpt tə]	sich an etw anpassen	
meet the needs [ˌmiːt ðə ˈniːdz]	den Bedarf decken	
edition [ɪˈdɪʃn]	Ausgabe	
obtain [əbˈteɪn]	erhalten	
valuable [ˈvæljuəbl]	wertvoll	
insight [ˈɪnsaɪt]	Einblick	

govern [ˈɡʌvən]	bestimmen, regeln	
transaction [trɑːnˈzækʃn]	(Geschäfts-)Vorgang, Transaktion	
feature [ˈfiːtʃə]	Eigenschaft, *(spezielle)* Funktion	
p.43 account settlement [ˈsetlmənt]	Abrechnung	
simplify [ˈsɪmplɪfaɪ]	vereinfachen	
billing [ˈbɪlɪŋ]	Fakturierung, Rechnungsstellung	
settling (of account) [ˈsetlɪŋ]	Abrechnung	
operate [ˈɒpəreɪt]	arbeiten	
replace [rɪˈpleɪs]	ersetzen	
invoicing [ˈɪnvɔɪsɪŋ]	Fakturierung, Rechnungsstellung	
T rare(ly) [ˈreəli]	selten	
suppose [səˈpəʊz]	annehmen, glauben	
manual [ˈmænjuəl]	Handbuch	
calculate [ˈkælkjuleɪt]	berechnen	
process [ˈprəʊses]	Verfahren, Ablauf	
comply with [kəmˈplaɪ wɪð]	*(Vorschriften)* entsprechen, *(Bedingungen)* erfüllen	
law [lɔː]	Gesetz, Recht	
applicable [əˈplɪkəbl]	gültig, geltend	
withstand sth [wɪðˈstænd]	etw aushalten, einer Sache standhalten	
customs official [ˌkʌstəmz əˈfɪʃl]	Zollbeamter/-in	
clear [klɪə]	*(Zoll:)* abfertigen	
import customs [ˈɪmpɔːt kʌstəmz]	Importzoll	
p.44 wide-body [ˌwaɪd bɒdi]	Großraum-	
aircraft [ˈeəkrɑːft]	Flugzeug	
cross-section [ˈkrɒs ˌsekʃn]	Querschnitt	
quantity [ˈkwɒntəti]	Menge	
effort [ˈefət]	Arbeit, Mühe, Anstrengung	
manifest [ˈmænɪfest]	Ladungsverzeichnis	
p.45 regulate [ˈreɡjuleɪt]	beaufsichtigen, regulieren, regeln	
convenience [kənˈviːniəns]	Zweckmäßigkeit, Komfort	
competitive [kəmˈpetətɪv]	konkurrenzfähig, wettbewerbsorientiert, *(Preis:)* günstig	
essential [ɪˈsenʃl]	wesentlich, unbedingt notwendig	
p.46 advise [ədˈvaɪz]	beraten, raten	
emergency order [ɪˈmɜːdʒənsi ɔːdə]	Eilauftrag	
tape [teɪp]	Band	
since [sɪns]	da, weil	
T recommend [ˌrekəˈmend]	empfehlen	
wonder [ˈwʌndə]	sich fragen	
advice [ədˈvaɪs]	*(guter)* Rat	

iː	ɪ	e	æ	ɑː	ɒ	ɔː	ʊ	uː	ʌ	ɜː	ə
see	sit	ten	bad	arm	got	saw	put	too	cut	bird	about

give advice — raten, beraten, Rat erteilen
[gɪv əd'vaɪs]
reasonably ['riːznəbli] — ziemlich
urgent ['ɜːdʒənt] — dringend, eilig
T perishable ['perɪʃəbl] — verderblich
turn up [ˌtɜːn 'ʌp] — auftauchen
stopover ['stɒpəʊvə] — Zwischenstopp
customs clearance — Zollabfertigung
[ˌkʌstəmz 'klɪərəns]
p.47 previous ['priːviəs] — vorherig, vorig
assistance [ə'sɪstəns] — Hilfe, Unterstützung
refer to sth [rɪ'fɜː tə] — unter/in etw nachschauen
enquiry [ɪn'kwaɪəri] — Anfrage
air waybill [ˌeə 'weɪbɪl] — Luftfrachtbrief
state [steɪt] — angeben, erklären, sagen
p.48 chargeable weight — frachtpflichtiges Gewicht,
[ˌtʃɑːdʒəbl 'weɪt] — gebührenpflichtiges
— Gewicht
charges ['tʃɑːdʒɪz] — Gebühren
take into consideration — in Betracht ziehen
[ˌteɪk ɪntə
kənˌsɪdə'reɪʃn]
departure [dɪ'pɑːtʃə] — Abfahrt, Abflug
duration [dju'reɪʃn] — Dauer
on time [ɒn 'taɪm] — pünktlich
issue ['ɪʃuː] — ausstellen, ausgeben
p.49 validity [və'lɪdəti] — Gültigkeit
routing ['ruːtɪŋ] — Routenplanung
collect [kə'lekt] — unfrei
signature ['sɪgnətʃə] — Unterschrift
p.50 placement ['pleɪsmənt] — Praktikum
on behalf of sb — in jds Namen
[ɒn bɪ'hɑːf əv]
consign [kən'saɪn] — übergeben
issuing bank — ausstellende Bank
['ɪʃuːɪŋ bæŋk]
up front [ʌp 'frʌnt] — im Voraus
dodgy ['dɒdʒi] — gefährlich, unsicher
Shipper's Letter of Instructions
[ʃɪpəz ˌletər əv — Absenderanweisung
ɪn'strʌkʃnz]
T handy ['hændi] — praktisch
current ['kʌrənt] — aktuell
check number — Prüfziffer
['tʃek nʌmbə]
divide by [dɪ'vaɪd baɪ] — teilen durch
issuing carrier — ausstellender Frachtführer
[ˌɪʃuːɪŋ 'kæriə]
receiving carrier — Empfangsspediteur
[rɪˌsiːvɪŋ 'kæriə]
beneficiary — Begünstigte/r,
[ˌbenɪ'fɪʃəri] — Empfänger/in
agree [ə'griː] — vereinbaren
sum [sʌm] — Betrag, Summe
transit document — Transitpapier,
['trænzɪt dɒkjumənt] — Versandschein (EU)

commercial invoice — Handelsrechnung
[kəˌmɜːʃl 'ɪnvɔɪs]
in favour of sb — zu jds Gunsten
[ɪn 'feɪvər əv]
seller ['selə] — Verkäufer/in
p.51 natural disaster — Naturkatastrophe
[ˌnætʃrəl dɪ'zɑːstə]
strike [straɪk] — zuschlagen
drug [drʌg] — Medikament, Arzneimittel
desperate ['despərət] — verzweifelt
hit [hɪt] — treffen, hier: betroffen
face sth [feɪs] — vor etw stehen, mit etw
— konfrontiert sein
competition — Konkurrenz,
[ˌkɒmpə'tɪʃn] — Wettbewerb(er)
chamber ['tʃeɪmbə] — Kammer
commerce ['kɒmɜːs] — Handel
enterprise ['entəpraɪz] — Unternehmen,
— Unternehmung
closure ['kləʊʒə] — Schließung
airspace ['eəspeɪs] — Luftraum
far-reaching — weitreichend
[ˌfɑː 'riːtʃɪŋ]
community — Gemeinschaft
[kə'mjuːnəti]
premature — zu früh
[ˌpremə'tʃʊə]
quantify ['kwɒntɪfaɪ] — in Zahlen ausdrücken,
— quantifizieren
rely on sth [rɪ'laɪ ɒn] — auf etw angewiesen sein,
— auf etw beruhen
physical ['fɪzɪkl] — physisch, körperlich
especially [ɪ'speʃəli] — besonders
suffer from sth — unter etw leiden
['sʌfə frəm]
inconvenience — Unannehmlichkeiten
[ˌɪnkən'viːniəns]
stranded ['strændɪd] — gestrandet
in terms of — was … angeht
[ɪn 'tɜːmz əv]
heavy ['hevi] — hier: stark
affect [ə'fekt] — betreffen
including [ɪn'kluːdɪŋ] — einschließlich
be at the mercy of sb — jdm ausgeliefert sein
[bi ət ðə 'mɜːsi əv]
difficulty ['dɪfɪkəlti] — Problem, Schwierigkeit
tight [taɪt] — knapp, eng
expiry date — Verfallsdatum
[ɪk'spaɪəri deɪt]
havoc ['hævək] — Chaos
delay [dɪ'leɪ] — Verzögerung, Verspätung
point out [ˌpɔɪnt 'aʊt] — hinweisen auf
deploy [dɪ'plɔɪ] — absenden
prolonged [prə'lɒŋd] — verlängert
bottleneck ['bɒtlnek] — Engpass, Engstelle,
— Nadelöhr
cause [kɔːz] — verursachen

tʃ	dʒ	ʃ	ʒ	θ	ð	ŋ	s	z	v	w
chips	jet	ship	garage	thing	the	ring	ice	as	very	wet

131

divert [daɪ'vɜːt]	umleiten	close [kləʊs]	nahe *(gelegen)*
lengthen ['leŋθən]	verlängern	harbour ['hɑːbə]	Hafen
		distance ['dɪstəns]	Entfernung
Unit 5		rough [rʌf]	rau
		threaten ['θretn]	bedrohen, drohen
p. 52 accident ['æksɪdənt]	Unfall	insurer [ɪn'ʃʊərə]	Versicherer
no matter [nəʊ 'mætə]	egal	total loss [ˌtəʊtl 'lɒs]	Totalschaden, Totalverlust
derail [diː'reɪl]	entgleisen	constructive total loss	konstruktiver
injure ['ɪndʒə]	verletzen	[kənˌstrʌktɪv	Totalverlust, ange-
capsize ['kæpsaɪz]	kentern	ˌtəʊtl 'lɒs]	nommener Totalschaden
crash landing	Bruchlandung	pollute [pə'luːt]	verschmutzen
[ˌkræʃ 'lændɪŋ]		contaminate	kontaminieren
consider [kən'sɪdə]	berücksichtigen,	[kən'tæmɪneɪt]	
	betrachten	fuel oil [ˌfjuːəl 'ɔɪl]	Schiffstreibstoff
damage ['dæmɪdʒ]	Schaden, Beschädigung	salvage ['sælvɪdʒ]	Bergung
injury ['ɪndʒəri]	Verletzung	contract salvage	Bergung laut Vertrag
p. 53 claim [kleɪm]	Forderung, Anspruch,	[ˌkɒntrækt 'sælvɪdʒ]	
	Antrag	salvor ['sælvə]	Berger
(make an) insurance	einen Versicherungs-	take sb/sth in tow	jdn/etw in Schlepptau
claim	anspruch *(geltend*	[ˌteɪk ɪn 'təʊ]	nehmen
[ɪn'ʃʊərəns kleɪm]	*machen)*	claimant ['kleɪmənt]	Antragsteller/in
beach [biːtʃ]	stranden, auf Grund	p. 54 shaky ['ʃeɪki]	wacklig, schwach
	laufen *(lassen)*	notify sb/sth ['nəʊtɪfaɪ]	jn/etw benachrichtigen
investigation	Untersuchung	policy ['pɒləsi]	(Versicherungs-)Police
[ɪnˌvestɪ'geɪʃn]		floating policy	offene Police
rescue service	Rettungsdienst	[ˌfləʊtɪŋ 'pɒləsi]	
['reskjuː sɜːvɪs]		voyage policy	Reisepolice
claim [kleɪm]	fordern, beanspruchen,	['vɔɪɪdʒ pɒləsi]	
	einen *(Versicherungs-)*	property ['prɒpəti]	Eigentum
	Anspruch geltend	own [əʊn]	besitzen
	machen	fixed [fɪkst]	fest, festgelegt
registered owner	eingetragene/r Besitzer/in	fee [fiː]	Gebühr, Honorar
[ˌredʒɪstəd 'əʊnə]		flotsam ['flɒtsəm]	Treibgut
damages ['dæmɪdʒɪz]	Schadenersatz	debris ['debriː]	Abfall, Trümmer,
finder's fee [ˌfaɪndəz 'fiː]	Finderlohn		Überbleibsel,
sanctuary ['sæŋktʃuəri]	Schutzgebiet		Bruchstücke
recompense	Entschädigung	shipwreck ['ʃɪprek]	Schiffbruch, Schiffswrack
['rekəmpens]		remain [rɪ'meɪn]	bleiben, verbleiben
port of registry	Heimathafen	jetsam ['dʒetsəm]	über Bord geworfene
[ˌpɔːt əv 'redʒɪstri]			Ladung
operator ['ɒpəreɪtə]	Linienreederei	deliberately	absichtlich
charter ['tʃɑːtə]	Mieten, Chartern	[dɪ'lɪbərətli]	
under charter to	verchartert an	jettison ['dʒetɪsn]	über Bord werfen
[ˌʌndə 'tʃɑːtə tə]		pure [pjʊə]	rein
weaken ['wiːkən]	schwächen	pure salvage	Besitzübergang im
overloaded	überladen	[ˌpjʊə 'sælvɪdʒ]	Schadensfall
[əʊvə'ləʊdɪd]		absence ['æbsəns]	Abwesenheit
rescue ['reskjuː]	retten	derelict ['derəlɪkt]	aufgegeben, verlassen
wash off the deck	von Deck spülen	p. 55 shipwrecked goods	Strandgut
[wɒʃ ˌɒf ðə 'dek]		[ˌʃɪprekt 'gʊdz]	
huge [hjuːdʒ]	enorm, riesig	wash up [ˌwɒʃ 'ʌp]	angespült werden
violent ['vaɪələnt]	heftig	treasure ['treʒə]	Schatz
distress call	Notruf, SOS-Ruf	treasure hunter	Schatzsucher
[dɪ'stres kɔːl]		['treʒə hʌntə]	
abandon sb/sth	jdn/etw verlassen	cask [kɑːsk]	Fass
[ə'bændən]		nappy ['næpi]	Windel
territorial water	Hoheitsgewässer	scattered ['skætəd]	verstreut
[terəˌtɔːriəl 'wɔːtə]			

iː	ɪ	e	æ	ɑː	ɒ	ɔː	ʊ	uː	ʌ	ɜː	ə
see	sit	ten	bad	arm	got	saw	put	too	cut	bird	about

close off [ˌkləʊz ˈɒf]	sperren	mature [məˈtʃʊə]	reifen
service [ˈsɜːvɪs]	(Geschirr:) Service	spirits [ˈspɪrɪts]	Spirituosen, Alkohol
convenient [kənˈviːniənt]	günstig, passend	appoint [əˈpɔɪnt]	benennen, ernennen
		distillery [dɪˈstɪləri]	Brennerei
smash sth open [ˌsmæʃ ˈəʊpən]	etw aufbrechen	examination [ɪgˌzæmɪˈneɪʃn]	Untersuchung
disgraceful [dɪsˈgreɪsfl]	skandalös, eine Schande	presumably [prɪˈzjuːməbli]	vermutlich
anger [ˈæŋgə]	Ärger	recover [rɪˈkʌvə]	wiedererlangen
legal position [ˌliːgl pəˈzɪʃn]	Gesetzeslage	destroyed [dɪˈstrɔɪd]	zerstört
That's the least of it. [ˌðæts ðə ˈliːst əv ɪt]	Das ist das geringste Problem!	cause [kɔːz]	Ursache
heirloom [ˈeəluːm]	Erbstück	locate sth [ləʊˈkeɪt]	etw orten, ausfindig machen
apology [əˈpɒlədʒi]	Entschuldigung	sea water [ˈsiː wɔːtə]	Meerwasser
realize sth [ˈrɪəlaɪz]	sich einer Sache klar/bewusst sein	(the) undersigned [ˌʌndəˈsaɪnd]	der/die Unterzeichnete, der/die Unterzeichnende
reimburse [ˌriːɪmˈbɜːs]	erstatten, entschädigen	write-off [ˈraɪtɒf]	Totalverlust, Totalschaden
commercial value [kəˌmɜːʃl ˈvæljuː]	Handelswert	amount [əˈmaʊnt]	Umfang
expedite [ˈekspədaɪt]	beschleunigen	moderate [ˈmɒdərət]	gemäßigt, mäßig
settlement [ˈsetlmənt]	Abwicklung, Regulierung	coastguard [ˈkəʊstɡɑːd]	Küstenwache
p. 56 break the news to sb [ˌbreɪk ðə ˈnjuːz tə]	jdm die Nachricht überbringen	determine [dɪˈtɜːmɪn]	festsetzen, bestimmen
regret [rɪˈgret]	bedauern	payable [ˈpeɪəbl]	zahlbar
flood [flʌd]	Überschwemmung	prejudice [ˈpredʒudɪs]	Vorurteil
serious [ˈsɪəriəs]	ernst, ernsthaft, hier: groß	without prejudice [wɪˌðaʊt ˈpredʒudɪs]	ohne Vorbehalt
mechanical breakdown [mɪˌkænɪkl ˈbreɪkdaʊn]	Maschinenschaden	for whom it may concern [fə ˌhuːm ɪt meɪ kənˈsɜːn]	an alle, die es angeht
circumstances [ˈsɜːkəmstɑːnsɪz]	Umstände	p. 59 enclosed [ɪnˈkləʊzd]	beigefügt
		credit [ˈkredɪt]	gutschreiben, überweisen
beyond [bɪˈjɒnd]	jenseits	undoubtedly [ʌnˈdaʊtɪdli]	zweifellos
upset [ˌʌpˈset]	verärgert		
solve [sɒlv]	lösen	hesitate [ˈhezɪteɪt]	zögern
apologize [əˈpɒlədʒaɪz]	sich entschuldigen	enclosure [ɪnˈkləʊʒə]	(Brief:) Anlage
reassure sb [ˌriːəˈʃʊə]	jdn beruhigen	p. 61 invest [ɪnˈvest]	investieren
trust [trʌst]	Vertrauen	merchant [ˈmɜːtʃənt]	Kaufmann, Händler
renowned [rɪˈnaʊnd]	berühmt, bekannt	share [ʃeə]	Anteil
neat [niːt]	ordentlich	underwrite [ˌʌndəˈraɪt]	(Risiko) versichern, übernehmen
queue [kjuː]	(Warte-)Schlange		
be apologetic for sth [bi əˌpɒləˈdʒetɪk fə]	sich für etw entschuldigen	attract [əˈtrækt]	anlocken
		underwriter [ˈʌndəraɪtə]	Versicherer
be sb's fault [bi ˌsʌmbədiz fɔːlt]	jds Schuld sein	establish [ɪˈstæblɪʃ]	aufstellen
p. 57 proposal [prəˈpəʊzl]	Antrag	conduct [kɒndʌkt]	(Geschäfts-)Gebaren
close-up [ˈkləʊs ʌp]	Nahaufnahme	grain of rice [ˌɡreɪn əv ˈraɪs]	Reiskorn
ripped [rɪpt]	gerissen	duke [djuːk]	Herzog
furious [ˈfjʊəriəs]	wütend	capture [ˈkæptʃə]	dingfest machen, einfangen
assess [əˈses]	bewerten, bemessen, festsetzen		
loss adjuster [ˌlɒs əˈdʒʌstə]	Schadenssachverständige/r	protect [prəˈtekt]	schützen
		heading [ˈhedɪŋ]	Überschrift
conduct [kənˈdʌkt]	durchführen, hier: erstellen	consumer [kənˈsjuːmə]	Verbraucher/in
survey (report) [ˈsɜːveɪ rɪpɔːt]	Gutachten	profit [ˈprɒfɪt]	Gewinn
		particular [pəˈtɪkjələ]	bestimmter/r/s
scene [siːn]	Ort (des Geschehens)	strange [streɪndʒ]	seltsam
p. 58 policy holder [ˈpɒləsi həʊldə]	Versicherungsnehmer/in		

tʃ	dʒ	ʃ	ʒ	θ	ð	ŋ	s	z	v	w
chips	jet	ship	garage	thing	the	ring	ice	as	very	wet

133

Unit 6

p.62	warehousing ['weəhaʊzɪŋ]	Lagerung, Lagerhaltung, Lagerwesen
	advancement [əd'vɑ:nsmənt]	Fortschritt
	process ['prəʊses]	Vorgang
	order form ['ɔ:də fɔ:m]	Bestellschein, Auftragsformular
	storage ['stɔ:rɪdʒ]	Lager, Lagerung
	rack [ræk]	Stapel
	bale [beɪl]	Ballen
	blister roll ['blɪstə rəʊl]	Folienrolle
	moisture ['mɔɪstʃə]	Feuchtigkeit
	forklift ['fɔ:klɪft]	Gabelstapler
	packer ['pækə]	Verpacker/in, Einpacker/in
	dust [dʌst]	Staub
	office supplies ['ɒfɪs səplaɪz]	Bürobedarf
	picker ['pɪkə]	Kommissionierer/in
p.63	trucker ['trʌkə]	Lastwagenfahrer/in
	ask for directions [,ɑ:sk fə də'rekʃnz]	nach dem Weg fragen
	scheduler ['ʃedju:lə]	Disponent/in, Terminsachbearbeiter/in
	SatNav ['sætnæv]	Navigationssystem
	break down [,breɪk 'daʊn]	kaputtgehen
	woollen ['wʊlən]	Woll-
	give directions [gɪv də'rekʃnz]	den Weg erklären
	turn around [,tɜ:n ə'raʊnd]	wenden
	narrow ['nærəʊ]	schmal
	turn into ['tɜ:n ɪntə]	einbiegen
	cemetery ['semətri]	Friedhof
T	straight ahead [,streɪt ə'hed]	geradeaus
	stretch [stretʃ]	Stück, Abschnitt
	turn-off ['tɜ:nɒf]	Abzweig
	petrol station ['petrəl steɪʃn]	Tankstelle
	crossroads ['krɒsrəʊdz]	Kreuzung
	junction ['dʒʌŋkʃn]	Kreuzung
	miss sth [mɪs]	etw verfehlen, verpassen
p.64	T-junction ['ti: dʒʌŋkʃn]	Einmündung
	insurance adjuster [ɪn'ʃʊərəns ədʒʌstə]	Schadensachverständige/r
	operating costs ['ɒpəreɪtɪŋ kɒsts]	Betriebskosten
p.65	stocktaking ['stɒkteɪkɪŋ]	Inventur
	update [,ʌp'deɪt]	aktualisieren
	record keeping ['rekɔ:d ki:pɪŋ]	Dokumentation
	accurate ['ækjərət]	genau
	receipt [rɪ'si:t]	Warenannahme, Wareneingang

	fingerprint ['fɪŋgəprɪnt]	Fingerabdruck
	store [stɔ:]	(Dateien) speichern
	checkout ['tʃekaʊt]	Kasse
	cashier [kæ'ʃɪə]	Kassierer/in
	spread [spred]	sich ausbreiten
	(RFID) tag [,ɑ:(r) ef aɪ 'di: tæg]	RFID-Etikett
	circuit ['sɜ:kɪt]	Schaltkreis, Schaltung
	radio ['reɪdiəʊ]	Funk
	frequency ['fri:kwənsi]	Frequenz
	unaffected by [,ʌnə'fektɪd baɪ]	unempfindlich gegen
p.66	be in charge of sth [bi ɪn 'tʃɑ:dʒ əv]	für etw zuständig sein
	receiving station [rɪ'si:vɪŋ steɪʃn]	hier: Warenannahme, Wareneingang
	delivery bay [dɪ'lɪvəri beɪ]	Ladebucht
	rear [rɪə]	hintere/r/s
	wedge [wedʒ]	Keil
	delivery note [dɪ'lɪvəri nəʊt]	Lieferschein
	handheld ['hændheld]	Handgerät
	pallet truck ['pælət trʌk]	Hubwagen
	cart [kɑ:t]	Wagen
	mezzanine ['mezəni:n]	Palettenlagerort
	shelf, shelves [ʃelf, ʃelvz]	Regal
	outsize ['aʊtsaɪz]	übergroß
	order picker ['ɔ:də pɪkə]	Kommissionierer
	picking station ['pɪkɪŋ steɪʃn]	Kommissionierposition
	pick [pɪk]	(Sendung) kommissionieren
	maintenance ['meɪntənəns]	Wartung, Instandhaltung
	conveyor system [kən'veɪə sɪstəm]	Förderanlage
	service ['sɜ:vɪs]	warten
	various ['veəriəs]	verschieden
p.67	palletized ['pælətaɪzd]	palettiert, auf Paletten
	aisle [aɪl]	Gang
	corridor ['kɒridɔ:]	Flur, Korridor
	press [pres]	drücken
	tray [treɪ]	Schale, Tablett
	board [bɔ:d]	Brett
	enthusiastic (about sth) [ɪn,θju:zi'æstɪk]	begeistert (von etw)
	dashboard ['dæʃbɔ:d]	Armaturenbrett
	technician [tek'nɪʃn]	Techniker/in
	picking order ['pɪkɪŋ ɔ:də]	Kommissionierauftrag
T	cash machine ['kæʃ məʃi:n]	Geldautomat
	steer [stɪə]	lenken, steuern

iː	ɪ	e	æ	ɑː	ɒ	ɔː	ʊ	uː	ʌ	ɜː	ə
see	sit	ten	bad	arm	got	saw	put	too	cut	bird	about

consumption [kən'sʌmpʃn] — Verbrauch

sit back [ˌsɪt 'bæk] — sich zurücklehnen

legally ['liːgəli] — von Rechts wegen

T engage [ɪn'geɪdʒ] — einschalten, auslösen, bedienen

controls [kən'trəʊlz] — Schalter, Regler, Steuerung

apply [ə'plaɪ] — anwenden, auslösen

emergency brake [ɪ'mɜːdʒənsi breɪk] — Notbremse

report [rɪ'pɔːt] — hier: Beurteilung

p.68 stress [stres] — Belastung

impact ['ɪmpækt] — Stoß, Aufprall

external [ɪk'stɜːnl] — Außen-, äußerlich

internal [ɪn'tɜːnl] — Innen-

adequate ['ædɪkwət] — angemessen, ausreichend

shipping label ['ʃɪpɪŋ leɪbl] — Versandetikett

palletizer ['pælətaɪzə] — Palettierer

shipping area ['ʃɪpɪŋ eəriə] — Versandbereich

strap [stræp] — Band

packaging area ['pækɪdʒɪŋ eəriə] — Verpackungsbereich

freight train ['freɪt treɪn] — Güterzug

case erector ['keɪs ɪrektə] — Kartonaufrichter

plastic film [ˌplæstɪk 'fɪlm] — Kunststofffolie

sorting area ['sɔːtɪŋ eəriə] — Sortierbereich

shrink wrap ['ʃrɪŋk ræp] — mit Schrumpffolie umwickeln

cutter ['kʌtə] — Schneidemaschine

tape sth [teɪp] — etw (mit Klebeband) zukleben

stick sth [stɪk] — etw kleben

wrapped [ræpt] — umwickelt, eingewickelt

stretch wrap film [ˌstretʃ ræp 'fɪlm] — Dehnfolie

p.69 wooden ['wʊdn] — aus Holz

framework ['freɪmwɜːk] — Konstruktion

sacking ['sækɪŋ] — Sackleinen

loose [luːs] — lose

widespread ['waɪdspred] — verbreitet

light bulb ['laɪtbʌlb] — Glühbirne

tea leaf, leaves ['tiː liːf, liːvz] — Teeblatt, -blätter

p.70 wheel rim ['wiːl rɪm] — Radfelge

slot [slɒt] — Schlitz, Aussparung

This way up [ˌðɪs weɪ 'ʌp] — Hier oben

clamp [klæmp] — Klammer

sling [slɪŋ] — Schlaufe, Schlinge

chain [tʃeɪn] — Kette

as indicated [əz 'ɪndɪkeɪtɪd] — wie gezeigt

fragile ['frædʒaɪl] — zerbrechlich

hand hook ['hænd hʊk] — Haken

centre of gravity [ˌsentər əv 'grævəti] — Schwerpunkt

dangerous goods [ˌdeɪndʒərəs 'gʊdz] — Gefahrengüter

handling regulations ['hændlɪŋ regjuleɪʃnz] — Handhabungsvorschriften

hazardous materials [ˌhæzədəs mə'tɪəriəlz] — Gefahrengüter

corrosive [kə'rəʊsɪv] — ätzend

environmentally hazardous [ɪnvaɪrən,mentəli 'hæzədəs] — umweltschädigend

flammable ['flæməbl] — entflammbar

harmful ['hɑːmfl] — gesundheitsschädlich

irritant ['ɪrɪtənt] — reizend

oxidizing ['ɒksɪdaɪzɪŋ] — oxidierend

p.71 Guelph Palace ['gwelf pæləs] — Welfenschloss

Brunswick ['brʌnzwɪk] — Braunschweig

equestrian monument [ɪˌkwestriən 'mɒnjumənt] — Reiterstandbild

destroy [dɪ'strɔɪ] — zerstören

copper ['kɒpə] — Kupfer

replica ['replɪkə] — Kopie, Nachbildung

thief, thieves [θiːf, θiːvz] — Dieb, Diebe

city council ['sɪti kaʊnsl] — Stadtrat

reconstruct sth [ˌriːkən'strʌkt] — etw rekonstruieren, wiedererrichten

chariot ['tʃæriət] — Streitwagen

cast [kɑːst] — gießen

foundry ['faʊndri] — Gießerei

failure ['feɪljə] — Fehlschlag

recast [ˌriː'kɑːst] — neu gießen

bring sb in [ˌbrɪŋ 'ɪn] — jdn hinzuziehen

examine sb/sth [ɪg'zæmɪn] — jn/etw untersuchen

level ['levl] — Niveau, hier: Stärke

Unit 7

p.72 construction kit [kən'strʌkʃn kɪt] — Bausatz

moulding ['məʊldɪŋ] — Formteil

primary producer [ˌpraɪməri prə'djuːsə] — Hersteller

keep sb in the know [kiːp ˌsʌmbədi ɪn **T** ðə 'nəʊ] — jdn auf dem Laufenden halten

join sb [dʒɔɪn] — bei jdm sein

dry land [ˌdraɪ 'lænd] — Festland

tʃ	dʒ	ʃ	ʒ	θ	ð	ŋ	s	z	v	w
chips	jet	ship	garage	thing	the	ring	ice	as	very	wet

T	frame [freɪm]	Rahmen
	get sth straight	etw klarstellen
	[ˌget 'streɪt]	
	premises ['premɪsɪz]	(Betriebs-)Gelände
p.73	**origin** ['ɒrɪdʒɪn]	Ursprungsort
	port of origin	Verschiffungshafen
	[ˌpɔːt əv 'ɒrɪdʒɪn]	
	port of destination	Bestimmungshafen
	[ˌpɔːt əv destɪ'neɪʃn]	
	weight estimate	Schätzgewicht
	['weɪt estɪmət]	
	require [rɪ'kwaɪə]	erfordern
	declared value	angegebener/erklärter
	[dɪˌkleəd 'væljuː]	Wert
p.74	**dispatch** [dɪ'spætʃ]	Versand
	advice of dispatch	Versandanzeige
	[ədˌvaɪs əv dɪ'spætʃ]	
	sail [seɪl]	(Schiff:) auslaufen, abfahren
p.75	**gap** [gæp]	Lücke
	structural damage	Bauschaden
	[ˌstrʌktʃərəl 'dæmɪdʒ]	
	collapse [kə'læps]	einbrechen, zusammenbrechen
p.76	**pro forma invoice**	Proformarechnung
	[ˌprəʊ 'fɔːmə ɪnvɔɪs]	
	in advance of sth	vor etw
	[ɪn əd'vɑːns əv]	
	note sth [nəʊt]	etw vermerken
	preliminary	vorläufig
	[prɪ'lɪmɪnəri]	
	quotation [kwəʊ'teɪʃn]	Kostenvoranschlag, Angebot
	importation	Einfuhr, Import
	[ˌɪmpɔː'teɪʃn]	
	bill to ['bɪl tə]	(im Formular:) Rechnungsempfänger
	payment term	Zahlungsfrist
	['peɪmənt tɜːm]	
	unit price [ˌjuːnɪt 'praɪs]	Preis pro Einheit
	say [seɪ]	(im Formular:) in Worten
	authorized signatory	Zeichnungsberechtigte/r
	[ˌɔːθəraɪzd 'sɪgnətri]	
p.77	**depart** [dɪ'pɑːt]	abfahren, abreisen
	certificate of origin	Ursprungszeugnis, Herkunftszeugnis
	[səˌtɪfɪkət əv 'ɒrɪdʒɪn]	
	release sth [rɪ'liːs]	etw herausgeben
	declaration	Erklärung
	[ˌdeklə'reɪʃn]	
	overleaf [ˌəʊvə'liːf]	umseitig
	means [miːnz]	Mittel
	thence [ðens]	hier: von dort
	certification	Bescheinigung, Beurkundung
	[ˌsɜːtɪfɪ'keɪʃn]	
	hereby [ˌhɪə'baɪ]	hiermit, hierdurch
	certify ['sɜːtɪfaɪ]	bescheinigen, beurkunden
	declare [dɪ'kleə]	erklären

p.78	**terms** [tɜːmz]	Bedingungen
	sales terms	Verkaufsbedingungen
	['seɪlz tɜːmz]	
	payment terms	Zahlungsbedingungen
	['peɪmənt tɜːmz]	
	export invoice	Ausfuhrrechnung
	['ekspɔːt ɪnvɔɪs]	
	purchase ['pɜːtʃəs]	Kauf
	export licence	Ausfuhrgenehmigung
	['ekspɔːt laɪsns]	
	bill of dispatch	Versandbescheinigung
	[ˌbɪl əv dɪ'spætʃ]	
	customs declaration	Zollerklärung
	[ˌkʌstəmz ˌdeklə'reɪʃn]	
	specific [spə'sɪfɪk]	bestimmt
	manufacture	Herstellung
	[ˌmænju'fæktʃə]	
	statement ['steɪtmənt]	Erklärung
	exchange [ɪks'tʃeɪndʒ]	austauschen
p.79	**negotiable bill of lading**	begebbares, handelbares, übertragbares Konnossement
	[nɪˌgəʊʃ(i)əbl ˌbɪl əv 'leɪdɪŋ]	
	possession [pə'zeʃn]	Besitz
	take possession of	in Besitz nehmen
	[teɪk pə'zeʃn əv]	
	fulfil [fʊl'fɪl]	erfüllen
	subject to	vorbehaltlich, gemäß
	['sʌbdʒekt tə]	
	notify address	Avisieranschrift, Benachrichtigungs- adresse
	['nəʊtɪfaɪ ədres]	
	timely ['taɪmli]	rechtzeitig
	take in charge	übernehmen
	[ˌteɪk ɪn 'tʃɑːdʒ]	
	apparent [ə'pærənt]	augenscheinlich
	order ['ɔːdə]	Ordnung
	herein [hɪər'ɪn]	hier
	surrender [sə'rendə]	aushändigen, übergeben
	duly ['djuːli]	ordnungsgemäß
	endorse [ɪn'dɔːs]	indossieren (mit einem Übertragungsvermerk versehen)
	witness ['wɪtnəs]	Zeuge/-in
	in witness whereof	zu Urkund wessen
	[ɪn ˌwɪtnəs weər'ɒv]	
	tenor ['tenə]	Inhalt, Sinn
	accomplish [ə'kʌmplɪʃ]	ausführen
	void [vɔɪd]	unwirksam, ungültig, nichtig
p.80	**oral** ['ɔːrəl]	mündlich
p.81	**bright** [braɪt]	(Farbe:) leuchtend, bunt
	ornament ['ɔːnəmənt]	Verzierung
	reflective [rɪ'flektɪv]	reflektierend
	side panel ['saɪd pænl]	Seitenwand
	landscape ['lændskeɪp]	Landschaft
	chassis ['ʃæsi]	Fahrgestell
	bump [bʌmp]	Bodenwelle, Buckel

iː	ɪ	e	æ	ɑː	ɒ	ɔː	ʊ	uː	ʌ	ɜː	ə
see	sit	ten	bad	arm	got	saw	put	too	cut	bird	about

cab [kæb]	Führerhaus	sales goal ['seɪlz gəʊl]	Verkaufsziel
treasure chest ['treʒə tʃest]	Schatztruhe	export clerk ['ekspɔːt klɑːk]	Exportsachbearbeiter/in
cover ['kʌvə]	hier: (mit Stoff) beziehen	customs entry ['kʌstəmz entri]	Zollerklärung
artificial [ˌɑːtɪ'fɪʃl]	künstlich	customs tariff [ˌkʌstəmz 'tærɪf]	Zolltarif
marigold ['mærigəʊld]	Ringelblume		
silk [sɪlk]	Seide	familiarity [fəˌmɪliærəti]	Vertrautheit
skilled [skɪld]	geschickt	apply for (a job) [ə'plaɪ fə]	sich (um eine Stelle) bewerben
transformation [ˌtrɑːnsfə'meɪʃn]	Umwandlung	p.85 curriculum vitae (CV) [kəˌrɪkjələm 'viːtaɪ]	Lebenslauf
expense [ɪk'spens]	Aufwand, Kosten	summarize ['sʌməraɪz]	zusammenfassen
hire ['haɪə]	mieten	sales brochure ['seɪlz brəʊʃə]	Verkaufsprospekt
illiterate [ɪ'lɪtərət]	Analphabet/in		
flamboyant [flæm'bɔɪənt]	extravagant, grell	unique selling point (USP) [juˌniːk 'selɪŋ pɔɪnt]	Alleinstellungs- merkmal
surface ['sɜːfɪs]	Oberfläche	objective [əb'dʒektɪv]	Ziel

Unit 8

p.82 importance [ɪm'pɔːtns]	Bedeutung	attention [ə'tenʃn]	Aufmerksamkeit
regard [rɪ'gɑːd]	betrachten, ansehen	capture ['kæptʃə]	fesseln
treaty ['triːti]	Abkommen, Vertrag	throughout [θruː'aʊt]	durchgehend, ständig
billion ['bɪliən]	Milliarde	factual ['fæktʃuəl]	sachlich
outnumber [ˌaʊt'nʌmbə]	(zahlenmäßig) übertreffen	reverse [rɪ'vɜːs]	umgekehrt
T		duties ['djuːtiz]	Aufgaben, Pflichten
ratio ['reɪʃiəʊ]	Verhältnis	responsibilites [rɪˌspɒnsə'bɪlətiz]	Aufgaben
reliable [rɪ'laɪəbl]	verlässlich	achievement [ə'tʃiːvmənt]	Leistung, Erfolg
p.83 scale [skeɪl]	Skala	brief(ly) ['briːfli]	knapp, kurz
rate sth [reɪt]	etw einordnen, bewerten	achieve [ə'tʃiːv]	erzielen
ability [ə'bɪləti]	Fähigkeit	attend [ə'tend]	(Schule) besuchen
penfriend ['penfrend]	Brieffreund/in	gain [geɪn]	erwerben
tuition [tjuː'ɪʃn]	Unterricht	data protection ['deɪtə prətekʃn]	Datenschutz
p.84 job hunting ['dʒɒb hʌntɪŋ]	Arbeitsuche, Stellensuche	referee [ˌrefə'riː]	Referenz (Person)
acquire [ə'kwaɪə]	erwerben	on request [ɒn rɪ'kwest]	auf Anfrage
sales executive ['seɪlz ɪgzekjətɪv]	Verkaufsmanager/in	permission [pə'mɪʃn]	Erlaubnis
salary ['sæləri]	Gehalt, Lohn	favourably ['feɪvərəbli]	wohlwollend, günstig
domestic [də'mestɪk]	inländisch, Inlands-, Binnen-	p.86 recommendation [ˌrekəmen'deɪʃn]	Empfehlung
exchange of goods [ɪks,tʃeɪndʒ əv 'gʊdz]	Warenaustausch	dishonest [dɪs'ɒnɪst]	unlauter, unehrlich
establish [ɪ'stæblɪʃ]	feststellen	sensible ['sensəbl]	verständlich
requirements [rɪ'kwaɪəmənts]	Bedürfnisse	recruitment process [rɪ'kruːtmənt prəʊses]	Einstellungsverfahren
implement ['ɪmplɪmənt]	umsetzen	discourage [dɪs'kʌrɪdʒ]	davon abraten
promotion [prə'məʊʃn]	Werbung	head-shot ['hed ʃɒt]	Portrait
required [rɪ'kwaɪəd]	erforderlich	draft [drɑːft]	Entwurf
self-motivate [ˌself 'məʊtɪveɪt]	sich motivieren	follow sth closely [ˌfɒləʊ 'kləʊsli]	sich streng an etw halten
self-manage [ˌself 'mænɪdʒ]	eigenverantwortlich tätig sein	grammar school ['græmə skuːl]	Gymnasium
crucial ['kruːʃl]	entscheidend, ausschlaggebend	export assistant ['ekspɔːt əsɪstənt]	Exportsachbearbeiter/in
manage ['mænɪdʒ]	regeln, organisieren	p.87 pursue [pə'sjuː]	verfolgen
work effort ['wɜːk efət]	Arbeitseinsatz	customer base ['kʌstəmə beɪs]	Kundenstamm
achieve [ə'tʃiːv]	(Ziel) erreichen		

tʃ	dʒ	ʃ	ʒ	θ	ð	ŋ	s	z	v	w	
chips	jet	ship	garage	thing	the	ring	ice	as	very	wet	137

vocational school [vəʊˌkeɪʃənl ˈskuːl]		Berufsschule
subject [ˈsʌbdʒekt]		(Schul-)Fach
conversational French [kɒnvəˌseɪʃənl ˈfrentʃ]		gesprochenes Französisch
p.88	**cover(ing) letter** [ˌkʌvərɪŋ ˈletə]	Anschreiben, Begleitbrief
	grammar school [ˈgræmə skuːl]	Gymnasium
	be raised [bi ˈreɪzd]	aufwachsen
	bilingually [ˌbaɪˈlɪŋgwəli]	zweisprachig
	have appeal [həv əˈpiːl]	ausgesprochen attraktiv sein
p.89	**fix** [fɪks]	*(Termin)* abmachen, vereinbaren
p.90	**handy** [ˈhændi]	griffbereit
	landline [ˈlændlaɪn]	Festnetzleitung
	static [ˈstætɪk]	atmosphärische Störungen, Rauschen
	applicant [ˈæplɪkənt]	Bewerber/in
	reveal [rɪˈviːl]	verraten, preisgeben, offenbaren

iː	ɪ	e	æ	ɑː	ɒ	ɔː	ʊ	uː	ʌ	ɜː	ə
see	sit	ten	bad	arm	got	saw	put	too	cut	bird	about

Alphabetical word list

Diese Liste enthält alle Wörter in alphabetischer Reihenfolge. Die Zahl nach dem Stichwort bezieht sich auf die Seite, auf der das Wort zum ersten Mal erscheint.
T = das Wort befindet sich in den Transcripts (Hörverständnisübungen).

A

abandon sb/sth *53* jdn/etw verlassen
ability *83* Fähigkeit
aboard *29* an Bord
about, be ~ *22T* da sein
absence *54* Abwesenheit
access *8* Zugriff, Zugang
accident *52* Unfall
accomplish *79* ausführen
accordance, in ~ with *27* in Übereinstimmung mit, nach
according to *32* gemäß, nach
according to plan *34* nach Plan
account operative *10T* Sachbearbeiter/in
account settlement *43* Abrechnung
accurate *65* genau
achieve *84 (Ziel)* erreichen; *85* erzielen
achievement *85* Leistung, Erfolg
acquire *15* akquirieren; *84* erwerben
adapt to sth *42* sich an etw anpassen
adaptability *42* Wandlungsfähigkeit
additional *39* zusätzlich, Zusatz-
adequate *68* angemessen, ausreichend
adjust *38* anpassen
administration, basic ~ *10T* elementare Verwaltungsaufgaben
administrative *10T* Verwaltungs-
advance, in ~ of sth *76* vor etw
advanced *8* modern, fortschrittlich
advancement *62* Fortschritt
advantage *28* Vorteil
advice *46T (guter)* Rat; **give ~** *46T* raten, beraten, Rat erteilen
advice of dispatch *74* Versandanzeige
advise *46* beraten, raten
aerial *86* Luft-
affect *33* sich auswirken auf, beeinflussen; *51* betreffen
afraid, I'm ~ *25* leider
aft *39* achtern, Achter-
agree *50* vereinbaren
agreement *36T* Vereinbarung, Übereinkunft
air cargo *42* Luftfracht
air cargo company *15* Luftfrachtgesellschaft

air compressor *39* Druckluftkompressor
aircraft *44* Flugzeug
air freight *10T* Luftfracht
airspace *51* Luftraum
air traffic *40* Luftverkehr
air waybill *47* Luftfrachtbrief
aisle *67* Gang
alliance *8* Bündnis, Allianz
alongside *31* neben
amount *14* Betrag, Menge; *58* Umfang
anger *55T* Ärger
apologetic, be ~ for sth *56* sich für etw entschuldigen
apologize *56* sich entschuldigen
apology *55T* Entschuldigung
apparent *79* augenscheinlich
appeal, have ~ *88* ausgesprochen attraktiv sein
applicable *43* gültig, geltend
applicant *90* Bewerber/in
application *40* Anwendung, *(Computer:)* Programm
apply *67T* anwenden, auslösen
apply for (a job) *84* sich *(um eine Stelle)* bewerben
appoint *58* benennen, ernennen
appointment *9* Termin
appraisal *16* Bewertung, Beurteilung
appreciate sth *20* etw zu schätzen wissen
apprentice *18* Auszubildende/r, Lehrling
apprenticeship *18T* Ausbildung, Lehre
approximately *33T* zirka, ungefähr
area *8* Fläche; *12T* Bereich
area of expertise *16* Fachgebiet
army supplies *10* Nachschub
around, be ~ *32* es geben
arrange *15* arrangieren, planen, festlegen; *20* regeln, arrangieren
arrival *27* Ankunft
articulated lorry (BE) *18T* Sattelschlepper, Sattelzug
artificial *81* künstlich
assess *57* bewerten, bemessen, festsetzen
assistance *47* Hilfe, Unterstützung
associated with *9* verbunden mit

assume *36T* annehmen, ausgehen
attack *33* Angriff
attend sth *20* an etw teilnehmen; *85 (Schule)* besuchen
attention *85* Aufmerksamkeit
attract *61* anlocken
authority *42* Behörde
authorized signatory *76* Zeichnungsberechtigte/r
available *20* verfügbar
avoid *13* vermeiden
axle *27* Achse

B

bale *62* Ballen
barge *29* Kahn, Lastkahn
barrel *29* Fass
beach *53* stranden, auf Grund laufen (lassen)
behalf, on ~ of sb *50* in jds Namen
belong *13* gehören
beneficiary *50* Begünstigte/r, Empfänger/in
beyond *56* jenseits
bilingually *88* zweisprachig
bill of dispatch *78* Versandbescheinigung
bill of lading (B/L) *33* Konnossement; **clean ~** *37* Konnossement ohne Einschränkung, reines Konnossement; **Combined Transport ~** *37* kombiniertes Transportkonnossement; **foul ~** *36* unreines Konnossement; **House ~** *37* Spediteurkonnossement; **negotiable ~** *81* begebbares, handelbares, übertragbares Konnossement; **Port to Port ~** *37* Port-to-Port Seekonnossement; **Received for Shipment ~** *37* Empfangskonnossement; **Shipped on Board ~** *37* Bordkonnossement
bill to *76 (im Formular:)* Rechnungsempfänger
billing *43* Fakturierung, Rechnungsstellung
billion *82T* Milliarde
blister roll *62* Folienrolle
board *67* Brett

bookkeeping 15 Buchhaltung, Buchführung
border 36T Grenze
border post 36T Grenzpfahl
bossy 13 rechthaberisch
bottleneck 51 Engpass, Engstelle, Nadelöhr
bound, be ~ to do sth 18T etw bestimmt tun
branch (of a company) 9T Niederlassung
break bulk 32 Sammelladung aufteilen, umpacken
break down 63 kaputtgehen
break the news to sb 56 jdm die Nachricht überbringen
breakage 32 Bruch, Bruchschaden
brief(ly) 85 knapp, kurz
bright 81 (Farbe:) leuchtend, bunt
bring sb in 71 jdn hinzuziehen
Brunswick 71 Braunschweig
bulk carrier 29 Massengutfrachter, Schüttgutfrachter
bulk container 31 Schüttgutcontainer
bulk load 18T Schüttladung
bulk loader 18T Schüttgutlader
bulk wagon 19 Schüttgutwagen
bulky 39 sperrig
bump 81 Bodenwelle, Buckel
by-product 38 Nebenprodukt

C

cab 81 Führerhaus
cabinet 22T Aktenschrank
calculate 43T berechnen
capacity 30 Fassungsvermögen, Volumen
capsize 52 kentern
capture 61 dingfest machen, einfangen; 85 fesseln
car transporter 19 Autotransportwagen
care 27 Sorgfalt
cargo 18T Fracht
cargo agent 42 Ladungsagent
cargo bay 39 Laderaum
cargo door 39 Ladeluke
cargo movement 15 Güterbeförderung
carriage 26 Transport; contract of ~ 36 Frachtvertrag, Beförderungsvertrag; main- ~ 24 Hauptlauf; on- ~ 24 Nachlauf
carrier 26 Frachtführer, Verfrachter
carry on 12T weitergehen, weitermachen
cart 66 Wagen

case erector 68 Kartonaufrichter
cash machine 67T Geldautomat
cashier 65 Kassierer/in
cask 55 Fass
cast 71 gießen
cause 58 Ursache; 51 verursachen
cemetery 63T Friedhof
centre of gravity 70 Schwerpunkt
certificate of origin 77 Ursprungszeugnis, Herkunftszeugnis
certification 77 Bescheinigung, Beurkundung
certify 79 bescheinigen, beurkunden
chain 70 Kette
chamber 51 Kammer
chance 10T Gelegenheit; by any ~ 22T zufällig
characteristics 32 Eigenschaften, Merkmale
charge 24 Gebühr, Preis; 48 frachtpflichtiges Gewicht, gebührenpflichtiges Gewicht
charge, be in ~ of sth 66 für etw zuständig sein
chargeable weight 48 frachtpflichtiges Gewicht, gebührenpflichtiges Gewicht
chariot 71 Streitwagen
charter 53 Mieten, Chartern; under ~ to 53 verchartert an
chartered 16 amtlich zugelassen
chassis 81 Fahrgestell
check number 50T Prüfziffer
checkout 65 Kasse
Chief Executive Officer (CEO) 34T Geschäftsführer/in, Vorstandsvorsitzende/r
chief quartermaster 10T
circuit 65 Schaltkreis, Schaltung
circumstances 56 Umstände
city council 71 Stadtrat
claim 53 fordern, beanspruchen, einen (Versicherungs-)Anspruch geltend machen
claim 53 Forderung, Anspruch, Antrag
claimant 53 Antragsteller/in
clamp 70 Klammer
clarify 22 klären, erläutern
clause 36 Klausel, Eintrag
clean bill of lading 37 Konnossement ohne Einschränkung, reines Konnssoement
clear 36T räumen; 43 (Zoll:) abfertigen
clearance 36 Durchfahrtsbreite
clerk 10T Sachbearbeiter/in
client 10T Kunde/-in

close 53 nahe (gelegen)
close off 55 sperren
close-up 57 Nahaufnahme
closing paragraph 24 Schlussabsatz
closure 51 Schließung
coal 19 Kohle
coastguard 58 Küstenwache
collapse 75 einbrechen, zusammenbrechen
collect 49 unfrei
collection 26 Inkasso, Einzug; 15 Abholung
colour spectrum 13 Farbspektrum
Combined Transport B/L 37 kombiniertes Transportkonnossement
come up with sth 34T sich etw einfallen lassen, sich etw ausdenken
commerce 51 Handel
commercial 10T Wirtschafts-
commercial invoice 50 Handelsrechnung
commercial value 55T Handelswert
common 30 verbreitet, üblich
community 51 Gemeinschaft
comparison 23 Vergleich
competition 51 Konkurrenz, Wettbewerb(er)
competitive 45 konkurrenzfähig, wettbewerbsorientiert, (Preis:) günstig
complaint 14 Reklamation, Beschwerde
complete 16 (Ausbildung) abschließen
complimentary close 24 Schlussformel (Brief)
comply with 43 (Vorschriften) entsprechen, (Bedingungen) erfüllen
component 34 Bauteil
comprehensive 42 umfassend
concern, for whom it may ~ 58 an alle, die es angeht
condition 25 Bedingung; 26 Zustand
conduct 61 (Geschäfts-)Gebaren; 57 durchführen, hier: erstellen
confirm 25 bestätigen
consider 24 berücksichtigen; 52 betrachten
considerably 32 beträchtlich
consideration, take into ~ 48 in Betracht ziehen, berücksichtigen
consign 11 senden, versenden; 50T übergeben

consignee *15* Empfänger/in, Adressat/in

consignment *8* Sendung, Lieferung

consignment note *14* Frachtbrief, Warenbegleitschein

consignor *15* Versender, Absender, Verlader

consolidation *32* Sammelladung, Zusammenfassung (von Lieferungen)

construction kit *72* Bausatz

construction machinery *18* Baumaschinen

construction site *27* Baustelle

constructive total loss *53* konstruktiver Totalverlust, angenommener Totalschaden

consumer *61* Verbraucher/in

consumption *67T* Verbrauch

contain *10T* enthalten

container load, FCL (full ~) *32* volle Containerladung; LCL (less than ~) *32* Teilladung

container trailer *18T* Container-chassis, Containertrailer

contaminate *53* kontaminieren

contents *32* Inhalt

contract *33* Vertrag

contract of carriage *36* Frachtvertrag, Beförderungsvertrag

contract salvage *53* Bergung laut Vertrag

contractor *36T* Dienstleister, Unternehmer/in

controls *67T* Schalter, Regler, Steuerung

convenience *45* Zweckmäßigkeit, Komfort

convenient *19* günstig, praktisch, passend

conversational French *87* gesprochenes Französisch

convert *30* umbauen

conveyor belt *8* Förderband

conveyor system *66* Förderanlage

cope *34* zurechtkommen

copper *71* Kupfer

copy *14* Exemplar; *12* abschreiben

corporate account sales manager *16* Geschäftskundenbetreuer/in

correspond to *27* entsprechen

correspondingly *30* dementsprechend

corridor *67* Flur, Korridor

corrosive *70* ätzend

corrugated *30* gewellt, Well-

course *10T* Lauf, Verlauf

cover *8* sich erstrecken über; *16* umfassen; *18T* abdecken, bedecken; *36T* decken; *81 (mit Stoff)* beziehen

coverage *42* Deckung

cover(ing) letter *88* Anschreiben, Begleitbrief

crane *29* Kran

crash landing *52* Bruchlandung

crate *29* Holzkiste

credit *59* gutschreiben, überweisen

crew *41* Mannschaft, Besatzung, Personal

Crimean War *10T* Krimkrieg (1853–56)

crisis team *35* Krisenstab

crossroads *63T* Kreuzung

cross-section *44* Querschnitt

crucial *84* entscheidend, ausschlaggebend

cube *30* Würfel

current(ly) *25* im Moment, aktuell

curriculum vitae (CV) *85* Lebenslauf

curtain-sided trailer *18T* Schiebe-planenauflieger, Gardinen-planenauflieger

customer base *87* Kundenstamm

customer records *11* Kundendaten

customer services *12* Kundendienst, Kundenbetreuung

customer services manager *20* Kundenberater/in

customs *21* Zoll

customs clearance *46T* Zoll-abfertigung

customs declaration *78* Zollerklärung

customs entry *84* Zollerklärung

customs official *43* Zollbeamter/-in

customs tariff *85* Zolltarif

cut *14* zuschneiden

cut costs *32* Kosten senken

cutter *68* Schneidemaschine

D

damage *30* Beschädigung; *52* Schaden

damages *53* Schadenersatz

dangerous goods *70* Gefahrengüter

dashboard *67T* Armaturenbrett

data protection *85* Datenschutz

deal with sth *10T* mit etw zu tun haben, für etw zuständig sein

debris *34* Abfall, Trümmer, Überbleibsel, Bruchstücke

declaration *77* Erklärung

declare *77* erklären

declared value *73* angegebener/erklärter Wert

dedicated *16* speziell

definitive *42* maßgeblich

delay *51* Verzögerung, Verspätung

delayed *14* verspätet, verzögert

deliberately *54* absichtlich

deliver *8* liefern, zustellen

delivery *8* Lieferung, Zustellung

delivery bay *66* Ladebucht

delivery note *62* Lieferschein

demolish *36* abreißen

depart *77* abfahren, abreisen

department *10T* Abteilung

departure *48* Abfahrt, Abflug

depend *10T* davon abhängen

depend on sth *16* von etw abhängen

depending on *19* je nach

deploy *51* absenden

derail *52* entgleisen

derelict *54* aufgegeben, verlassen

designed for sb *42* für jdn gedacht

desperate *51* verzweifelt

destination *15* Zielort, Bestimmungsort

destroy *71* zerstören

destroyed *58* zerstört

detailed *36* genau

details *22* Einzelheiten, Angaben, Daten

determine *58* festsetzen, bestimmen

development *16* Entwicklung, Weiterbildung

diameter *33T* Durchmesser

difficulty *51* Problem, Schwierigkeit

dig sth up *36* etw aufgraben, *(Straße)* aufreißen

digit *22* Ziffer

directions, ask for ~ *63* nach dem Weg fragen; give ~ *63T* den Weg erklären

director *9* Leiter/in

disadvantage *28* Nachteil

disaster *10T* Katastrophe

discourage *86* davon abraten

disgraceful *55T* skandalös, eine Schande

dishonest *86* unlauter, unehrlich

dispatch *74* Versand

distance *53* Entfernung

distance-learning course *16* Fernkurs

distillery *58* Brennerei

distress call *53* Notruf, SOS-Ruf

distribution *16* Vertrieb, Versand

divert *51* umleiten

divide by *50T* teilen durch

divide up *10T* aufteilen
division *21* Abteilung, Sparte
do *33T* *hier:* ausreichen
docking charge *24* Dockgebühren, Löschgeld
document of title *36* Inhaberpapier, Besitzurkunde
documentary evidence *36* Belege, Nachweis
dodgy *50T* gefährlich, unsicher
domestic *84* inländisch, Inlands-, Binnen-
downriver *34T* flussabwärts
draft *86* Entwurf
drug *51* Medikament, Arzneimittel
drum *29* Fass
dry land *72T* Festland
duke *61* Herzog
duly *79* ordnungsgemäß
duration *48* Dauer
dust *62* Staub
duties *85* Aufgaben, Pflichten

E
economical *32* wirtschaftlich
edition *42* Ausgabe
efficient *8* effizient
effort *44* Arbeit, Mühe, Anstrengung
emergency brake *67T* Notbremse
emergency order *46T* Eilauftrag
employ *8* beschäftigen
employee *8* Angestellte/r
empty space *14* Leerraum
enclosed *59* beigefügt
enclosure *59* *(Brief:)* Anlage
endorse *79* indossieren *(mit einem Übertragungsvermerk versehen)*
engage *15* beauftragen, *67T* einschalten, auslösen, bedienen
enquiry *47* Anfrage
ensure *16* sicherstellen, gewährleisten
enter *12T* *(Gebäude)* betreten; *15* *(Daten)* eingeben
enterprise *51* Unternehmen, Unternehmung
enthusiastic (about sth) *67* begeistert (von etw)
entrance *7* Eingang
environment *42* *hier:* Umfeld
environmental *39* Umwelt-
environmentally hazardous *70* umweltschädigend
equestrian monument *71* Reiterstandbild
equip *34* ausrüsten, ausstatten
equipment *18T* *Gerät(e)*, Ausrüstung

equivalent *38* Entsprechung
escort *36T* Eskorte
especially *51* besonders
essential *45* wesentlich, unbedingt notwendig
establish *61* aufstellen; *84* feststellen
estimation *33T* Schätzung
evidence *36* Nachweis
examination *58* Untersuchung
examine sb/sth *71* jn/etw untersuchen
excellent *8* hervorragend, ausgezeichnet
exchange *78* austauschen
exchange of goods *84* Warenaustausch
existing customer *15* Bestandskunde/-in
excited, not get ~ about sth *10T* sich nicht zu viele Hoffnungen machen
expansion *12T* Erweiterung
expedite *55T* beschleunigen
expense *81* Aufwand, Kosten
expiry date *51* Verfallsdatum
explosive *39* Sprengstoff
export assistant *86* Exportsachbearbeiter/in
export clearance *24* Ausfuhrabfertigung
export clerk *84* Exportsachbearbeiter/in
export invoice *78* Ausfuhrrechnung
export licence *78* Ausfuhrgenehmigung
extend over *16* sich erstrecken über
extensive *27* umfangreich
external *68* Außen-, äußerlich

F
face sth *51* vor etw stehen, mit etw konfrontiert sein
facilities *33* Anlagen, Einrichtungen
facility *27* Anlage
factual *85* sachlich
failure *71* Fehlschlag
fairly *30* relativ, ziemlich
familiar *17* vertraut
familiarity *84* Vertrautheit
family-owned business *8* Familienbetrieb
far-reaching *51* weitreichend
fault, be sb's ~ *56* jds Schuld sein
favour, in ~ of sb *50* zu jds Gunsten
favourably *85* wohlwollend, günstig
FCL (full container load) *32* volle Containerladung
feasible *35* machbar, durchführbar

feature *42* Eigenschaft, *(spezielle)* Funktion
fee *54* Gebühr, Honorar
ferry *25* Fähre
ferry port *27* Fährhafen
ferry service *33* Fährverbindung, Fährverkehr
fertilizer *29* Dünger
figure *8* Zahl, Ziffer
final *32* endgültig
finance *12* Finanzen, Finanzabteilung
finder's fee *53* Finderlohn
findings *25* Ergebnisse
fingerprint *65* Fingerabdruck
finish sth *34T* etw fertigstellen
fix *27* befestigen, anbringen; *89* *(Termin)* abmachen, vereinbaren
fixed *54* fest, festgelegt
flamboyant *81* extravagant, grell
flammable *70* entflammbar
flat car *19* Flachwagen
flat rack container *31* Flachgestellcontainer, Flat
flatbed trailer *34T* Flachbettauflieger
flight attendant *41* Flugbegleiter/in
float *29* gleiten lassen
floating policy *54* offene Police
flood *56* Überschwemmung
floor *12T* Stockwerk, Etage
flotsam *54* Treibgut
follow, as ~s *24* wie folgt
follow sth closely *86* sich streng an etw halten
forklift *62* Gabelstapler
form of transport *10T* Transportart
forward sth *10T* etw versenden, verschicken
forwarding agency *8* Spedition
foul bill of lading *36* unreines Konnossement
found *9* gründen
foundry *71* Gießerei
fragile *70* zerbrechlich
frame *72T* Rahmen
framework *69* Konstruktion
freight *10T* Fracht
freight forwarder *15* Spediteur
freight forwarding agency *15* Spedition
freight handling *40* Frachtumschlag
freight manager *18* Speditionskaufmann/-frau
freight term *22T* Frachtklausel
freight train *68* Güterzug
frequency *65* Frequenz
fuel *18T* Brennstoff, Treibstoff, Benzin
fuel cell *38* Brennstoffzelle

fuel oil *53* Schiffstreibstoff
fulfil *79* erfüllen
fundamental to *40* grundlegend für,
  wesentlich für
furious *57* wütend
furnish *37* zur Verfügung stellen
fuselage *39* (Flugzeug-)Rumpf

G

gain *85* erwerben
gap *75* Lücke
general sales agent *42*
  Generalvertreter/in
global *8* weltweit *(tätig)*
go one's way *36T* klappen
goods *10T* Güter, Waren
govern *42* bestimmen, regeln
gradient *36* Steigung
grain *29* Getreide
grain of rice *61* Reiskorn
grammar school *86* Gymnasium
grease *39* Schmierfett
gross *37* brutto
gross weight *31* Bruttogewicht
ground crew *41* Bodenpersonal
ground floor *12* Erdgeschoss
groupage container *32*
  Sammelcontainer
grow into sth *8* sich zu etw
  entwickeln
guarantee *8* Garantie; *9* garantieren
Guelph Palace *71* Welfenschloss

H

hand, at first ~ *12T* mit eigenen
  Augen
hand hook *70* Haken
handheld *66* Handgerät
handle *8* umschlagen, bearbeiten,
  erledigen
handling charge *24* Rollgebühren
handling regulations *70* Handhabungsvorschriften
handy *50T* praktisch; *90* griffbereit
harbour *53* Hafen
harmful *38* schädlich, gefährlich;
  70 gesundheitsschädlich
haulage company *18* (Straßen-)
  Spedition(sfirma),
  Frachtfuhrunternehmen
haulier *37* (Straßen-)Spediteur
havoc *51* Chaos
hazardous materials *70*
  Gefahrengüter
head *12* Chef/in, Leiter/in
heading *61* Überschrift
head-shot *86* Portrait

heavy *51* *hier:* stark
heavy-duty *18T* strapazierfähig
heavy-lift crane *34T* Schwerlastkran
heavy-lift ship *29* Schwerlastschiff
height *30* Höhe
heirloom *55T* Erbstück
hereby *77* hiermit, hierdurch
herein *79* hier
hesitate *59* zögern
hire *81* mieten
hit *51* treffen, *hier:* betroffen
hold (on) *35* *(Telefon:)* dranbleiben
hold-up *34* Verzögerung
hopper wagon (BE) *19*
  Schüttgutwagen
House B/L *37* Spediteur-
  konnossement
hub *32* Knotenpunkt
huge *53* enorm, riesig
hull *38* (Schiffs-)Rumpf
Human Resources *12*
  Personal(abteilung)
hydrogen *38* Wasserstoff
hyphen *22* Bindestrich

I

identify *17* bestimmen
identifying mark *36*
  Erkennungszeichen
illiterate *81* Analphabet/in
impact *68* Stoß, Aufprall
implement *84* umsetzen
import customs *43* Importzoll
importance *82* Bedeutung
importation *76* Einfuhr, Import
impression *13* Eindruck
inch *31* Zoll
include *10T* enthalten
including *51* einschließlich
inconvenience *51* Unannehmlichkeiten
increase *29* zunehmen, steigen;
  36T *(Zeit)* verlängern
incur *36T* *(Kosten:)* anfallen
indeed *22T* in der Tat, tatsächlich
indicate, as ~d *70* wie gezeigt
indivisible *27* unteilbar
injure *52* verletzen
injury *52* Verletzung
inland *32* Binnen-
insight *42* Einblick
inspect *33* inspizieren
insurance *21* Versicherung
insurance adjuster *64*
  Schadenssachverständige/r
insurance claim *53*
  Vesicherungsanspruch

insurer *53* Versicherer
intend *38* vorhaben
intended for *40* dazu gedacht
intermediate *27* Zwischen-
intermodal container *30* Container
  für den kombinierten Verkehr
internal *68* Innen-
International Standards Organization
  (ISO) *30* Internationale Organisation
  für Normung
internship *7* Praktikum
interrupt *33* unterbrechen, stören
introduce sb/sth *9* jdn/etw vorstellen
introductions *13* Vorstellung
invest *61* investieren
investigation *53* Untersuchung
invoice *15* Rechnung
invoicing *43T* Fakturierung,
  Rechnungsstellung
involve *14* mit sich bringen,
  beinhalten; *35* nach sich ziehen
involved *36T* beteiligt
irritant *70* reizend
issue *48* ausstellen, ausgeben
issuing bank *50T* ausstellende Bank
issuing carrier *50T* ausstellender
  Frachtführer
item *14* Artikel
item of furniture *20* Möbelstück

J

jetsam *54* über Bord geworfene
  Ladung
jettison *54* über Bord werfen
job hunting *84* Arbeitssuche,
  Stellensuche
join sb *72T* bei jdm sein
journey time *36T* Fahrzeit
junction *63T* Kreuzung

K

keep sb in the know *72T* jdn auf
  dem Laufenden halten
key *7* *hier:* (Karten-)Legende
key figures *8* Kennzahlen

L

label sth *14* etw etikettieren
landing gear *39* Fahrwerk
landline *90* Festnetzleitung
landscape *81* Landschaft
landslide *34* Erdrutsch
latest, at the ~ *20* spätestens
law *43* Gesetz, Recht
lay *27* *(Gleise)* verlegen
LCL (less than container load)
  32 Teilladung

leader 16 Führungskraft
leadership 16 Führung, Leitung
least, That's the ~ of it. 55T Das ist das geringste Problem!
legal position 55T Gesetzeslage
legally 67T von Rechts wegen
length 8 Länge; 31 Tiefe
lengthen 51 verlängern
lengthy 40 sehr lang
letter of credit 36 Akkreditiv
level 71 Niveau, hier: Stärke
lift 29 heben, hieven
light bulb 69 Glühbirne
liquid 18T Flüssigkeit
liver 39 Leber
livestock 19 Vieh
live-stock car 19 Viehtransportwagen
load 41 Ladung; 10T laden
loading 31 Verladung
loading ramp 39 Laderampe
locate sth 58 etw orten, ausfindig machen
location 40 Ort, Standort
look forward to sth 10T sich auf etw freuen
loose 69 lose
loss 30 Verlust; constructive total ~ 53 konstruktiver Totalverlust, angenommener Totalschaden; total 53 Totalschaden, Totalverlust
loss adjuster 57 Schaden-sachverständige/r
low loader 18T Tieflader

M

main 7 Haupt-
main body 24 Haupttext
main-carriage 24 Weiterbeförderung
maintain 14 (Daten etc.) pflegen, verwalten
maintenance 66 Wartung, Instandhaltung
major 8 bedeutend, wichtig, größer
majority 17 Mehrheit, Großteil
make it 36T es schaffen
manage 22T es schaffen; 84 regeln, organisieren
managing director 12 Geschäftsführer/in
manifest 44 Ladungsverzeichnis
manoeuvre 36T manövrieren
manual 43T Handbuch
manufacture 78 Herstellung
manufacturer 15 Hersteller/in
map out 28 kartographieren, in eine Karte eintragen
marigold 81 Ringelblume

marine shipping company 15 Schifffahrtsgesellschaft, Reederei
marine surveyor 34T Seesachverständige/r
maritime 28 See-
mature 58 reifen
means 77 Mittel
measure 14 messen
measurement 30 Maß
mechanical breakdown 56 Maschinenschaden
medical aid 39 medizinische Hilfsgüter
meet 36T (Kosten:) begleichen
meet the needs 42 den Bedarf decken
member 17 Mitglied
mention 12 erwähnen, nennen
mention, not to ~ 73T ganz zu schweigen von
merchant 61 Kaufmann, Händler
mercy, be at the ~ of sb 51 jdm ausgeliefert sein
mezzanine 66 Palettenlager(ort)
mind 23 etwas dagegen haben
miss sb/sth 23 jdn/etw verpassen; 63T etw verfehlen
missing, be ~ 12 fehlen
mixture 10T Mischung
moderate 58 gemäßigt, mäßig
modification 36T Veränderung
moisture 62 Feuchtigkeit
moulding 72 Formteil
movement 11 Bewegung, Fortbewegung
multi-country 32 länderübergreifend

N

nappy 55 Windel
narrow 63T schmal
natural disaster 51 Naturkatastrophe
nature 19 Art
neat 56 ordentlich
negotiable 36 übertragbar, handelbar, begebbar
negotiable bill of lading 79 begebbares, handelbares, übertragbares Konnossement
neighbouring 36T Nachbar-
net weight 31 Nettogewicht
news, break the ~ to sb 56 jdm die Nachricht überbringen
next door 12T neben, nebenan
nightmare 14 Alptraum
no matter 52 egal
non-negotiable 37 nicht übertragbar, nicht handelbar

not until 30 erst
note 76 vermerken
notice 36T (es) bemerken
notify sb/sth 54 jn/etw benachrichtigen
notify address 79 Avisieranschrift, Benachrichtigungsadresse

O

objective 85 Ziel
obtain 42 erhalten
ocean vessel 34 Seeschiff
office supplies 62 Bürobedarf
off-the-job training 16 schulische Ausbildung, Weiterbildung
on-carriage 24 Nachlauf
on-the-job training 16 innerbetriebliche Ausbildung
operate 14 funktionieren; 43 arbeiten
operating costs 64 Betriebskosten
operation 8 Betrieb, Geschäft
operational area 16 Geschäftsbereich
operations 40 Betrieb
operations manager 34 Einsatz-leiter/in
operator 53 Linienreederei
opportunity 16 Gelegenheit, Möglichkeit
oral 80 mündlich
order 8 Auftrag, Bestellung; 13 Reihenfolge; 25 Befehl; 79 Ordnung; 13 bestellen
order form 62 Bestellschein, Auftragsformular
order picker 66 Kommissionierer
ore 29 Erz
organizational chart 12 Organigramm
origin 73 Ursprungsort
ornament 81 Verzierung
outnumber 82T (zahlenmäßig) übertreffen
outsize 66 übergroß
overleaf 77 umseitig
overloaded 53 überladen
overnight 27 über Nacht
overseas 14 Auslands-, in Übersee
own 54 besitzen
oxidizing 70 oxidierend

P

pack 11 etwas verpacken
package 9 Paket, Verpackung
packaging 10T Verpackung
packaging area 68 Verpackungs-bereich

packer *62* Verpacker/in, Einpacker/in
packing list *14* Packliste, Versandliste
pallet *29* Palette
pallet truck *66* Hubwagen
palletized *67* palettiert, auf Paletten
palletizer *68* Palettierer
paperwork *21* Formalitäten,
  Papierkram
particular *61* bestimmter/r/s
particulars *37* Angaben, Einzelheiten
partly *12T* zum Teil, teilweise
past sth *36T* an etw vorbei
pattern *40* Muster, Schema
payable *58* zahlbar
payload *31* Ladegewicht, Nutzlast
payment *36* Zahlung
payment term *76* Zahlungsfrist
payment terms *78* Zahlungsbedingungen
penfriend *83* Brieffreund/in
people management *16*
  Personalführung
percentage *28* Anteil, Prozentsatz
performance *16* Leistung
perishable *46T* verderblich
permission *85* Erlaubnis
petrol *18T* Benzin
petrol station *63T* Tankstelle
physical *51* physisch, körperlich
pick *66 (Sendung)* kommissionieren
pick up *22T* abholen; *27* aufnehmen,
  aufladen
pick-up *15* Abholung
picker *62* Kommissionierer/in
picking order *67T* Kommissionier-
  auftrag
picking station *66*
  Kommissionierposition
pipe *18T* Rohr, Röhre
place *8 (Auftrag)* erteilen,
  (Bestellung) aufgeben; *27* legen,
  platzieren
placement *50* Praktikum
plant *36T* Fabrik, Betrieb
plant manager *34T* Betriebsleiter/in
plastic film *68* Kunststofffolie
pleasure *13* Freude, Vergnügen
point out *51* hinweisen auf
policy *54* (Versicherungs-)Police
policy holder *58*
  Versicherungsnehmer/in
politeness *25* Höflichkeit
pollutant *38* Schadstoff
pollute *53* verschmutzen
poor *21 hier:* schlecht
pop in *12T* vorbeischauen
popularity *33* Beliebtheit

port *24* Hafen
port of destination *73* Bestimmungshafen
port of discharge *25* Entladehafen
port of loading *26* (Ver)ladehafen
port of origin *73* Verschiffungshafen
port of registry *53* Heimathafen
Port to Port B/L *37* Port-to-Port
  Seekonnossement
position *24* Stellung
possession *79* Besitz; take ~ of *79* in
  Besitz nehmen
power *38* antreiben, mit Energie
  versorgen
power cable *36T* Stromkabel
pre-carriage *24* Vorlauf
precise *22T* genau, präzise
prejudice *58* Vorurteil; without ~
  58 ohne Vorbehalt
preliminary *76* vorläufig
premature *51* zu früh
premises *72T* (Betriebs-)Gelände
prepaid *26* vorausbezahlt
preparation *27* Vorbereitung
press *67* drücken
pressure, put ~ on sb *34T* auf jdn
  Druck ausüben
presumably *58* vermutlich
previous *47* vorherig, vorig
primary producer *76* Hersteller
priority *21* Vorrang, Priorität
pro forma invoice *76* Proforma-
  rechnung
procedure *41* Maßnahm
process *15* bearbeiten *43* Verfahren,
  Ablauf; *62* Vorgang;
producer *10T* Hersteller, Produzent
production manager *33T*
  Produktionsleiter/in
production plant *27*
  Produktionsstätte, Fabrik
production site *33* Produktionsstätte,
  Betriebsgelände
professional *16* beruflich, Berufs-;
  42 (in einer bestimmten Branche)
  Berufstätige/r
profit *61* Gewinn
progress *33* Fortschritt
prolonged *51* verlängert
promote *40* fördern, voranbringen
promotion *84* Werbung
prop sth up *36T* etw aufbauen,
  aufschlagen
proper(ly) *13* richtig
property *54* Eigentum
proposal *57* Antrag
propulsion *38* Schub, Antrieb

protect *61* schützen
protection *30* Schutz
prove *32* sich erweisen als
provide *36* bieten, zur Verfügung
  stellen
public *10T* öffentlich
purchase *78* Kauf
pure *54* rein
pure salvage *54* Besitzübergang im
  Schadensfall
purpose *40* Zweck
pursue *87* verfolgen
put pressure on sb *34T* auf jdn
  Druck ausüben

Q
quantify *51* in Zahlen ausdrücken,
  quantifizieren
quantity *44* Menge
query *14* Anfrage
queue *56* (Warte-)Schlange
quotation *76* Kostenvoranschlag,
  Angebot
quote *20* Kostenvoranschlag,
  Angebot; *10T* zitieren

R
rack *62* Stapel
radio *65* Funk
rail *10* Schiene
rail freight *10* Bahnfracht
rail gauge *27* Spurweite
rail pusher *27* Schienen-
  schiebevorrichtung
rail rolling stock *19* rollendes Material
  (Waggons und Lokomotiven)
railing *36T* Geländer
raised, be ~ *88* aufwachsen
range *16* Reihe, Auswahl, Bandbreite
rare(ly) *43T* selten
rate *33* Rate, Satz, Preis; *83* etw
  einordnen, bewerten
ratio *82T* Verhältnis
realize sth *55T* sich einer Sache klar/
  bewusst sein
rear *66* hintere/r/s
reasonable *34T* akzeptabel,
  angemessen
reasonably *46T* ziemlich
reassure sb *56* jdn beruhigen
rebuild *36* neu bauen
recast *71* neu gießen
receipt *36* Empfangsbestätigung,
  Quittung; *65* Warenannahme,
  Wareneingang
receive *7* erhalten, bekommen; *37*
  entgegennehmen

Received for Shipment B/L *37*
Empfangskonnossement
receiving carrier *50T* Empfangsspediteur
receiving station *32* Empfangs-
station, Empfangsbahnhof; *66 hier:*
Warenannahme, Wareneingang
reception *12* Empfang
recipient *24* Empfänger
recommend *46T* empfehlen
recommendation *86* Empfehlung
recompense *53* Entschädigung
reconstruct sth *71* etw
rekonstruieren, wiedererrichten
record keeping *65* Dokumentation
records *11* Unterlagen, Daten
recover *58* wiedererlangen
recruitment *16* Einstellung,
Personalbeschaffung
recruitment process *86*
Einstellungsverfahren
reefer *31* Kühlcontainer
refer to sb/sth *20* von jdm/etw
sprechen, jdn/etw erwähnen;
47 unter/in etw nachschauen
referee *85* Referenz *(Person)*
reference line *24* Betreffzeile
reflective *81* reflektierend
refugee *39* Flüchtling
regard *82* betrachten, ansehen
regard sb/sth as sth *25* jdn/etw als
etw erachten, jdn/etw für etw halten
regarding *42* bezüglich, betreffend
regards *20* Grüße
registered owner *53* eingetragene/r
Besitzer/in
regret *56* bedauern
regular, on a ~ basis *42* regelmäßig
regulate *45* beaufsichtigen,
regulieren, regeln
regulations *42* Bestimmungen
reimburse *55T* erstatten,
entschädigen
release *38* ablassen
release sth *77* herausgeben
relevant (to) *16* wichtig *(für)*
reliability *31* Zuverlässigkeit
reliable *20* zuverlässig; *82T*
verlässlich
reload *27* wieder/erneut laden
rely on sth *51* auf etw angewiesen
sein, auf etw beruhen
remain *54* bleiben, verbleiben
remark *26* Bemerkung
reminder *33* Mahnung, Erinnerung
remove *11* entfernen
renewable *38* erneuerbar

renowned *56* berühmt, bekannt
replace *36T* wieder aufstellen;
43 ersetzen
replica *71* Kopie, Nachbildung
report *67T hier:* Beurteilung
representative *36T* Vertreter/in
reputation *41* Ruf
request *25* Bitte, Anfrage; on ~
85 auf Anfrage
require *73* erfordern
required *84* erforderlich
requirements *84* Bedürfnisse
rescue *53* retten
rescue service *53* Rettungsdienst
respond to sth *13* auf etw reagieren,
auf etw antworten
responsibilites *85* Aufgaben
responsible for *10T* verantwortlich
für, zuständig für
retailer *15* Einzelhändler
reveal *90* verraten, preisgeben,
offenbaren
reverse *85* umgekehrt
RFID tag *65* RFID-Etikett
rigid *18T* starr
ripped *57* gerissen
rise *38 (Preis etc.:)* steigen
road construction company *36T*
Straßenbaufirma
road freight *10T* Lkw-Ladung,
Lkw-Transport, Straßengüter-
transport
road haulage *15* Straßentransport
road works *36* Straßenbauarbeiten
rolling stock *19* rollendes Material
(Waggons und Lokomotiven)
rope *18T* Seil
rough *53* rau
roughly *27* ungefähr
round-trip *27* Hin- und Rückfahrt
route *15* Route, Strecke
routing *49* Routenplanung
rude *25* unhöflich, unverschämt
rules *40* Bestimmungen

S
sacking *69* Sackleinen
safety margin *34T* Sicherheits-
spielraum
sail *74 (Schiff:)* auslaufen, abfahren
salary *84* Gehalt, Lohn
sale *8* Vertrieb
sales *12* Vertrieb(sabteilung)
sales adviser *15* Vertriebsberater/in
sales brochure *85* Verkaufsprospekt
sales executive *84* Verkaufs-
manager/in

sales goal *84* Verkaufsziel
sales terms *78* Verkaufsbedingungen
salutation *24* Anrede *(Brief)*
salvage *53* Bergung
salvor *53* Berger
sanctuary *53* Schutzgebiet
SatNav *63* Navigationssystem
say *76 (im Formular:)* in Worten
scale *83* Skala
scattered *55* verstreut
scene *57* Ort *(des Geschehens)*
schedule *27* Plan, Zeitplan,
Terminplan, Fahrplan
scheduled *40* planmäßig
scheduler *63* Disponent/in,
Terminsachbearbeiter/in
scrap metal *18T* Schrott, Altmetall
sea freight *10T* Seefracht
sea port *28* Seehafen
sea water *58* Meerwasser
sea waybill *36* Seefrachtbrief
sea-going barge *29* Hochseebarge,
Frachtkahn
seal *14* zukleben; *30* versiegeln,
verschließen, abdichten
section *11* Teil, Abteilung; *27*
Abschnitt, Teil(stück)
secure sth *18T* etw befestigen
self-manage *84* eigenverantwortlich
tätig sein
self-motivate *84* sich motivieren
seller *50* Verkäufer/in
sender *24* Absender
senior management *12T*
Betriebsleitung, leitende Angestellte,
Direktion
sense *10T* Sinn
sensible *10T* vernünftig; *86*
verständlich
sensitive *18T* empfindlich
serious *56* ernst, ernsthaft, *hier:* groß
serve *40* dienen
service *55 (Geschirr:)* Service; *66*
warten
set *30* festsetzen
settling (of account) *43* Abrechnung
settlement *55T* Abwicklung,
Regulierung
severe *33 (Unwetter etc.)* heftig
shaky *54* wacklig, schwach
share *61* Anteil
shelf, shelves *66* Regal
shift *27* schieben, verschieben
shipment *20* Versand
Shipped on Board B/L *37*
Bordkonnossement
shipper *15* Versender

Shipper's Letter of Instructions *50T* Absenderanweisung

shipping area *68* Versandbereich, Ladebucht

shipping label *68* Versandetikett

shipping route *28* Schifffahrtsweg

shipwreck *54* Schiffbruch, Schiffswrack

shipwrecked goods *55* Strandgut

short notice *22T* kurzfristig

shorten *32* verkürzen

shrink wrap *68* mit Schrumpffolie umwickeln

shunt *27* *(Eisenbahn:)* rangieren

side loader *18T* Seitenlader

side panel *81* Seitenwand

sign *15* unterschreiben

signature *49* Unterschrift

significant(ly) *32* erheblich

silk *81* Seide

simplify *43* vereinfachen

sit back *67T* sich zurücklehnen

site plan *7* Lageplan

sketch *12* skizzieren

skilled *81* geschickt

slash *22* Schrägstrich

sleeper *19* *(Eisenbahn:)* Bahnschwelle

slender *38* schlank

sliding door *18T* Schiebetür

sling *70* Schlaufe, Schlinge

slot *70* Schlitz, Aussparung

smash sth open *55T* etw aufbrechen

smooth *34* reibungslos

solar *38* Sonnen-

solve *56* lösen

sorting area *68* Sortierbereich

sound *10T* klingen

source *38* Quelle

specialist *36T* Spezial-, spezialisiert

specialize in sth *10T* sich auf etw spezialisieren

specially *29* speziell, eigens, für etw (gedacht)

specific *78* bestimmt

specifically *10T* genau, im Einzelnen

spirits *58* Spirituosen, Alkohol

split *10T* aufteilen

spread *65* sich ausbreiten

staff *10T* Angestellte/r, Personal

standardize *40* normen

state *17* Staat, Land; *47* angeben, erklären, sagen

statement *78* Erklärung

state-of-the-art *27* modern, auf dem neuesten Stand der Technik

static *90* atmosphärische Störungen, Rauschen

stationery *10T* Schreibwaren, Bürobedarf

statistics *33T* Statistik, statistische Daten

steel *18* Stahl

steelworks *27* Stahlwerk(e)

steer *67T* lenken, steuern

step frame *18T* Tieflader

stern *29* Heck

stick sth *68* etw kleben

stock car *19* Viehtransportwagen

stocked *8* lagernd, gelagert

stocktaking *65* Inventur

stopover *46T* Zwischenstopp

storage *10T* Lagerung; *62* Lager

store *10T* lagern; *65* *(Dateien)* speichern

straight, get sth ~ *72T* etw klarstellen

straight ahead *63T* geradeaus

stranded *51* gestrandet

strange *61* seltsam

strap *68* Band

stress *68* Belastung

stretch *63T* Stück, Abschnitt

stretch wrap film *68* Dehnfolie

strike *25* Streik; *51* zuschlagen

strip *32* *(Container)* entladen

structural damage *75* Bauschaden

stuff *32* *(Container)* beladen

subject *87* (Schul-)Fach

subject to *79* vorbehaltlich, gemäß

suffer from sth *51* unter etw leiden

suitable *24* passend

sum *50* Betrag, Summe

summarize *85* zusammenfassen

supplies, army ~ *10T* Nachschub

supply chain *15* Lieferkette, Zulieferkette

support *38* Unterstützung, Stütz-

suppose *43T* annehmen, glauben

surface *81* Oberfläche

surplus *30* überschüssig, überzählig

surrender *79* aushändigen, übergeben

survey (report) *57* Gutachten

swing down *18T* (sich) herunterklappen *(lassen)*

T

tail fin *39* Heckflosse

tailor *21* *(auf etw)* zuschneiden

take in charge *79* übernehmen

take into consideration *48* in Betracht ziehen, berücksichtigen

take over *26* übernehmen

take possession of *81* in Besitz nehmen

take sb/sth in tow *53* jdn/etw in Schlepptau nehmen

tank wagon *19* Tankwagen

tape *46T* Band

tape sth *68* etw *(mit Klebeband)* zukleben

tare weight *31* Taragewicht

tarpaulin *18T* Plane

tautliner *18T* Schiebeplanenauflieger, Gardinenplanenauflieger

tea leaf, leaves *69* Teeblatt, -blätter

technically *8* technisch

technician *67T* Techniker/in

tenor *79* Inhalt, Sinn

term, in ~s of *51* was … angeht

terms *78* Bedingungen

territorial water *53* Hoheitsgewässer

theft *31* Diebstahl

thence *77* hier: von dort

thief, thieves *71* Dieb, Diebe

This way up *70* Hier oben

threaten *53* bedrohen, drohen

throughout *85* durchgehend, ständig

tie down *41* (am Boden) festzurren

tight *51* knapp, eng

(a) tight fit *36T* eine knappe Sache

tilt *18T* kippen

timber *18T* (Nutz-)Holz

time, on ~ *48* pünktlich

timely *79* rechtzeitig

T-junction *64* Einmündung

tool *29* Werkzeug

total *22T* Gesamt-

total loss *53* Totalschaden, Totalverlust

touch, get in ~ with sb *22T* sich mit jdm in Verbindung setzen

tow *34T* schleppen

tow, take sb/sth in ~ *53* jdn/etw in Schlepptau nehmen

trace *14* (eine Sendung) orten

track *27* Gleis; *14* *(eine Sendung)* verfolgen

trade *28* Handel

trade body *40* Handelsorganisation

trailer *18T* Anhänger, Sattelauflieger

trainee *7* Auszubildende/r

trainer *16* Ausbilder/in

training *16* Ausbildung

tramp *29* Trampschiff

transaction *42* (Geschäfts-)Vorgang, Transaktion

transformation *81* Umwandlung

transit document *50* Transitpapier, Versandschein (EU)

transit time *32* Beförderungszeit, Laufzeit

transload *32* umladen
transplant *39* Transplantation
transport clerk *15* Transport-
  sachbearbeiter/in
transport mode *26* Beförderungsart
tray *67* Schale, Tablett
treasure *55* Schatz
treasure chest *81* Schatztruhe
treasure hunter *55* Schatzsucher
treat sb *9* jdn behandeln
treaty *82* Abkommen, Vertrag
trucker *63* Lastwagenfahrer/in
trust *56* Vertrauen
tug boat *34T* Schlepper
tuition *83* Unterricht
turn around *63T* wenden
turn into *63T* einbiegen
turn-off *63T* Abzweig
turn out to be sth *36T* sich als etw
  erweisen
turn up *46T* auftauchen
tyre *35* Reifen

U

unaffected by *65* unempfindlich
  gegen
unclean *36* unrein
under charter to *53* verchartert an
under construction *33T* im Bau
underscore *22* Unterstrich
(the) undersigned *58* der/die
  Unterzeichnete, der/die
  Unterzeichnende
undertake *36T* ausführen,
  vornehmen
underwrite *61* *(Risiko)* versichern,
  übernehmen
underwriter *61* Versicherer
undoubtedly *59* zweifellos
uneventful *34* ohne Zwischenfälle
uniform *40* einheitlich
unique selling point (USP) *85*
  Alleinstellungsmerkmal
unit loading device (ULD) *41*
  Luftfrachtcontainer
unit price *76* Preis pro Einheit
unload *10T* abladen, ausladen,
  entladen
unloading *31* Entladung
unpleasant *36T* unerfreulich,
  unangenehm
unsafe *13* gefährlich, nicht sicher
until, not ~ *30* erst
update *65* aktualisieren

up front *50T* im Voraus
upset *56* verärgert
urgent *46T* dringend, eilig

V

validity *49* Gültigkeit
valuable *42* wertvoll
value *26* Wert
value sth *41* etw schätzen
van *8* Lieferwagen
various *66* verschieden
vary *30* schwanken, variieren
VAT (value added tax) *24*
  Mehrwertsteuer
vehicle *11* Fahrzeug
vessel *26* Schiff
violent *53* heftig
vocational school *87* Berufsschule
void *79* unwirksam, ungültig, nichtig
volume *18T* Menge, Volumen
voyage policy *54* Reisepolice

W

warehouse *7* Lager(halle)
warehouse worker *10T*
  Lagerarbeiter/in
warehousing *62* Lagerung,
  Lagerhaltung, Lagerwesen
wash off the deck *53* von Deck spülen
wash up *55* angespült werden
waste paper *29* Altpapier
wastepaper basket *22T* Papierkorb
waterproof *18T* wasserdicht
weaken *53* schwächen
wedge *66* Keil
weigh *22T* wiegen
weight *19* Gewicht
weight estimate *73* Schätzgewicht
wheat *29* Weizen
wheel rim *70* Radfelge
wholesaler *39* Großhändler,
  Großhandel
wide *33T* breit
wide-body *44* Großraum-
widespread *69* verbreitet
width *31* Breite
wing *12T* Flügel
wire cable *19* Drahtkabel
without prejudice *58* ohne Vorbehalt
withstand sth *43* etw aushalten, einer
  Sache standhalten
witness *79* Zeuge/-in; in ~ whereof
  79 zu Urkund wessen
wonder *46T* sich fragen
wood chips *18T* Holzspäne
wooden *69* aus Holz
woollen *63T* Woll-

work effort *84* Arbeitseinsatz
work one's way through sth *16* sich
  durch etw hindurcharbeiten
workplace *16* Arbeitsplatz
wrapped *68* umwickelt, eingewickelt
write-off *58* Totalverlust,
  Totalschaden

Y

yard *18T* Hof

Irregular verbs

be – was/were – been — *sein*
beat – beat – beaten — *schlagen, besiegen*
become – became – become — *werden*
begin – began – begun — *anfangen, beginnen*
bleed – bled – bled — *bluten*
break – broke – broken — *brechen*
bring – brought – brought — *bringen*
build – built – built — *bauen*
burn – burnt – burnt — *(ver)brennen*
buy – bought – bought — *kaufen*
catch – caught – caught — *fangen*
choose – chose – chosen — *wählen*
come – came – come — *kommen*
cost – cost – cost — *kosten*
cut – cut – cut — *schneiden*
do – did – done — *tun, machen*
draw – drew – drawn — *zeichnen*
dream – dreamt/dreamed – dreamt/dreamed — *träumen*
drink – drank – drunk — *trinken*
drive – drove – driven — *fahren*
eat – ate – eaten — *essen*
fall – fell – fallen — *fallen*
feed – fed – fed — *füttern, ernähren*
feel – felt – felt — *(sich) fühlen, empfinden*
fight – fought – fought — *kämpfen*
find – found – found — *finden*
fit – fit/fitted – fit/fitted — *passen*
fly – flew – flown — *fliegen*
forget – forgot – forgotten — *vergessen*
freeze – froze – frozen — *frieren*
get – got – got (*AE* gotten) — *bekommen*
give – gave – given — *geben*
go – went – gone — *gehen, fahren*
grow – grew – grown — *wachsen*
hang – hung – hung — *hängen*
have – had – had — *haben*
hear – heard – heard — *hören*
hide – hid – hidden — *(sich) verstecken*
hit – hit – hit — *schlagen*
hold – held – held — *halten, festhalten*
keep – kept – kept — *behalten*
know – knew – known — *kennen, wissen*
lay – laid – laid — *legen*
lean – leant/leaned – leant/leaned — *(sich) lehnen, neigen*
learn – learnt/learned – learnt/learned — *lernen*
leave – left – left — *abfahren, verlassen, weggehen*
let – let – let — *lassen*
lie – lay – lain — *liegen*
light – lit – lit — *anzünden, beleuchten, anmachen*

lose – lost – lost — *verlieren*
make – made – made — *machen*
mean – meant – meant — *meinen, bedeuten*
meet – met – met — *treffen*
pay – paid – paid — *bezahlen*
put – put – put — *setzen, stellen, legen*
quit – quit/quitted – quit/quitted — *verlassen, aufhören*
read – read – read — *lesen*
ride – rode – ridden — *reiten, fahren*
rise – rose – risen — *(an)steigen*
run – ran – run — *laufen, rennen*
say – said – said — *sagen*
see – saw – seen — *sehen*
sell – sold – sold — *verkaufen*
send – sent – sent — *senden, schicken*
set – set – set — *setzen, stellen*
show – showed – shown — *zeigen*
shut – shut – shut — *schließen*
sing – sang – sung — *singen*
sit – sat – sat — *sitzen*
sleep – slept – slept — *schlafen*
smell – smelt/smelled – smelt/smelled — *riechen*
speak – spoke – spoken — *sprechen*
spell – spelt/spelled – spelt/spelled — *buchstabieren*
spend – spent – spent — *ausgeben, verbringen*
stand – stood – stood — *stehen*
steal – stole – stolen — *stehlen*
swim – swam – swum — *schwimmen*
take – took – taken — *nehmen*
teach – taught – taught — *unterrichten, beibringen*
tear – tore – torn — *zerreißen*
tell – told – told — *sagen, erzählen*
think – thought – thought — *denken*
throw – threw – thrown — *werfen*
understand – understood – understood — *verstehen*
wake – woke – woken — *aufwachen/aufwecken*
wear – wore – worn — *tragen (Kleidung)*
win – won – won — *gewinnen*
write – wrote – written — *schreiben*

European countries

Albania [æl'beɪnɪə]	Albanien
Andorra [æn'dɒrə]	Andorra
Armenia [ɑː'miːnɪə]	Armenien
Austria ['ɒstrɪə]	Österreich
Azerbaijan [æzəbaɪ'dʒɑːn]	Aserbaidschan
Belarus [ˌbela'ruːs]	Weißrussland
Belgium ['beldʒəm]	Belgien
Bosnia & Herzegovina [bɒznɪə ænd hɜːtsəgə'viːnə]	Bosnien und Herzegowina
Bulgaria [bʌl'geərɪə]	Bulgarien
Croatia [krəʊ'eɪʃə]	Kroatien
Cyprus ['saɪprəs]	Zypern
Czech Republic [ðə ˌtʃek rɪ'pʌblɪk]	Tschechien
Denmark ['denmɑrk]	Dänemark
Estonia [es'təʊnɪə]	Estland
Finland ['fɪnlənd]	Finnland
France ['frɑːns]	Frankreich
Georgia ['dʒɔːrdʒə]	Georgien
Germany ['dʒɜːməni]	Deutschland
Greece ['griːs]	Griechenland
Hungary [hʌ'ŋgəri]	Ungarn
Iceland ['aɪslənd]	Island
Ireland ['aɪələnd]	Irland
Italy ['ɪtəli]	Italien
Kosovo ['kɒsəvəʊ]	Kosovo
Latvia ['lætvɪə]	Lettland
Liechtenstein ['lɪktənstaɪn]	Liechtenstein
Lithuania [lɪθu'eɪnɪə]	Litauen
Luxembourg ['lʌksəmbɜrg]	Luxemburg
Macedonia [mæsə'dəʊnɪə]	Makedonien
Malta ['mɒltə]	Malta
Moldova [mɒl'dəʊvə]	Moldawien
Monaco ['mɒnəkəʊ]	Monaco
Montenegro [mɒntə'neɪgrəʊ]	Montenegro
The Netherlands [ðə 'neðələndz]	Holland
Norway ['nɔːrweɪ]	Norwegen
Poland ['pəʊlənd]	Polen
Portugal ['pɔːrtʃuəgl]	Portugal
Romania [rəʊ'meɪnɪə]	Rumänien
Russia ['rʌʃə]	Russland
San Marino [sæn mə'riːnəʊ]	San Marino
Serbia ['sɜrbɪə]	Serbien
Slovakia [sləʊ'vækɪə]	Slowakei
Slovenia [sləʊ'viːnɪə]	Slowenien
Spain ['speɪn]	Spanien
Sweden ['swiːdən]	Schweden
Switzerland ['swɪtsələnd]	die Schweiz
Turkey ['tɜrki]	die Türkei
Ukraine [ju'kreɪn]	Ukraine
United Kingdom [ðə juˌnaɪtɪd 'kɪŋdəm]	Vereinigtes Königreich
Vatican City [ðə 'vætɪkən ˌsɪti]	Vatikanstadt

Acknowledgements

RF Fotos:

Fotolia: S. 10, S. 16, S. 114;
Istockphoto: S. 15 / oben, S. 19/a/b/c/d/e, S. 28 / oben, S. 39 / oben, S. 41, S. 62/1, S. 62/2, S. 66/2, S. 68, S. 72 / oben, S. 112;
Shutterstock: S. 17, S. 18/e, S. 20, S. 21, S. 30, S. 34, S. 58, S. 82, S. 87, S. 89, S. 106, S. 107, S. 109, S. 111, S. 119;
Wikipedia: S. 18/b, S. 18/c, S19/f, S. 29/a, S. 31/a/b/c/d/e, S. 65, S. 69/1–4, S. 72;

RM Fotos:

Alamy: S. 14 / 1 / ImageSource IE318, S. 14 / 2 / Shoosh, S. 18 / a / Alvery&Towers Picture Library, S. 18 / d / Industrial, S. 27 / Ria Novosti, S. 29 / b / L. Smak, S. 29 / c / Dan Lee, S. 29 / d / M. Eveleigh, S. 29 / e /GeoPic, S. 50 / Denkou Business2, S. 54 / M. Passmore, S. 63 / M. Lavrenow, S. 66 / 1 / Fancy Veer Set 19, S. 66 / 3 / Image Source / IS356, S. 66 / 4 / image100, S. 82 / 1 / Eddie Linssen, S. 82/2/PCL, S. 82 / 3 / Jack Cox, S. 82 / 4 / M. Wojtkowiak, S. 84 / Look / H. Eisenberger;
Fotofinder: S. 18 / f / Caro / Giessen, S. 44 / 1 / photothek / U. Grabowsky;
PictureAlliance: S. 29/f, S. 52 / a / epa / Justin Lane, S. 52 / b / Sören Stache, S. 52 / c / A. Devlin, S. 52 / d / S. Puchner, S. 53 / A. Devlin, S. 55/stf, S. 61 / Mary Evans Picture Library, S. 71 / Oliver Krause;

Illustrationen:

Thomas Malangeri / S. 11; Gabriele Heinisch / S. 15, S. 39, S. 44, S. 56, S. 67, S. 69 / oben, S. 70 / oben; Kaluza / Kölzsch / Gastner / Blasius / S. 28; Oxford Designers & Illustrators / S. 48; Berufsgenossenschaft Nahrungsmittel und Gastgewerbe / S. 70 unten

Mit freundlicher Unterstützung: Firma Lyreco Deutschland GmbH, Barsinghausen / S. 7, S. 9; Firma Fagioli / S. 36; Wallenius Wilhelmsen Logistics, E/S Orcelle / S. 38; Cathay Pacific Airways Ltd Frankfurt / S. 47; www.careersinlogistics.co.uk / S. 84;

Textquellen:

S. 16 / based on information from www.lyreco.co.uk, S. 27 / adapted from World Magazine No. 2 / 2005 / Kuehne + Nagel, S. 32 / based on information from World Magazine No. 2 / 2005 / Kuehne + Nagel, S. 38 / based on information from www.2wglobal.com/www/pdf/Green-Flagship.pdf, S. 42 / www.iata.org/ ps/publications/Pages/air-cargo-tariff-aspx, S. 51 / adapted from www.timesofmalta.com, 22. April 2010, S. 114 / adapted from http://www.eurotunnel.com/uk/conditions-of-carriage/

Nicht alle Copyright-Inhaber konnten ermittelt werden; deren Urheberrechte werden hiermit vorsorglich und ausdrücklich anerkannt.

Danksagung:

Wir bedanken uns bei Lyreco Deutschland GmbH sowie bei allen anderen Instituten, Firmen und Personen, die uns freundlicherweise Material für dieses Lehrwerk zur Verfügung gestellt haben.

THE WORLD

New Zealand

Papua New Guinea

Australia

Sydney

Philippines

Indonesia

Jakarta

Malaysia

Kuala Lumpur

Taiwan

Hong Kong

Vietnam

Cam-bodia

Laos

Thai-land

Myan-mar

Bangla-desh

Japan

Tokyo

Yokohama

North Korea

South Korea

Shanghai

China

Beijing

Mongolia

Nepal

India

Sri Lanka

Kyrgystan

Tajikistan

Pakistan

Mumbai

Kazakhstan

Uzbekistan

Turkmenistan

Afghanistan

Iran

Oman

Dubai

UAE

Saudi Arabia

Kuwait

Irak

Jemen

Georgia

Turkey

Greece

Ukraine

Russia

Moscow

Finland

Sweden

Norway

United Kingdom

Leeds

London

Ireland

Iceland

Germany

Paris

France

Italy

Spain

Portugal

Somalia

Ethiopia

Eritrea

Sudan

Egypt

Libya

Tunisia

Algeria

Morocco

Sahara

Mauretania

Mali

Niger

Chad

Central African Rep.

Nigeria

Cameroon

Burkina Faso

Senegal

Guinea

Sierra Leone

Liberia

Côte d'Ivoire

Ghana

Uganda

Kenya

Tanzania

Malawi

Mo-sam-bique

Zim-babwe

Zambia

Bots-wana

Swaziland

Lesotho

South Africa

Namibia

Angola

Dem. Rep. of Kongo

Gabun

Kongo

Madagascar

Indian Ocean

Greenland

Canada

United States of America

San Francisco

Las Vegas

Montreal

New York

Mexico

Mexico City

Guatemala

El Salvador

Honduras

Nicaragua

Costa Rica

Panama

Bahamas

Cuba

Jamaica

Haiti

Dominican Rep.

Puerto Rico

Venezuela

Columbia

Ecuador

Peru

Bolivia

Brasil

Guyana

Surinam

Fr.-Guyana

Rio de Janeiro

Paraguay

Uruguay

Buenos Aires

Argentina

Chile

Atlantic Ocean

Pacific Ocean

Pacific Ocean

Stand: 2008